The Wisconsin Story

The Wisconsin Story

**150 People, Places, and Turning Points
that Shaped the Badger State**

Dennis McCann

WISCONSIN HISTORICAL SOCIETY PRESS

Published by the Wisconsin Historical Society Press

Publishers since 1855

The Wisconsin Historical Society helps people connect to the past
by collecting, preserving, and sharing stories. Founded in 1846,
the Society is one of the nation's finest historical institutions.
Join the Wisconsin Historical Society: wisconsinhistory.org/membership

Front cover images: clockwise from top left: Hank Aaron, WHI Image ID
26365; Dr. Kate Newcomb, WHI Image ID 115801; Chromolithograph
portrait of Old Abe, 1865, WHI Image ID 79132; Harry Houdini, WHI Image
ID 3629; and John Muir, 1899, WHI Image ID 3948.
Back cover image: Wisconsin cheese billboard, 1942, WHI Image ID 2039.

Printed in the United States of America

Cover Design by Mayfly Design. Typesetting by Diana Boger.

23 22 21 20 19   1 2 3 4 5

Library of Congress Cataloging-in-Publication Data
Names: McCann, Dennis, 1950– author.
Title: The Wisconsin story : 150 people, places, and turning points that
   shaped the Badger State / Dennis McCann.
Description: Madison, WI : Wisconsin Historical Society Press, [2019] |
   Originally published: Milwaukee : Milwaukee Journal Sentinel, 1998. |
   Includes index.
Identifiers: LCCN 2019011062 | ISBN 9780870209314 (pbk. : alk. paper) |
   ISBN 9780870209321 (ebook)
Subjects: LCSH: Wisconsin—History. | Wisconsin—Biography.
Classification: LCC F581 .M45 2019 | DDC 977.5—dc23 LC record
   available at https://lccn.loc.gov/2019011062

For Barbara, who treasures Wisconsin as I do.

Contents

Introduction

As Wisconsin's 150th birthday approached in 1997, sesquicentennial fever began spreading through communities all across the state. While a governor-appointed commission took on the task of planning the official party to be held at the State Capitol on May 29, 1998, local historical societies, elected officials, and all manner of organizations in communities big and small began devising their own ways to take part in the observance.

My newspaper at the time, the *Milwaukee Journal Sentinel*, also wanted in on the festivities, and editors were barnstorming ideas. One night, while driving to Madison to catch a Wisconsin Badger basketball game, my editor, Marty Kaiser, told me they were thinking of having a writer paddle the Wisconsin River from its source at Lac Vieux Desert to the place near Prairie du Chien where it empties into the Mississippi River, spinning tales along the way. And he said my name had come up as the guy to send.

Great, I thought, 430 miles in a canoe suffering sunburn and mosquitos and with no place to carry golf clubs, and my name came up first.

For whatever reason, that idea quietly evaporated when editors decided instead to publish 150 historical essays in honor of Wisconsin's 150 years, running one each day for 150 days in the newspaper and then all of them together in book form as our lasting gift to the birthday state. Again, my name came up first and that time I was delighted. Given my personal interest in state history, the opportunity to wander at will through Wisconsin's long and proud past and retell this great state's stories was more privilege than duty. And for a longtime newspaperman whose best work nonetheless suffered the indignity of almost instant recycling, the opportunity to write something as permanent as a book was the assignment of a lifetime. As it happened, the first copies of the book were delivered from the printer to my hotel room in Madison the very day of the sesquicentennial and I carried them with me to the cake-and-bunting bash on the Capitol steps.

During the following year, I toured the state, giving book talks and sharing state history until it was time to be a newspaper columnist again. Eventually the last of the books sold and it seemed *The Wisconsin Story: 150 Stories/150 Years* was a part of my past. And for nearly 20 years it was, until one day in 2017 Kathy Borkowski, the director of the Wisconsin Historical Society Press at the time, first saw the book while visiting my home in Bayfield and almost immediately wondered if the Society Press, for which I had already written three other books, should publish a new edition of *The Wisconsin Story*. When the answer turned out to be yes, I was as delighted as that first day I was spared a long, buggy, sweaty paddle on the state's namesake river.

Thanks must go to Kathy and to Kate Thompson, the Press's current director, for seeing merit in this new edition. And now, as then, thanks to those who helped make the first edition possible, especially Paula Haubrich of the *Journal Sentinel*'s News Information Center for all the research help and the late Don Walker, editor extraordinaire, who shaped the 150 essays as needed and oversaw their publication in book form.

The basis for a number of these stories was the *Wisconsin Magazine of History*, which should be on the reading list of anyone interested in events that shaped this state. Special thanks to previous magazine editors Paul H. Hass and Jack O. Holzhueter for contributing ideas and for sending me in the right direction. Thanks also to Bill Meindl, publisher of *Voyageur*, northeast Wisconsin's fine historical review, who willingly shared good stories. A tip of the hat as well to directors of historical societies and museums throughout the state who responded to entreaties with tips on local events of pride or importance.

Many of the stories included in this book were assembled from longer accounts in dozens of books about Wisconsin, including but certainly not limited to the following: *The New Richmond Tornado of 1899* by Anna P. Epley, *The Wisconsin Story* by Russell Austin, *Gangster Holidays* by Thomas Hollatz, *The Badger State: A Documentary History of Wisconsin* by Barbara and Justus Paul, *Wisconsin: The Story of the Badger State* by Norman K. Risjord, *The Lake Superior County in History and in Story* by Guy M. Burhnam, *Long Live the Hodag* by Kurt Daniel Kortenhof, *I Had a Hammer* by Henry Aaron, *Ghost Towns of Wisconsin* by William F. Stark, *Leading Events of Wisconsin History* by Henry E. Legler, *Wisconsin: A History* by Robert C. Nesbit, *On Wisconsin Women* by Genevieve McBride, *The Romance of Wisconsin Place Names* by Robert E. Gard and L. G. Sorden, *Wisconsin: The Way We Were* by Mary A. Shafer, *Badger Saints and Sinners* and *Old World Wisconsin* by Fred Holmes, and two special guides: "Brevet's Wisconsin Historical Markers and Sites" and "Wisconsin Literary Travel Guide."

Asaph Whittlesey,
Ashland's Snowshoe Legislator

Modern-day lawmakers from the cold reaches of northern Wisconsin often complain about the rigors of travel to distant Madison—at worst a long drive, at best a short flight.

But for sheer dedication and perseverance, no modern officeholder can hold a candle to Asaph Whittlesey, whose first trip to the capital was on snowshoes.

Most impressive, Asaph Whittlesey's trek occurred long before state lawmakers awarded themselves mileage and expenses.

Whittlesey dressed for his long, cold journey from Ashland to Madison.
WHI IMAGE ID 36714

In January 1860, five years after he and a partner founded the city of Ashland, Whittlesey was selected to represent the remote Lake Superior country, still a full wilderness away from Madison, in the Wisconsin Legislature.

It was the heart of winter, but Whittlesey took his duty seriously. The north needed a voice. So, because the closest train depot was 240 miles away in Sparta, Whittlesey armed himself, strapped on long snowshoes and set of on foot by Indian trail, accompanied by one other man and two dogs.

A photograph taken en route showed Whittlesey wearing goggles to fend off snow blindness, with a tin drinking cup strapped to his waist. He carried his possessions in a backpack but left his overcoat behind in Ashland so its bulk would not slow him down.

A man who was at the tavern in Sparta where Whittlesey sough comfort upon arrival later recalled that the stranger who straggled in from the cold that January night looked anything but statesmanlike.

"He was dressed in buckskin, carried a pack and an immense pair of snowshoes which, to me, had the appearance of long, drawn-out fish nets," wrote J. S. Buck.

"He looked very much like the pictures of trappers that are sometimes seen on the covers of dime novels."

The men at the tavern were so impressed with Whittlesey's dogged determination to represent the north country that they helped him come up with a suit of ready-made clothing in which he would not be embarrassed to present himself to the governor.

"The clothes were slightly large and bagged considerably," Buck wrote, "but all in all the suit was an improvement on buckskins."

Thanks to his new friends, Whittlesey was suddenly blessed with more clothing than he could wear at one time so, about to forsake the Indian trail for the train, he also bought a trunk.

On the outside he painted "Hon. Asaph Whittlesey" in bold letters. The snowshoes, unfortunately, were too long for the trunk and had to be left in Sparta, but the newly-suited Whittlesey set out for Madison, where he presented the governor with a petition to establish the new county of Ashland.

H. H. Bennett
and the Wisconsin Dells

Before Tommy Bartlett and his bumper stickers, there was Henry Hamilton Bennett and his photographs.

In a sense, even before there was the Wisconsin Dells, there was H. H. Bennett, who opened the shutter in his cigar-box camera and revealed the enchanting hidden gulches, sandstone bluffs and winding waters to the world.

Think of him as the father of the Wisconsin postcard, but of so much more as well.

The modern Dells was still Kilbourn City when Bennett returned from the Civil War and became a portrait photographer. Like other communities, Kilbourn City was chasing industry, damming its river to provide power. But Bennett turned the city in a different direction.

Portraits did not keep a photographer busy in the 1860s, so Bennett filled his time with landscape photography. The art was in its infancy then, which made Bennett's accomplishments seem all the more amazing. Technology was so limited that he had to cart not just his bulky camera, tripod and glass plate, into dark canyons and onto the river he was shooting, he also had to tow a darkroom in order to develop his plates at once.

Bennett used cigar boxes to achieve a three-dimensional effect, taking two photos of a scene from slightly different vantages. The stereoscopic views of the beautiful Wisconsin River dells he produced were viewed in parlors across the country, and by the 1870s tourists began to seek out this countryside in person.

Some of the earliest tours included Bennett's studio, where visitors would purchase his images.

And why not? He has an artist's eye and a magician's touch. One of his most famous photographs, taken with the help of cigar boxes and rubber bands, caught a rope suspended in mid-air as a logger threw it to shore. It was so advanced that many thought it trick photography.

Bennett rowed his boat up and down the river, poking into caves and gulches and recording their mysteries. He rode timber rafts to catch the live action, persuaded leery Ho-Chunk neighbors to sit for portraits—in the process recording history along with the lined faces of his neighbors—and made pictures of the many tourist-crammed steamers that visited his river, in no small part lured by his photographs.

As Bennett became recognized as one of the finest landscape pictorialists of his time, he was in demand to travel and share his talent. His 1887 photos of fireworks in St. Paul are said to be the first of their kind, and Bennett visited Milwaukee and Chicago often to record city scenes.

But what became Wisconsin Dells was his home, and for 40 years he returned to the pine country and his familiar subjects. Bennett died on New Year's Day in 1908, but thousands of images survived him and have been used in many shows, even in recent years. In 1976, his studio, which was taken over by family members, was placed on the National Register of Historic Places. The studio is now a historic site operated by the Wisconsin Historical Society.

FACING: H. H. Bennett (holding a camera) and Ruth Bennett on shore near Sugar Bowl. WHI IMAGE ID 8264

"Fighting Bob" Ushered in the Progressive Era

The man inaugurated as governor on January 7, 1901, could have come from frontier central casting. Robert Marion La Follette, born in a log cabin in Dane County in 1855, was the state's first home-grown governor, a University of Wisconsin law school graduate, three-term member of Congress—its youngest member in 1885 at a tender 29—and an oratorical master.

Yet he was "Bob" to voters, and even when he lost his congressional job in 1891 he stayed active.

When he ran for governor a decade later on a reform platform, he won the largest vote yet cast in Wisconsin.

The progressive movement that gained force in the 1890s was premised on restoring to "the people" the influence and privilege that had been absorbed by big business and corporate interests, and by political machines such as the Republicans then in power.

In seeking the party's nominations, La Follette argued for taxes on powerful railroads and utilities and favored direct primaries to give voters more say.

Whether from the back of a farm wagon or at a formal dais, he was an energetic campaigner. Scorning party bosses and machine politics, he conducted Wisconsin's first whistle-stop campaign, covering 6,000 miles and delivering 208 speeches in 61 counties.

The press called his inauguration the biggest in history, a day of bands, parades and a ball that attracted a disparate crowd of "swells" and "rabble."

The chairman of arrangements called the swearing in of the state's first native son a great day for Wisconsin.

Outgoing Governor Edward Scofield was noticeably cool, but university students who lined the gallery at the old Capitol, feet dangling over railings, contributed "the university raw-raw."

Carriages swarmed around the university gymnasium for the inaugural ball, which the papers said drew 10,000 people.

Alas, it was also noted that Governor La Follette, however agile on the stump, was a flop on the dance floor.

Once he stepped on his wife's train and when he missed his steps in a complicated quadrille he "threw up his hands in disgust." He was greatly relieved when the caller got to "seat your partners."

As for the crowd, "There were evening suits and décolleté gowns and there were sweaters and jerseys. There was the bud of youth and the wrinkles of old age; there were professors and politicians and pugs. It was a motley crowd.

La Follette Sr., when he became governor of Wisconsin.
WHI IMAGE ID 10900

"The rabble stood near the door. . . . Gradually, however, those in sweaters, some wearing hats and some holding the hands of their best girls, approached the swells and before the grand march the whole immense room was filled with an interested mass of American people."

La Follette would be governor until 1906, when he became a US senator.

The Christmas Tree Ship Disaster

This is what it had come to for the proud sailing ships of the Great Lakes. In the decades after the Civil War, thousands of cargoes of wheat and white pine were shipped on schooners from busy Great Lakes ports, but as wheat faded as a cash crop and the forests were stripped clean these ships were left to scour ports for work.

The Milwaukee-built *Rouse Simmons* was one of these tramp steamers. For more than 20 years the three-masted schooner—125 feet in length and weighing 200 tons—had carried cargo between Muskegon (Michigan) and Chicago. But as business fell off, the ship was sold in 1893 and passed from captain to captain as work allowed.

In 1910, Captain Herman Schuenemann, who with his brother, August, had made a livelihood by hauling Christmas trees each

The *Rouse Simmons*. WHI IMAGE ID 111297

November from Michigan to Chicago, acquired an interest in the *Simmons*.

Thus, the tramp became the Christmas Tree Ship, sailing from the northern woods with evergreens on deck, lashed to masts and rigging. Families would arrive to greet her in Chicago for the pleasure of buying her trees. This seasonal business was so good that in 1912, every available nook was crammed with evergreens, including November 12, when the ship left Thompson Harbor near Manistique, Michigan.

November is the deadliest month on the Great Lakes, and some who watched the *Rouse Simmons* depart that day in a rising wind under gray skies were said to have feared for her safety. Correctly, as it turned out. The temperature dropped and snow began to fall as the ship left its tug escorts and headed into open water. Off the Kewaunee Coast Guard Station the next day, the ship was flying distress signals.

A power boat, *Tuscarora*, rushed to the ship but was hampered by the fierce storm. The *Simmons* was seen covered in ice, sails in tatters, but before the *Tuscarora* could reach its side, snow swirled and contact was lost.

And so was the Christmas Tree Ship. A bottle found later near Sheboygan carried Schuenemann's last written words: "Everybody good-by. I guess we are thru. Leaking bad. Endwald and Steve fell overboard. God help us."

Water-logged evergreens surfaced near the site of the sinking off Two Rivers for years after, but the wreckage of the *Rouse Simmons* was not discovered until 1971, when a scuba diver inspecting another wreck happened upon it. It still contained hundreds of trees, and 59 years after the sinking, two trees—obviously without needles—were brought to Milwaukee, where one was displayed in the lobby of the Marine National Exchange Bank.

The anchor of the *Rouse Simmons* was also retrieved; it stands today at the entrance to the Milwaukee Yacht Club.

W. D. Hoard,
the Dairy Cow's Friend

He was a governor of Wisconsin, a country editor, a university regent, a gifted orator, and a champion of the dairy business who as much as any single figure helped give this state its identity as America's Dairyland.

"Speak to a cow as you would a lady," was Hoard's famous advice to farmers, "and you'll more often get what you want."

Is it not fitting for a man so wise to have a shrine yet today?

Wheat was a weakened king in Wisconsin when Hoard began his efforts to move dairying from an exercise in farm-by-farm self-sufficiency to a nationally-recognized commercial enterprise.

A New York native, he came to Wisconsin in 1857. In 1870, he founded the *Jefferson County Union* newspaper at Fort Atkinson, which preached Hoard's gospel of soil conservation, proper fertilization and better animal care even before he began dairying's new bible, *Hoard's Dairyman* magazine, in 1885.

He envisioned his magazines would compose a library of knowledge for farmers who, he believed, desperately needed to become more professional. Too many farmers, he said, were "using 15 cents worth of knowledge to do $1,000 worth of business."

Hoard was one of the "Seven Wise Men" who in 1872 formed the Wisconsin Dairymen's Association, the first statewide milk producers organization. It fought the good fight on behalf of Wisconsin cheese and butter, vehemently opposed legalization of oleo margarine and engaged in political battles on behalf of the always busy and often solitary dairy farmer.

Hoard eventually entered politics himself and in 1888 ran for governor as a Republican, much to the amusement of some who worried about a chief executive with manure on his boots.

He became known as "the cow candidate." And one newspaper smirked that if he went to Madison, legislators would "draw their biennial plunder" in cheese and silage and the Park Hotel would be required to keep buttermilk on tap.

William Dempster Hoard in 1912.
WHI IMAGE ID 26649

But Hoard won the office, and while leading all the people of Wisconsin, he especially continued to fight dairying's battles.

Today, W. D. Hoard's accomplishment are documented at the Hoard Dairy Shrine and Museum in Fort Atkinson, where the magazine he began continues to preach the need for more professional, better educated dairy managers.

"My life has been devoted to a special effort of demonstrating dairy truth," he wrote a friend in 1906. "Everywhere I am confronted with the fact that fully one-third of farmers do not believe farming is an intellectual pursuit."

Farmers' minds, believed W. D. Hoard, needed fertilizing as much as their fields.

One Last Toast
Greeted Prohibition

It was the day the high life—at least legally—left Wisconsin. On January 16, 1920, Prohibition signaled last call for 9,656 Wisconsin saloons, and the $67,000 the state chapter of the Anti-Saloon League of American had spent in pushing for a ban on beer and booze had paid off.

At $6.93 per shuttered saloon, the league said, the high price of living couldn't touch "the low cost of dying for saloons. Let 'em die while the dying is cheap!"

Of course, rumors of drinking's death were greatly exaggerated.

Wisconsin was dragged kicking and screaming into temperance. Milwaukee breweries employed 6,000 workers and slaked a major share of the nation's thirst for beer. For the many immigrants from beer-drinking countries (78.3% of state residents "had an inherited wet predilection," dry forces calculated) beer-drinking was a cultural pleasure, not the vice opponents saw.

But World War I tipped the balance by putting all Germans under suspicion, even those who cared only about hops, not the Kaiser. True patriots argued grain should be made into bread for fighting men and not for liquor. Still, even as national laws made dry throats appear inevitable, the fight over ratification of the 18th amendment was biting.

The brewing industry argued taxes on liquor were paying for more of the war effort than liberty bonds; the Anti-Saloon League called Milwaukee brewers "the worst of all our German enemies" and dubbed their beer "Kaiser brew."

Governor Emmanuel Philipp ratifying the 18th Amendment on January 17, 1919. From left to right: Executive Messenger Samuel Banks; Senator George B. Skogmo; Secretary. L. C. Whittet; Secretary of State Merlin Hull; Governor E. L. Philipp; and Lieutenant Governor E. F. Dithmar.
WHI IMAGE ID 43009

The Volstead Act banned intoxicating spirits in June 1919 and the 18th Amendment followed. Recognizing the noose had tightened around John Barleycorn's neck, Wisconsin gave its assent—but only grudgingly. Ratification took the votes of 36 states; Wisconsin's was the 39th.

Few expected Prohibition to last, but the last night of legal drinking was special nonetheless. Parties were also wakes; revelers, not yet dry, sang "How Dry I Am," and of course "Taps" was heard.

But the ink on the new law was all that stayed dry. Low-alcohol beer was available, doctors wrote so many prescriptions for "medicinal" spirits it seemed an epidemic had broken out and home brew and bathtub gin were everywhere. Speakeasies sprang up, moonshine stills were built everywhere in rural areas, officials were paid to look the other way and the law was widely ignored.

In 1925 State Senator Bernard Gettelman of Milwaukee, who vociferously defended home brewing as legal, dared Prohibition agents to arrest him.

"Let them come in. Let them taste some of my wine," he said. "They can't prosecute me and they won't try. . . . The joke is on the Anti-Saloon League."

"It must be terrible wine," a league official replied. "They tell me he makes it out of raisins and yeast and potatoes. I can't imagine how he can drink it. Such courage should be applied to legitimate ends."

How Dry We Aren't—
the End of the "Noble Experiment"

For 13 years, the grand experiment that was Prohibition staggered and teetered like the drunks it was supposed to have made extinct, forcing thirsty Americans to improvise but seldom to go without.

Ultimately, it was the dry law that disappeared.

The 1920s experience was not Wisconsin's first experience with controls on drink.

In 1851, prohibitionists had forced a statewide referendum on the issue and won, 27,519 to 24,109.

The Legislature declined to go along, however, and liquor remained legal until the nationwide ban 70 years later.

But colorful as the era of bootleggers and "The Untouchables" seemed years later, Eliot Ness and all the G-men in America couldn't keep the spigots closed. By the early 1930s, beer was on its way back.

Just as anti-German sentiment had added to the push for Prohibition, efforts to fight the ravages of the Great Depression helped bring it to an end. In Milwaukee, legal beer brewing would mean thousands of jobs, first for low-alcohol beer and later for the real stuff. Breweries geared up, even as politicians and wet and dry forces here and in Washington continued to haggle.

When Milwaukeean Mary Eggert, still arguing for temperance, referred to "poisonous alcohol" at a 1931 hearing, Antigo Senator James Barker objected.

"Lady," he said, "I've been drinking alcohol for 55 years and I'm not poisoned."

Celebrating the end of Prohibition (note the people setting fire to the sign).
WHI IMAGE ID 9426

"You wouldn't act like that," Mary Eggert replied, "if you weren't poisoned mentally."

Others sweated the details, whether the percentage of alcohol that would be set or the rate of tax. Some feared too high a tax would make the nickel glass of beer impossible. Hundreds attended hearings on beer regulation.

But brewers, and many beer drinkers, kept their eye on the big picture and were more than ready when low-alcohol beer was legalized again on April 7, 1933.

Lines formed early outside breweries, waiting for beer by the glass and by the barrel.

Others stood outside their favorite former taverns, waiting for them to be transformed again. At 12:01, deliveries began, taps were opened, factory whistles blew and the party began.

Trains and trucks began beer shipments within minutes, returning Milwaukee to its rightful status as brewer to America, and beer was even flown from Milwaukee that night to President Roosevelt in Washington. On April 17, when the city officially celebrated the end of this long, national nightmare, 20,000 people squeezed into the Auditorium to rejoice.

As state Senator H. W. Bolens had said during debate in Madison:

"I am glad that the people of Wisconsin have returned to their senses. . . .

"Happy days are here again."

Super Bowl I
Went to Titletown

The first Super Bowl wasn't officially "Super." It was merely billed on game programs as the "AFL-NFL World Championship Game" of professional football, but then it was played in the days before Roman numerals, back in those understated days when Green Bay Packer fans didn't paint their barns green, shave a G in their dog's hide and tattoo their devotion on bald spots and other bare flesh.

How quaint it all seems now.

On January 15, 1967, at the not-even-sold-out Los Angeles Coliseum, the National Football League's Packers bested the American Football League's Kansas City Chiefs, 35–10, overcoming a slow start to prove their pregame status as heavy (13½ points) favorites had not been an embarrassing miscalculation. (It would be up to Joe Namath in 1969 to turn that applecart upside down.)

A Green Bay Packers sticker.
WHI IMAGE ID 81762

Bart Starr, the hero quarterback, was named the first game's most valuable player, but the great coach Vince Lombardi got the game ball. Max McGee was the talk of the country for his unexpected appearance off the bench—not to mention his sensational touchdown catches—and there were celebrations of other legendary Packers as well.

Three challenge games were played between the champions of the two leagues before the rival leagues agreed to merge on May 17, 1969. No one, of course, could foresee what the Super Bowl would become—a near-official national holiday marked by every manner of corporate excess but seldom a game for the ages—but then as now America's newspapers felled entire forests to publish their assessments.

In comments that would come in handy in future Januarys, Pete Waldmeir of the *Detroit News* called the game "overemphasized and overexposed" and concluded it proved nothing.

Steve Weller of the *Buffalo Evening News* griped that it went too much according to script, right down to the release of thousands of pigeons that promptly flew away. "It would have been a better story," he wrote, "if the pigeons or the Packers had made a mistake."

And the *Milwaukee Journal's* Oliver Kuechle, noting almost one-third of the 93,000 seats were empty, wrote that "the future of the game now is in some doubt." He more correctly touched on the winner's share of $15,000 per player and said "a new chapter has been opened in modern professional football history—the Gravy Bowl."

Even then, by the way, the modern Packers' famous follow-them-anywhere faithful made their mark.

A fan at the top of the stands behind the Kansas City end zone held a sign that read:

"Canal Zone for G. B."

The Siege at Gresham

The 1975 takeover of a remote Wisconsin novitiate was an Indian rebellion for TV times, a long-running standoff with moments of drama, violence, comedy and, ultimately, tragedy. It was waged against the backdrop of 1970s activism that rocked American life, but its lasting effects are difficult to trace.

The facility on the Red River near Gresham, in Shawano County, had been built as a mansion for an East Coast executive. It later was bought by the Alexian Brothers, a Catholic order, who added a 64-room novitiate, but it was empty when heavily armed American Indians seized it on New Year's Day.

The Menominee Warriors Society, as they were called, demanded that the estate be turned over for use as a tribal health facility.

"We are prepared to die," a warrior vowed. "Let me make sure you know that."

They were indeed taken seriously. Society members carrying rifles patrolled the building's roof and grounds, while county and state officials established a military-style noose around the property. Checkpoints were set up and hundreds of National Guard members bolstered the force outside while activists from national Indian groups came to lend their aid.

But a settlement eluded negotiators.

The takeover force had not prepared well. Needing food, several of the protestors went from the novitiate to a nearby supermarket. When Guardsmen refused them re-entry, a newspaper remarked, "Indian uprisings just aren't what they used to be."

Wisconsin National Guard and an armored personnel carrier at the Novitiate during the siege. WHI IMAGE ID 83076

On January 31, a deadline for Indian evacuation, actor Marlon Brando and James Groppi, the Milwaukee priest and civil rights leader, arrived in Shawano, joined in a drum ceremony and then entered the novitiate, Groppi with sleeping bag in hand.

The takeover was not without flash points. Gunfire was reported often. Snowmobilers slipped through the barricades one night and fired shots at the novitiate, and a group of white citizens angered by the protracted dispute threatened to attack if Guardsmen would not.

Said Brando later: "It was a little like Disneyland in the beginning. And then when we were up on the roof and the bullets started to fly all around us, then there was a certain kind of reality."

The takeover ended February 4. An agreement called for the Menominees to purchase the facility at some point, but it never happened. Months later, arson gutted the mansion, and various plans for the heavily damaged facility have all fallen through.

Five Menominees faced charges; one died in a shootout with police before trial. Takeover leader Michael Sturdevant was convicted of nine felonies and sentenced to prison, but not without a final twist.

At sentencing, one of his character witnesses was Hugh Simonson, the National Guard colonel who had led the troops outside.

August Derleth
and the Wisconsin River

It stretches the truth only slightly to suggest that in the time it takes to read the story of August Derleth, Derleth could have written three more.

The sage of Sauk City, who worked and walked his entire life along his beloved Wisconsin River, was Wisconsin's most prolific writer, "a one-man fiction factory" as he was sometimes called.

Derleth published more than 150 books, ranging from poetry and historical novels to the macabre. He wrote thousands of articles and short stories and sometimes pumped out 10,000 words a day. He also lectured on writing and operated his own publishing houses, but in his heart he was a writer.

Many of his works were set in the "fictional" small town of Sac Prairie, which everyone knew as a synthesis of Sauk City and its riverside twin, Prairie du Sac. Though nominally fiction, the dozens of works in this "Sac Prairie Saga" told of the joys and often unrealized hopes and dreams of Derleth and his neighbors who served as stand-ins for small towns everywhere.

But nature, and especially the Wisconsin River, were constants in his work. It gave him his sense of place, and so it was only right that Derleth was selected to tell the river's story for the "Rivers of America" series of books commissioned during the Great Depression.

In the summer of 1941, he and illustrator John Steuart Curry roamed the river's fishing holes and sand bars and swimming spots, and eventually he wrote:

August Derleth in 1942. WHI IMAGE ID 45660

"There is something about running water that has an enduring magic for a man.

"A brook or small river is an intimate thing; strangely, perhaps because of its many beautiful islands and its heavily wooded shores in those regions away from the power dams, the Wisconsin is an intimate river, though it is not a small river in any sense of the word.

"The river remembers past things, the aspects of life gone by forever—the Indians, the black robes, the voyageurs and the engagés, and traders; the redcoats moving along this wilderness route to seize the fort at Prairie du Chien; the raftsmen and the lumberjacks, the lead miners, the steamboats, and the river pilots who battled ceaselessly against the shifting islands and the sand . . .

"The wing dams are overgrown with willows and cottonwoods: the haunt of fishermen now; the highways and the railroads carry the commerce that once the Wisconsin bore on its surface; but the essential river has changed perhaps less than many rivers its size on the North American continent.

"The river of a thousand isles . . ." he called the Wisconsin.

His river, but not only his. No one he spoke to about the Wisconsin ever called it *our* river, he noted, but always my river.

It was proof, he said, of the Wisconsin's hold on its people. And especially on him.

The Shooting of Teddy Roosevelt

On the train taking him to his new home in Oshkosh, erstwhile New York bartender John Schrank was enjoying the countryside when someone asked whether he liked to hunt.

"Only Bull Moose," he replied. And hadn't he just tried to kill the biggest Bull Moose of all?

Theodore Roosevelt, the former president, was running for president again when he came to Milwaukee on October 14, 1912, for an appearance at the Milwaukee Auditorium. Shortly after 8 p.m., he tucked his thick speech into his breast pocket and departed the Gilpatrick Hotel.

Schrank, a 36-year-old Bavarian immigrant who had stalked the candidate for weeks, was waiting outside. He pulled a revolver from his coat and fired. The bullet smacked Roosevelt in the chest, but first it plowed through his heavy coat, lengthy speech and glasses case. One or all likely saved Roosevelt. While staggered by the bullet, he lost neither consciousness nor his famous bluster.

"Where you hit?" his aide, Henry Cochems, asked.

"He pinked me, Henry," Roosevelt said.

Though he was bleeding and his backers advised immediate treatment, Roosevelt insisted on delivering his message to Milwaukee. At the Auditorium, he suffered a doctor's examination, covered the wound with a handkerchief and took the stage.

Some in the audience were shocked to hear Roosevelt had been an assassin's target; others would not believe it. But the visibly bloodstained shirt was persuasive and not a bad dramatic device. A few minutes later, Roosevelt faltered but steadied himself and again denied pleas to cancel the speech.

Teddy Roosevelt leaving the Chicago and North Western depot after arriving in Milwaukee on his October 14th, 1912, visit, during which he was shot and wounded. WHI IMAGE ID 2096

"It takes more than one bullet to kill a Bull Moose," he said, and he proceeded to speak for an hour.

Roosevelt died with Schrank's bullet in his chest, but not for some years and then of other causes. He was rushed from the speech to a Milwaukee hospital, still saying he was not seriously wounded, but doctors insisted on taking him to a Chicago expert for care and recuperation.

"I don't want Milwaukee to feel badly about this," he was quoted in an account of the shooting by Stan Gores. "It wasn't the city's fault."

Despite the political upside that goes with surviving an assassination attempt, Roosevelt lost the election to Woodrow Wilson. If his marksmanship was a disappointment, the results should have pleased Schrank, whose half-addled explanation for the shooting was that he had not wanted to kill Roosevelt the man, only "Roosevelt the third termer."

Schrank resented a panel's finding that he was a lunatic, but his protestations of sanity could not save him from a life sentence to an Oshkosh hospital for the insane. And when a newsman inquired about his sanity en route to the hospital, Schrank hinted that he wasn't all that different from many in Wisconsin.

"The doctors say I am not and I say I am," he said. "I'm not worrying, though. The only thing I have to complain about is that they don't sell bottled beer on this train. I'm thirsty."

Schrank died, still in the asylum, in 1943.

John Deitz and
the Battle of Cameron Dam

John Deitz was Wisconsin's David, a little man with a Winchester rifle, who warred with lumber giants. Highly romanticized hero to supporters, gun-crazy anarchist to opponents, "The Defender of Cameron Dam" caught the nation's eye—and its fancy—in the waning days of the timber era.

His Goliath was the Chippewa Lumber and Boom Co., part of the giant Weyerhaeuser umbrella. Deitz bought 160 acres near the company's Cameron dam on the Thornapple River in Sawyer County and in 1940 moved his family there.

But tangled papers and Deitz's stubborn, contrary nature conspired to turn his dreams into melodramatic tragedy. First, the farm deed incorrectly omitted the company's dam and flowage rights. Then, when Deitz felt wronged by the company's denial of money he felt he was owed for back wages and for spring flood damage on his land, he demanded a toll on all logs that passed through the dam. The company refused, and when crews reached Cameron dam in 1904, Deitz was there with his Winchester.

For two years Deitz kept at bay not only lumber crews, but lawyers, the sheriff, various marshals and others who tried to intervene. Supporters, including his sons Clarence and Leslie, helped him guard the dam, ignoring every legal and emotional plea to end a standoff that had far outgrown its roots.

"DEITZ WILL FIGHT TO DEATH," read newspaper headlines, further building the image of the poor man wronged by the forces of wealth and power.

The Deitz family, 1906. WHI IMAGE ID 26626

The romance turned bloody on July 25, 1906, when the Sawyer County sheriff and an armed posse from Milwaukee—dressed as local militia—surprised Deitz and his family. A shot parted Clarence's hair, leaving him bloodied, and one intruder was also wounded.

The legend was truly aloft. While the sheriff told the press, "The only way to take Deitz is to kill the whole family . . . ," others rallied to the man who had been beset by company-hired thugs. What had begun as a misguided dispute over property rights was suddenly a national rallying point in the class struggle.

Sympathetic reporters from all over deified Deitz. Letters of support flooded the governor's office, discouraging further use of force. Milwaukee socialists especially rushed to his support; a Milwaukee theatrical agent offered to put Deitz on stage, even promising bail money if he was arrested.

Eventually, Deitz settled with the company for back wages and his battle should have ended. But in 1910, a fight broke out in town and Dietz, ever the combatant, shot and almost killed his antagonist. In attempting to serve an arrest warrant, authorities wounded Deitz's daughter and arrested his son, and Deitz's last stand was on.

Faced with a force of nearly 75 men, Deitz resisted again. During a fantastic shootout, hundreds of bullets hit the cabin where he and his family sought cover. Far fewer shots were returned, but one killed Deputy Oscar Harp.

Light years from the property rights tussle that had lit the fuse, Deitz was tried for murder. Despite public sympathy, again in large portion from Milwaukee, he was convicted. His life sentence was later reduced, and he rejoined his family in Milwaukee, where he died in 1924.

The lumber era preceded him in death.

High on Milk—the Saga
of Elm Farm Ollie

Among the many notable "firsts" recorded by Wisconsin natives this feat might not make the top 10, but it was a high achievement nonetheless.

It occurred on February 18, 1930, when dairy interests found an eye-catching way to promote milk at the St. Louis International Air Exposition. As the proud, if partisan, *Milwaukee Journal* reported on its front page:

"Elsworth W. Bunce, former *Journal* carrier and graduate of West Division High School, has the distinction of being the first man to milk a cow in an airplane flight."

Ollie, the first cow milked on an airplane. BARRY LEVENSON

It was, of course, a first for cows, as well. Her name was Elm Farm Ollie, a Guernsey whose nickname became "Sky Queen" after her historic flight.

Accompanied by reporters, her mission was "to blaze a trail for the transportation of livestock by air," said a St. Louis newspaper, by allowing scientists to observe the effects of flight on her demeanor and milk production.

Elm Farm Ollie was fed and milked during the 72-mile flight from Bismarck, Missouri, to St. Louis. Her milk was sealed in paper containers and dropped over the city of St. Louis.

Ollie's stunt proved so popular that a large crowd, apparently thirsty for milk, gathered on the field where her plane was to land, forcing it to be diverted.

Bunce was chosen for the airborne breakthrough not for his paper carrying skills but because he worked for the American Guernsey Cattle Club. The flying cow's singular achievement is still celebrated by a small group of Madison residents who belong to the Elm Farm Ollie Fan Club, which once commissioned an operetta about the event. They called it "Moocini's *Madam Butterfat.*"

Dr. Kate, the Angel on Snowshoes

She was called simply "Dr. Kate," and this was her life. Born in Kansas in 1886, raised in Boston and trained in Buffalo, Kate Pelham Newcomb began her medical career in the poor neighborhoods of New York, where she delivered hundreds of babies, and later worked in Detroit.

But it was in the northern Wisconsin community of Woodruff where she became an angel. Newcomb had moved to the woods with her husband, William, in hopes fresh air would help her minister to his health problems.

Dr. Kate had once rejected marriage to a man who wanted a country practice, so naturally she was pressed into a practice that involved not only country but remote forests, as well. It wasn't exactly wilderness in 1931 when she began treating the ills of northern Wisconsin residents, but 70 square miles of woods was far from the world she had known.

Dr. Kate with the "World's Biggest Penny." DR. KATE MUSEUM, WOODRUFF, WI

She didn't adjust, she thrived. On snowshoes, by canoe, by long treks through snowy logging roads, Dr. Kate reached patients who had summoned her with, "Come quick, Doc!" Her Ford Model T was fitted with skis.

She was often the only doctor available for 7,000 residents and many more thousands of summer visitors.

"Self-sufficient in so many ways, they need help badly at times," she once said. But if she was their medical godmother, she had no illusions about her powers. She always remembered a physician-teacher's admonition.

" 'Never go into a sick room without a prayer on your lips.' To this day I still do," she said.

The area had a doctor but desperately needed a hospital. So with just $3,000 in hand, a hospital was begun, again with a prayer for help. It came in the form of a million-penny campaign involving local children, a feel-good story irresistible to newspapers of the day. Donations poured in.

The hospital was still $30,000 in debt when Dr. Kate's story went Hollywood. Lured to Hollywood for what she thought would be a conference, Dr. Kate instead found herself on the popular *This Is Your Life* program, where host Ralph Edwards appealed to viewers to help the "Angel on Snowshoes" pay for her hospital.

"Aid for State's 'Dr. Kate' Swamping Tiny Post Office," a *Milwaukee Journal* headline read days later. Mail had fallen like snow on Woodruff. Workers used bushel baskets, banana crates and cardboard boxes to store the 82 pouches of mail that ultimately yielded more than $100,000.

When Dr. Kate arrived home, driving a new car presented to her on the TV show, she was a bigger heroine than ever. The second annual "Penny Parade" in 1954 was called the largest in northern Wisconsin history, with 90 floats and 15 bands marching before an estimated 25,000 people.

Not long after, Dr. Kate's funeral procession was also of storied proportions. She fell in 1956 and broke a hip, underwent surgery but suffered complications. It surprised no one to hear a doctor say that a tired heart muscle had failed their doctor. At the age of 69 she had given so much of it to them.

Jesse James Strang,
Wisconsin's Own King

In just the eighth year of Wisconsin statehood, its first king died and was buried near Burlington, where a stone marker still describes his vanished kingdom.

Of course, not every knee bowed to "King" James Jesse Strang, but his bizarre and charismatic style drew enough followers—and wives—to make him one of early Wisconsin's most fascinating characters.

Strang came to Burlington from New York in 1843, where he soon joined the thriving Mormon community there. He was personally baptized by Mormon founder and prophet Joseph Smith in Illinois and immediately returned to establish a Mormon settlement near the White River in Walworth County.

He named his new paradise Voree, which he said meant "garden of peace," and began recruiting followers. A short time later, when Smith and his brother were killed by a mob, Strang pulled off his ultimate recruitment. He produced a letter, which he said Smith had written just days before his death, naming none other than James Jesse Strang the next Mormon prophet.

Smelling a rat, elders drummed Strang from the fold, but he returned to Burlington undaunted. In September 1844, he led followers to what he named the Hill of Promise and directed them to dig. Amazingly, they found copper plates covered with strange writing. Even more amazing, only Strang could interpret the symbols as bolstering his status as prophet.

Some followers had had enough, but believing converts by the hundreds streamed to Voree. Strang, who already published

Strang in 1855. WHI IMAGE ID 125396

a newspaper, ordered construction of a vast marble "Temple of Zion" and other grand structures, but even as his community was growing he sensed the resentment of non-Mormons nearby and decided to move.

In 1847, he declared the Lord had directed the community to move to Beaver Island in Lake Michigan, and so the residents of Voree left Racine harbor to build what would become the new village of St. James.

New rules applied there. Strang declared St. James a kingdom, and he was its king. Coronation came on July 8, 1850, when Strang, wearing an old actor's red cape and metal crown studded with stars, paraded before his subjects as "King James I of Beaver Island, apostle, seer, revelator and translator."

To the dismay of non-Mormons in the area, Strang reversed his earlier opposition to polygamy and took several new wives, although his first wife immediately left him. But Strang was certainly not despised by everyone; he was twice elected to the Michigan legislature.

The king's raging ego and dictatorial style caused his demise, however. On June 16, 1856, Strang was ambushed by two disgruntled subjects. Wounded, apparently dying, Strang asked to be returned to Voree, and so two of his wives—Betsy and Phoebe—took him down Lake Michigan, then by wagon to Burlington.

Strang died in Voree on July 9, in a house across the road from where the marker still stands, and most of what has been his "garden of peace" eventually disappeared.

The Hodag and the Hoaxer
—Eugene Shepard

The Hodag, like Paul Bunyan, grew out of the can-you-top-this storytelling of rough and tumble lumber camps, where outlying the next man was both accomplishment and evening's entertainment.

In that circle, not many could top the silver-tongued Eugene Shepard, a master at cruising timber stands and estimating their worth. He was also a land speculator, surveyor, resort owner and, when his spending was under control, one of Rhinelander's wealthiest men. Shepard became a North Woods legend when he raised the Hodag up from lumberjack lore by "capturing" one and offering it to the world at large.

And the world lined up to look.

Shepard's life of pranks led some to call him "the P. T. Barnum of northern Wisconsin." When he owned a resort at Star Lake, he would rig wooden muskies with wires and make them jump, the better to encourage guests to stay another day.

The exotic scented moss he charged tourists two bits to smell, or more to buy, was later found to be regular moss sprayed with cheap perfume. He imported a pair of moose from Minnesota to pull him through town in a horse buggy.

Shepard did not invent the Hodag, which was already known in lumberjack stories as the horned beast that grew from the ashes of a cremated logging ox. (Logging oxen, of course, had to be cremated to rid their souls of the considerable profanity directed their way by lumberjacks.) The Hodag that grew from the ashes

A staged hodag capture. WHI IMAGE ID 36382

was large, mean, horned, fanged, green-eyed and smelled like a combination of buzzard meat and skunk perfume.

If Shepard did not invent the legend, however, he invented the first Hodag anyone ever saw.

In 1896, the Oneida County Fair was hurting for big attractions when organizers wondered whether Shepard had any ideas.

Did he? Shepard arranged the carving of a Hodag from a wood stump, fitted it with hide and horns and announced this beast captured near Lake Creek outside Rhinelander would be displayed at the fair. Come one, come all.

The Hodag was kept in a dark cage in dim light, but hundreds came to see what they could, paying their hard-earned 10 cents each to hear Shepard describe the capture. The ruse was so successful he took the Hodag on the road, first to other county fairs but once to the Wisconsin State Fair.

Travelers began seeking out Shepard's house. When they arrived, his sons would sneak into the Hodag's quarters, move its limbs with wires, growl and moan and rattle a fence to suggest the animal's ferocity. Some say P. T. Barnum himself came to view the Hodag and offered to buy it, but one Shepard biographer suggests the Barnum angle was just another layer of the escalating hoax.

Oddly, the Hodag remained an attraction after the ruse was revealed and continued to draw tourists. So Shepard continued telling the story, ever enhancing the grisly details, no matter that each new story contradicted the last.

Shepard's Hodag eventually was lost in a fire, but Rhinelander remains Hodag Country to this day. The myth, captured, became real.

Margarethe Schurz and
the First Kindergarten

Kindergarten, Margarethe Meyer Schurz once explained, was a garden for the crop called children.

She was passionate about the point. And, if not for this German-born woman who made Wisconsin her home, children might have forever started their education in the numerically correct—but nurturingly inappropriate—first grade.

Margarethe Meyer was born in Hamburg in 1833 to a prominent family that encouraged her to pursue the arts and education. There she was exposed as a teenager to the teachings of kindergarten founder and advocate Friedrich Froebel. When Meyer came to America—by then married to Carl Schurz, who would gain his own fame for political activism in Wisconsin—she carried Froebel's ideas with her.

They settled in Watertown in 1856. There, the story goes, Margarethe employed Froebel's philosophy while caring for her daughter, Agathe, and four neighbor children, leading them in games and songs and group activities that channeled their energy while preparing them for school at the same time.

Other parents were so impressed at the results that they prevailed upon Schurz to help their children, so she opened a small kindergarten, the first in the United States.

The idea began to spread, in part because Schurz would accompany her husband on his political travels and preach kindergarten's benefits. When a mother once complimented Agathe's behavior and leadership of other children as nothing short of a miracle, Schurz demurred.

Margarethe Meyer Schurz. WHI IMAGE ID 4681

"No miracle," she said. "Just brought up in a kindergarten."

She later said that Froebel credited her with expressing his views better than his own books had. Her work certainly gained an audience; kindergarten became an accepted and integral part of American education and an accepted course of study for elementary teachers.

Margarethe was troubled with poor health her entire life. In 1876, just 42 years old, she died at her family's home in New York.

In Watertown, the building that housed her first kindergarten was restored, and today it is identified by a historical marker even a 5-year-old could appreciate.

Laura Ingalls Wilder
and the Wisconsin Frontier

Laura Ingalls Wilder, whose stories of frontier life in Wisconsin began with *Little House in the Big Woods*, was always surprised that her books sold so well.

"Children who read it wrote to me begging for more," she said.

"I was amazed because I didn't know how to write. I went to little red schoolhouses all over the west and I never was graduated from anything."

She was too modest. She told stories very well, and the tales she didn't begin sharing until age 65 graduated her from a mere senior citizen with captivating experiences to bestselling author.

Children with an interest in log cabin life owe her a debt of gratitude, as did the actor Michael Landon and his television cast.

Laura Ingalls was born in 1867 in a cabin at Pepin, a Mississippi River village in western Wisconsin. She spent her early childhood there, absorbing memories that would become literature decades later, before her father decided the area was becoming crowded with settlers and moved the family to Kansas in the early 1870s.

She continued to move about, to Minnesota, South Dakota and, after her marriage to Almanzo Wilder in 1885 when she was 18, to a farm near Mansfield, Missouri.

A former teacher, she had written articles for farm magazines before her daughter, Rose, urged her to record her family experiences. After *Little House in the Big Woods* was published in 1935, the reading public's appetite for more stories was such that an entire "Little House" series followed. The books were somewhat

Carrie, Mary, and Laura Ingalls, ca. 1880, six years after leaving
Wisconsin. LAURA INGALLS WILDER HISTORIC HOME AND MUSEUM

fictionalized but largely autobiographical, describing the joys and
hardships of her childhood frontier life in Wisconsin and her
family's travels west.

Wilder won many awards for her books, which remain popular today, no doubt in part because of the *Little House* TV series.
A park and memorial museum are operated near Pepin today for
summer visitors, and while she lived in the cabin for just her early
years, it is the appropriate spot for her memory to be preserved.

"For Laura, this is where it all began—in the Big Woods of
Wisconsin," wrote her biographer, Donald Zochert.

"In winter, snow flew through the long night. By morning's light it gleamed and crackled in giant drifts against the walls of Pa's house. In spring the flowers came bright and bountiful. Then the little clearing in the Big Woods rang with the sound of Pa's axe and the barking of a brindle bulldog named Jack . . ."

Laura Ingalls Wilder died in 1957.

First Snowmobile
Born in Sayner

Long before it was associated with winter fun and became an integral part of the northern economy—and before ever-increasing speeds and often foolhardy behavior revealed the sport's dark side—the snowmobile had true Wisconsin roots.

It was invented by a hunter with bad feet, a man who only wanted to keep up with his party.

"Even when someone else was breaking a trail, I was always several blocks behind," Carl Eliason once explained.

That was in the early 1920s in Sayner, in northern Wisconsin's Vilas County, where long winters allowed time for dealing with such problems.

In his workshop, Eliason took a pair of skis, mounted a small motor on them and added other parts from a Model T Ford. Using bicycle parts from Milwaukee, a rope-controlled steering device and various other make-do parts, Eliason produced in 1924 the first engine-powered ski machine.

Suddenly, Eliason was faster than his buddies on snowshoes. Over the next few years he patented his invention, even as he continued to increase its size and power.

Neighbors, of course, soon wanted sleds of their own. So Eliason began building them during winter months, employing men who would come in after deer season and work until spring came. He charged about $350 for the sleds, though no two were alike.

In the early 1930s, *Popular Mechanics* magazine spread word of his creation far and wide and more orders poured in. And, as

Winter scene of an early snowmobile race at Rangeline Lake, January 31, 1926. WHI IMAGE ID 113685

happens, man found a way to use something designed for one purpose in quite another pursuit—war.

When an order for 200 machines came from the Finnish government, just one of a number of countries said to have realized the snow sled's potential in winter combat—Eliason realized demand had outstripped his ability to produce. He sold patent rights to the Four Wheel Drive Company of Clintonville, which assembled machines in Appleton and, later, in Canada. Eliason went on to produce other inventions, including patented weedless fish hooks.

Eliason's original sled is in Sayner yet today, where a marker describes his contribution to northern life.

It also notes that the first snowmobile race was held in Three Lakes in 1926. More than 100 "snow buggies" took part.

Pearling in Wisconsin

It was Wisconsin's iridescent era, those years of underwater prospecting when Prairie du Chien was a national "Pearl Capital."

The city that sits where the Wisconsin River is introduced to the Mississippi was for several decades the center of a long-gone but colorful era of commercial clamming.

Clamming took place on other rivers, as well, including the Sugar, Pecatonica and Rock. But from about 1890 to 1920, fortune seekers engaged in large-scale pearl hunting on the Mississippi. Fashion had created an appetite for pearl adornments, and many could be found hidden in the mud and muck of Wisconsin rivers.

"In the summer," wrote M. J. Dyrud in the *Wisconsin Magazine of History*, "clammers' tents lined the Mississippi River shore.

"An enterprising Prairie du Chien grocer operated a store launch, delivering food and supplies to river customers. This service was welcomed by the rivermen, who were up at dawn and worked until dusk, raking clams into their boats after each floating pass across the submerged clam beds."

The boatmen would drag the bottom with rods hung with many small hooks; as the hooks caught in open shells of feeding clams or mussels the clams would react by closing their mouths, thus becoming hooked. The clams were steamed in large boilers and, when the meat was removed, inspected for pearls.

Clam shells sold to button factories created significant income; tons of shells were sold during good years. But pearls were the lure, and pearl buyers competed for the pink, salmon, green, black and multishaded prizes.

A clam fisher in a boat on the Mississippi River near Prairie du Chien, September 1928. WHI IMAGE ID 64433

The "Genoa pearl," named for the bed in which it was found, was nearly 1 inch in diameter. Veteran buyer John Peacock once paid a clammer $1,500 for a pearl he called the most beautiful he had ever seen and later sold it to a Chicago dealer for $5,000, who sold it to a New York buyer for $10,000, who in turn sold it in England for $20,000.

Wisconsin exhibited $150,000 worth of freshwater pearls at the 1893 Columbian Exposition, a collection later purchased by Tiffany and Co. of New York.

But all good things, even pearling, come to an end. Exhausted beds and the advent of cultured pearls brought an end to clamming in Wisconsin.

Louis Harvey,
the Governor Lost in War

Every state engaged in the bloody business that was this nation's Civil War suffered terrible casualties, but how many lost an elected governor with so many young men?

Such was the unusual fate of Wisconsin Governor Louis P. Harvey, a civilian who had wanted only to come to the aid of his state's suffering soldiers, not to join them in death.

In 1862, Wisconsin soldiers fought at the battle of Shiloh, where superior numbers of Confederate troops extracted a high price in dead and wounded.

Fighting was especially fierce for the 18th Wisconsin Regiment, which had arrived at the front after departing Milwaukee only a week earlier.

All were new to battle; some were even new to firearms.

"Many of the men," Harvey wrote from the battlefield just days later, "heard the order to load and fire for the first time in their lives in the presence of the enemy."

Harvey had rushed to Tennessee on a mission of mercy. When word of Wisconsin's troops' heavy losses reached Madison, Harvey appealed for medical supplies and led the expedition to the scene. He and his party accompanied a train car filled with supplies, ministered to constituent soldiers and arranged to have some sent home.

But Harvey would not go home alive.

On the rainy night of April 19, 1862, just 73 days after taking office, Harvey was aboard the steamer *Dunleith* attempting to transfer to another steamer, the *Minnehaha*, when he lost his

Portrait of Republican Louis P. Harvey, while he was Wisconsin's secretary of state (1860–1861).
WHI IMAGE ID 37904

footing and fell. His companions were unable to save him or to find his body; it was recovered more than 60 miles down the Tennessee River a few days later and returned to Wisconsin for burial.

Harvey's widow, Cordelia, then joined her husband's relief effort despite the tragic turn it had taken.

She began working with wounded soldiers and became a much-recognized hospital visitor and nurse. Soldiers were said to have dubbed her "the Wisconsin angel."

Cordelia Harvey carried her campaign right to the top. She met with President Lincoln and persuaded him to authorize soldiers' hospitals in the North, where conditions would be more sanitary and hospitable.

Three were eventually established in Wisconsin, at Madison, Milwaukee and Prairie du Chien. The Madison facility was named Harvey Soldiers' Hospital in 1863. When it later became an orphanage for soldiers' children, Cordelia Harvey became its first superintendent.

Louis Harvey was buried in Forest Hill Cemetery in Madison, where other prominent political figures joined him.

In a bit of wartime irony, Forest Hill also became the resting place of 140 Confederate soldiers, all prisoners of war who had died while being held in Madison. Harvey's remains lie not far from "Confederate Rest."

The Utopian Experiment
at Ceresco

Wisconsin was still four years from statehood when a group of farmers decided to build a Utopian settlement, an experimental society of collective living, shared labor, resources and profits.

Less than two years into statehood, they abandoned the effort.

The interesting thing was, by most accounts their efforts were a success.

The Utopian community that established a settlement in Fond du Lac County, in what today is Ripon, was one of many that sprang up in the mid-1800s across the country.

Its founders, mostly farmers from near Southport (now Kenosha) were influenced by the teachings of Charles Fourier, a French socialist, who had written a complex set of rules for establishing such communities. His plan had gotten much attention during economic downturns when suffering workers looked for a better way.

In May 1844, the 20 founding families purchased the land, built the first houses and set to work to build a farming operation that would support them.

The communal village was named Ceresco, after Ceres the goddess of agriculture. Its most notable feature, after its philosophy, was the "longhouse"—32 feet wide by more than 200 feet long—which offered living space, a community dining hall and kitchen.

Support buildings—a mill, school and other structures—were added. By 1846, the community had grown to 180 residents and was generally following Fourier's precepts for living—and getting along—together.

View of "Long House," one of the Ceresco buildings, 1910. WHI IMAGE ID 39675

There was payment for work by each member, and skilled workers were rewarded with extra allowances. Careful records were kept. The first year workers performed 102,760 hours of labor, and the return was good for the times.

There were strict rules for behavior—liquor, for example, was not allowed—and property was owned in common. And by most accounts the rules led to an agreeable community, unlike some other Utopian experiments that ended badly, with little dissension or unhappiness. It probably helped that profits were good.

But success was not enough. By most accounts, the lifestyle was not exciting enough to suit all residents. Some families began withdrawing from communal meals and other activities, then from the community altogether as opportunities elsewhere appeared more enticing.

The new state of Wisconsin was still taking its first shaky steps when the community was disbanded. Ripon's Ceresco Park commemorates what is left of Utopia.

Aldo Leopold,
Father of Conservation

The world is neatly divided into two camps, Aldo Leopold knew, as he also knew his side was a decided minority.

In his preface to his famous *A Sand County Almanac*, he wrote:

"There are some who can live without wild things and some who cannot. These essays are the delights and dilemmas of one who cannot."

The delights and dilemmas Leopold found at his Sauk County farm, sometimes at 3:30 a.m. when he left his shack with notebook and coffee cup in hand to listen and learn, became an environmental primer when *Almanac* was published in 1949, after his death.

Leopold's observations on land-use management and appeals for a land ethic made him the father of conservationism. The University of Wisconsin–Madison dedicated a wildlife management chair to him in 1933. He understood the intricate interconnections of wild things, but Leopold's lessons were as basic as a sore back suffered for a good cause:

"Acts of creation," he wrote in his *Almanac*, "are ordinarily reserved for gods and poets, but humbler folk may circumvent this restriction if they know how. To plant a pine, for example, one need be neither god nor poet; one need only own a shovel. By virtue of this curious loophole in the rules, any clodhopper may say: Let there be a tree—and there will be one."

Leopold's refuge was near Baraboo along the Wisconsin River, which since 1968 has been part of the 1,300-acre Leopold

Aldo Leopold inspecting white pine at his Wisconsin River retreat, 1946.
WHI IMAGE ID 93909

Memorial Reserve. The property includes his old shack, now listed on the National Register of Historic Places.

That was where Leopold would watch the dance of the woodcock at nightfall, or eagerly await the return of the geese each year.

"One swallow does not make a summer," he said, "but one skein of geese, cleaving the murk of a March thaw, is the spring.

"A March morning is only as drab as he who walks in it without a glance skyward, ear cocked for geese. I once knew an educated lady, banded by Phi Beta Kappa, who told me that she had never heard or seen the geese that twice a year proclaim the revolving seasons to her well-insulated roof.

"Is education possibly a process of trading awareness for things of lesser worth? The goose who trades his is soon a pile of feathers."

Leopold often wished to be a muskrat, the better to savor the sounds and special moments of the marsh he so loved. But Leopold enjoyed his sand country and the streams that ran through it. After a spectacular streamside episode in which he filled his creel with wily trout, he wrote:

"I shall now confess to you that none of those three trout had to be beheaded, or folded double, to fit their casket. What was big was not the trout, but the chance. What was full was not my creel, but my memory."

Daniel Hale Williams,
First Heart Surgeon

Before he turned to medicine, Daniel H. Williams trimmed heads. And but for the generosity of a Wisconsin man, the black doctor who won worldwide fame for conducting the first open-heart surgery might never have traded in his scissors for scalpels.

It would be the good fortune of one James Cornish that Williams got the boost he needed.

Williams came to Wisconsin from Baltimore, where he had been an apprentice shoemaker, and at age 17 opened a barbershop in Edgerton.

He later moved to Janesville, where he worked in a barbershop operated by Harry Anderson and lived in Anderson's home. But his interest was soon to turn to medicine. At 22, he became an apprentice to a Janesville doctor, Henry Palmer.

With Palmer's help, Williams entered medical studies in Chicago, at what later would become Northwestern University's medical school. It was his former boss, Anderson, who supported Williams with loans during his studies, allowing him to concentrate on medicine instead of having to work as well.

Daniel Hale Williams.
NORTHWESTERN UNIVERSITY
ARCHIVES

"I hate to ask for it," he once wrote to Anderson, "but what am I to do?"

In 1883, at age 27, Williams graduated and began a successful practice in Chicago, where he also advocated for better medical care for blacks and for the establishment of a hospital where black and white doctors could work side by side.

Thus began Provident Hospital, where Cornish was brought one late July night in 1893 with a chest stab wound suffered in a tavern brawl.

At first, the wound did not appear serious, but Williams soon saw that Cornish was suffering pain and was in shock, and he decided an operation was his only recourse.

Ignoring traditional treatment, Williams opened up Cornish's chest and found a puncture of the sac enclosing the heart. He sewed up the wound with sutures, left the heart wall alone and closed Cornish back up.

Cornish remained in critical condition for several days, and a second surgery was needed to remove a buildup of fluids, but recovery then began. Two months later, he was released from the hospital in good health.

It was the world's first recorded heart surgery. For Cornish, it was the ultimate close shave. For Williams, it was history.

Legal Oleo Ended
Wisconsin's Smuggling Era

As Wisconsin would take up arms today to defend green and gold, friends of the dairy cow once defended butter yellow. Indeed, the long battle over colored oleo in America's Dairyland inspired its own William Jennings Bryan moments.

Legalizing oleo, Representative Frank Nikolay once declared, would "crucify the family size farmer on a cross of oleo-margarine."

But butter's protected era, and decades of otherwise law-abiding Wisconsin residents sneaking across state borders for colored oleo, would soon be over.

Wisconsin was the last state to allow sale of yellow oleo. The ban was put in place in 1895; in 1931, 5,000 farmers marched on Madison demanding a tax even on unappetizing-looking white oleo.

Once 32 states had such restrictions. But all had melted away by the mid-1960s as changes in diet and demographics increased the public's appetite for butter's imitator.

Pressure here was growing.

Bootlegging, the first crime witnessed by generations of state youngsters, was rampant. The Federation of Women's Clubs demanded oleo, and urban lawmakers were for it.

Butter was still sacred to some in the land of small farms and dairy economy, but its pedestal was rocking. First a major dairy cooperative, and then the powerful Wisconsin Farm Bureau Federation declared legal oleo inevitable and surrendered. But butter remained a modern Alamo for a few rural lawmakers.

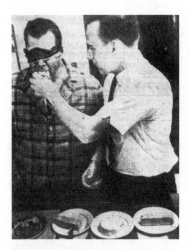

Senator Roseleip taking the oleo/
butter taste test, administered by
Senator Martin Schreiber, June 24,
1965. WHI IMAGE ID 1844

None was more vociferous than the blustery patriot Gordon Roseleip, a 270-pound Darlington Republican who festooned his Senate desk with small flags of red, white and blue—not, he pointed out, yellow.

"Why did God Almighty manufacture butter?" he asked in 1967. "To build good bodies for the future of this nation."

Patting his own frame, he said, "It's all muscle, and it's all from eating farm products. Butter gave me the strength to stand up here and fight for the farmer."

But Roseleip's cause had stumbled in 1965—during June Dairy Month, of all times—when he flunked a blind taste test, identifying oleo as butter. He said later he was "a greenhorn from the fields of southwestern Wisconsin" tricked by city slickers. But the damage was done.

After his death, his daughter revealed that butter's champion might have failed because his family had secretly been slipping him oleo to help control his weight.

In 1967, oleo won final approval, and on May 24, surrounded by women in yellow dresses—including his wife in gold earrings and yellow hose—Governor Warren Knowles inked the repeal with a yellow pen.

"The deed is done," he said.

On May 25, the *Sentinel* published Dorothy Knowles' "Can't Fail Unless . . ." cookie recipe. It included a half-cup of oleo.

Putting the Fight in "On, Wisconsin!"

Almost everything that is known about "On, Wisconsin!" is called baloney by some, except this:

The University of Wisconsin's touchdown torch song, according to no less than Professor Michael Leckrone, whose marching bands have played it a million times, has "a good shake to it."

Well, maybe 100,000 times. See the problem?

UW–Madison's official explanation say the tune was composed in 1909 by New Yorker William Purdy, then living in Chicago, for a song contest at the University of Minnesota.

On, Wisconsin!, first printed edition, 1909. UW ARCHIVES

But William E. Studwell, a Northern Illinois University professor who specializes in school fight songs, later insisted the Gopher angle was folklore, that the song was always intended for Wisconsin.

Purdy's roommate, Carl Beck, was credited with writing the lyrics and with suggesting the song be offered to Wisconsin instead, where Beck had once studied.

But years later, Purdy's relatives say Beck had inflated his contributions. Beck "could not even carry a tune," Purdy's daughter said in 1959.

Whatever its true roots, the rousing song was an instant hit on campus and, with changes in lyrics to fit different locales, across the country. Military bands loved the tune. In 1959, "On, Wisconsin!" was proclaimed the official state song.

However, controversy erupted anew in 1979 when it was reported that Beatle Paul McCartney had acquired the rights to Wisconsin's famous song, and many others, and was receiving royalty payments.

A Brit getting rich on Wisconsin? Governor Lee Dreyfus wrote McCartney, asking that he surrender the rights to Wisconsin as a memorial gesture for the slain John Lennon. The suggestion was turned down by McCartney's lawyer.

But Purdy's daughter, Marylois Purdy Vega, then denied McCartney's connection, saying the copyright had been sold to Flanner and Hafsoos, a Milwaukee music publishing company. However, that company then said it had given the rights to the university many years earlier.

A university lawyer who waded into the brouhaha in 1981 determined that McCartney did not own song rights to "On, Wisconsin" after all, only some sheet music rights through a company he bought.

Anyway, the lawyer said, all rights would soon expire and the song would be in the public domain.

But another music historian in Madison then appeared, saying no, no, no. The song had been in the public domain since 1915, he argued, when it was published without a copyright mark.

Whatever. In 1990, Professor Studwell ranked our feisty—and fight-provoking—anthem the third best college fight song in the land.

But, and this will surprise no one, some here thought it deserved first.

Alex Raineri
and Hurley's Last Gasp

Decades after Hurley's rowdy days had made it synonymous with sin, most Wisconsin residents assumed the city had long ago turned off its red lights, and the party was finally over.

But in 1980, old Hurley roused itself for one racy last gasp.

Or, as one paper said, a sleazy last gasp:

"It is like a wrinkled old stripper wiggling out of her scruffy underwear one last time, and nobody wants to watch."

Especially in Hurley. It had long been said that in northern Wisconsin's early days the "four toughest places in the world are Cumberland, Hayward, Hurley, and Hell"—all linked, either in the before or after, with saloons, gambling and whores.

Even so, the new scandal had an aura all its own.

The man on trial in federal court on abetting prostitution charges was Iron County's judge, Alex Raineri.

Raineri had been charged with five counts of promoting prostitution, lying to a grand jury and obstructing justice.

The activity involved the Show Bar on Hurley's famous Silver Street, although the bar had burned to the ground under suspicious circumstances before the trial began.

A parade of witnesses more accustomed to the darkness of a nightclub paraded into federal court in Madison late that fall over 15 days of testimony.

Cira Gasbarri, the Cuban-born owner of the Show Bar, told how Raineri had urged her to let dancers work the customers in the shadows of booths and that he personally handled the bar's finances. She said she and the judge were lovers—he denied it

View up Silver Street in Hurley, 1942. WHI IMAGE ID 84280

when he testified—but others, including several prostitutes, supported her testimony.

The legal soap opera also featured hints of various threats that had been made, a bullet fired in anger, cheap but high-priced champagne that brought its buyer special favors and other seamy elements.

In the end, Raineri was convicted by a jury on all counts and removed from office. When appeals failed, Raineri went to federal prison; the wrinkled old stripper, and all the other witnesses, went home.

One witness, it might be noted, was the Show Bar's former $60-a-week janitor.

He also, in keeping with old Hurley's tradition of looking the other way, was the town's retired police chief.

Spring Storm
Unearthed a Mastodon

The Dosch boys were delighted. In 1897, after swift and severe storms had rushed through their farm near Boaz in Richland County, Chris, Harry, Clyde and Verne were sent by their father to inspect a floodgate. They found a large bone sticking out of the eroded bank of Mill Creek.

They found another bone, and another, and eventually had unearthed almost all the structural bones of a giant animal that was later identified as a mastodon. They found a quartzite spear point, as well.

Boys being boys, they said nothing at first, but they couldn't resist piling the bones along fence posts to amaze passers-by.

The stunned mailman told everyone on his route, and soon people from all over Richland County were coming to witness the boys' amazing discovery.

The mastodon was a forest dweller that lived in eastern North America during the Ice Age. Related to modern elephants, it was large and hairy, stood 9 feet tall and weighed up to 8 tons. It is estimated that mastodons moved into Wisconsin 13,000 years ago and lived here for 4,000 years, when they became extinct.

Mastodon teeth and other bones have since been found in other places, but the Dosch boys had made the first recorded discovery of mastodon bones in Wisconsin. After moving the bones from building to building to keep them from prying visitors, the family sold the skeleton to the state.

The discovery of the spear point especially intrigued scientists because it appeared to establish that the Boaz mastodon had been

The mastodon on display at the University of Wisconsin
Geology Museum. UW GEOLOGY MUSEUM

hunted and killed by man. In 1915, Professors M. G. Mehl and
G. M. Schwartz—using plaster replicas where pieces of bone were
missing—restored the Boaz mastodon. Later, UW researchers
using more sophisticated tests determined that the bones actually
came from two animals—one from Boaz and the other from a
former settlement called Anderson Mills.

Many years later some of the Dosch family descendants urged
the university to return the mastodon to Richland Center, where
they wanted it displayed in a warehouse designed by Frank Lloyd
Wright. When that wasn't done, a replica was donated instead.

The Boaz mastodon is on exhibit at the Geology Museum at
the University of Wisconsin–Madison.

Father Mazzuchelli, Church Builder

Deep in southwestern Wisconsin, in the pinprick community of New Diggings, a special Mass is said each autumn in a weathered wooden church. It was built during Wisconsin's infancy by Samuel Mazzuchelli, the Italian-born Catholic priest whom his admirers view as a saint.

The little church was far from his only accomplishment.

Mazzuchelli, born in 1806, was the 16th of 17 children of a Milan banker and merchant, but he passed up the family business in favor of a religious life. At 17 he entered a novitiate and eventually became a Dominican priest.

He learned French, as well, which would stand him in good stead in his assignment to the New World. In 1830, he came to Mackinac Island to minister to the considerable spiritual needs of French Canadian trappers and voyageurs. He was then the only priest in the area just west of Lake Michigan, including Wisconsin, Iowa, Minnesota and northern Illinois.

He was 23, but undaunted. In 1831 he helped design what would become St. John the Evangelist church in Green Bay, the first Catholic church in Wisconsin.

He was a friend and associate of James Doty, the

Father Samuel Mazzuchelli.
WHI IMAGE ID 2787

71

territorial judge and developer, and of Henry Dodge, the territorial governor, but such lofty friendships did not keep him from working with often-neglected Native people as well.

He established a school for the Ho-Chunk and compiled a catechism in their language. He also developed the Chippewa Almanac, a work so rare the only known copy is in the rare book collection of the Library of Congress.

By 1835 Mazzuchelli was sent to the booming southwestern lead region, where his accomplishments would range from the construction of dozens of churches to the lessons he would teach in schools he established. Some of his parishioners, miners from Ireland or England had trouble with his tongue twister of a name and simply called him Father Matthew Kelly, which rhymed with his name.

Mazzuchelli served as chaplain for the first Wisconsin territorial legislature, an honor that impressed even him.

It was rare to find in any country's history, he said, "a legislative assembly where Protestants, outnumbering Catholics 18 to 1, have nevertheless conferred the office of chaplain on a priest."

In 1844 he purchased the Sinsinawa Mound in the southwestern corner of the state, where he would establish the College of St. Thomas for men and the Congregation of Dominican Sisters of Sinsinawa, a community of teaching nuns. Such were Mazzuchelli's contributions to early education—he taught science, philosophy, history and religion—that he was credited with introducing laboratory education in Wisconsin.

He died in 1864 and was buried behind his church in Benton, Wisconsin, far from Milan and the comfortable life he had eschewed. Mazzuchelli's supporters work yet today for his beatification.

The Capitol Fire of 1904

The second Wisconsin Capitol suffered its share of cost overruns and delays, but upon its completion in 1872, it was an imposing structure.

One state newspaper boasted in 1881, "There are few states in the Union possessing a neater, more imposing or more convenient capitol building."

But its conveniences, which included sprinklers and supposedly advanced fire safety features, were insufficient to save the sprawling structure one cold night in 1904.

After the generator was shut down for the night, the only lights burning late on February 26 were two gas jets that served night watchmen. At 2 a.m., watchman Nat Crampton smelled smoke and traced the odor to a newly varnished ceiling near one gaslight in the Assembly post office. A pail of water he threw on the flames did nothing, so while a second watchman arrived with a hose—only to discover there was no water pressure—the Madison Fire Department was called.

But firefighters, too, found almost no water pressure. The fire was spreading, so Governor Robert M. La Follette telegraphed Janesville and Milwaukee for help. In Milwaukee, fire officials rushed to an arriving train and asked how long it would take to reach the emergency.

The engineer replied that he could cover the 96 miles in 96 minutes "if the locomotive fireman holds out," and the target was indeed met. Unfortunately, when the pumper arrived, firefighters learned it had frozen during the subzero ride.

Wisconsin State Capitol fire, February 27, 1904. Some of the contents of the building are already in wagons ready to be hauled away. WHI IMAGE ID 23107

La Follette himself was at the Capitol by then, directing efforts that included almost 200 university students as well as firefighters. La Follette was among those entering the burning building to salvage important papers. Ladders were raised against the Capitol walls, and books from the State Law Library were tossed into snowbanks; later, Supreme Court Justice R. D. Marshall personally formed a hand-to-hand student brigade passing the books to safety.

Not all contributions were so positive, however. A witness later described seeing a few young people running down State Street with typewriters and other looted objects.

Efforts to control the fire weren't helped when flames reached a commissary and set off rounds of powder and rifle cartridges, but it was a mostly losing battle anyway. Fire raged through the west and east wings, the rotunda and upper level of the south wing, sparing only the north wing where firefighters had massed.

The fire was declared out by 10 p.m. the next day, 20 hours after its discovery. The loss was estimated at between $800,000 and $1 million, but that did not include the $7.5 million that would eventually be spent on a new Capitol, the grand white granite, classical-revival building that stands proudly on the Capitol Square today.

And the loss estimated did not include items for which there was no dollar value. Among the "casualties" was the stuffed carcass of Old Abe the eagle, the celebrated Civil War mascot who had, coincidentally, died in an earlier Capitol fire.

Victor Berger, Socialist Champion

In 1910, Wisconsin's Victor Berger became the first Socialist elected to Congress. It would not be his only lonely position. When he was barred from the House of Representatives in 1919, the vote was 311–1.

No opponent of World War I paid a steeper price than Victor Berger. The father of the Milwaukee Socialist legacy, Berger was born in 1860 in Austria and came to Milwaukee to teach in 1881. Later he became an ardent advocate of socialism and a newspaper publisher before he was sent to Congress.

Berger was vociferously anti-war, and both his statements and editorials in his Milwaukee Leader were deemed so inflammatory the post office revoked its mailing privileges.

Berger was charged in an indictment with violating the Espionage Act, which infuriated "patriots" elsewhere but did not sway voters in Milwaukee. In November 1918, they returned him to Congress just six days before the war ended. A month later in Chicago, Berger and four other Socialists were put on trial for conspiracy to hinder the war effort.

After four weeks of testimony, all five were convicted, and Berger was sentenced by Judge Kenesaw Mountain

Victor Berger, 1923.
WHI IMAGE ID 123863

Landis—later the commissioner of baseball—to 20 years at Fort Leavenworth. The sentence was stayed during appeal, but a short time later another judge declared Berger's paper "a hostile or enemy publication" and said those who read it were similarly disloyal.

Against that backdrop, and as America's "Red Scare" further inflamed opinions, Berger went to Washington to be sworn in.

Members refused to admit him. Despite Berger's continued backing at home, a nine-member committee reviewed his case and declared him in violation of his previous congressional oath for giving aid or comfort to the enemy.

Berger refused to recant his views and insisted he be seated.

"Remember, gentlemen, you may exclude me once. You may exclude me twice," Berger said. "But the 5th District of Wisconsin can not [*sic*] permit you to dictate what kind of man is to represent it."

He could not prevent the lopsided vote, however. And while the national press almost unanimously supported the action, Berger's constituents nominated him to yet another term. The campaign was ugly, but he won handily and was again excluded from Congress.

A rare supporter, Representative Edward Voigt, of Milwaukee, defended Berger in a House speech, saying: "You may say that Victor Berger is a traitor, but if you do, you have got to say that there are 25,000 traitors in the 5th District of Wisconsin."

Another member cried, "There are." This time the vote was 330–6.

Berger found redemption, however. Though he was defeated in 1920, his conviction was thrown out on a technicality. In 1922, he was again elected to Congress, and this time, the Red Scare having eased, he was welcomed in and seated.

Berger died in 1929 after being struck by a Milwaukee streetcar. He was praised as a man of the people, and a large throng paid its respects when his body was lying in state at City Hall.

Leading the Way
in Unemployment Pay

In 1932, when the harshness of the Great Depression was squeezing American life, hundreds of needy Milwaukee men crowded the corridors of City Hall.

They would have preferred to be looking for jobs, but in the absence of work they were seeking the benefits newly awarded to the deserving jobless.

Wisconsin was first in the nation to approve unemployment compensation, an action that became a model for other states and was eventually used in developing federal laws. US Supreme Court Justice Louis Brandeis later called Wisconsin "a single courageous state" for charting the way, but this groundbreaking step had not come easily.

Great Britain had established a compulsory national system as early as 1911, but even serious recessions from 1914–15 and 1920–21 failed to turn debate into action in this country.

Eventually it took the severity of the 1930s Depression, which proved "relief" through property taxes and charity inadequate to deal with widespread unemployment, to make more Americans receptive to government involvement. And it required decades of prodding by university professors, graduate students, labor advocates, Milwaukee socialists and others in the Progressive movement.

Versions of the landmark unemployment insurance bill signed into law by Governor Philip F. La Follette on January 28, 1932, had died many deaths in the Legislature in the decade before it was finally approved.

Professor John R. Commons and several colleagues who would become notable themselves, including Paul Raushenbush and his wife, Elizabeth Brandeis, the justice's daughter, had worked for years to craft a law that would protect workers during down periods, not unduly offend rural interests, not overtax employers and still contribute to workplace security.

Commons, generally called the father of unemployment laws, argued that joblessness was a cause of labor unrest and that by preventing it through unemployment insurance, employers would gain better labor-management relations, increased production and greater profits.

It took severe unemployment to finally turn the tide, but a statewide campaign in 1930–31 persuaded lawmakers to make history. The Assembly passed a "reserves bill" in December 1931, and the Senate followed on January 8.

"It was a thrilling experience to live in Wisconsin in these years," Elizabeth Brandeis later said, "to feel that there was a program under way, that government was playing a constructive part, that real things were being planned and done."

UW—Yes, UW—
Won Basketball Crown

In the 1970s, as college basketball was moving from mere sport to a televised month of madness, the then-Warriors of Marquette University rode Coach Al McGuire's big city street smarts and Irish moxie to a national title.

It was a game of run and gun by then, of centers as big as aircraft carriers and, in McGuire's eccentric vision, of seashells and balloons. The celebration in 1977 was joyous.

But then Marquette learned what its intrastate rivals at the University of Wisconsin had learned four decades earlier, back when shorts were still short and box scores separated hook shots from old-fashioned pushes.

Enjoy every second of every moment, was the lesson. Repeating won't be easy.

UW's first—and only—basketball title came in 1941, as war clouds were forming half a world away from the safety and security of a college gym. The team would be called the "Cinderella" Badgers because then—as, alas, ever since—few thought they could win it all.

Yet the Badgers, a *Milwaukee Journal* sportswriter would say, were "the team that refuses to be licked."

"Wisconsin didn't give a hoot for any of the dope."

Led by All-Americans Gene Englund and John Kotz and coached by Harold "Bud" Foster, Wisconsin opened the season with three victories before losing three of their next five.

But through the rest of the season, they rolled the table and earned their first National Collegiate Athletic Association playoff

The starting line up included (from l to r): Ted Strain, Gene Englund, Charles Epperson, Johnny Kotz, and Fred Rehm. UW ARCHIVES

games. They hosted the first two, defeating Dartmouth, 51–50, on March 21, before 12,500 fans, and Pittsburgh, 36–30, the next day before a crowd of 14,000.

The national title game in Kansas City on Saturday, March 29, was far from the heavily gambled inflated-price phenomenon it has become. It drew a crowd of 8,000, but 2,000 seats were empty when Wisconsin tipped off against the Washington State Cougars.

The Cougars were 6-point favorites, but Wisconsin, the *Journal* would say, "scoffed at the role of underdog. . . ." It scored the first six points, covered Washington's dangerous 6-foot-7 center "like a leech" and won comfortably, 39–34.

"Everybody was hugging everybody else," the paper said. "It was the awakening after a happy dream which wasn't a dream after all."

A roaring throng of 12,000 fans greeted the team's train in Madison shortly after midnight on Monday.

Curfew for female students was moved back one hour to 1:30 am to allow for celebration, but many stayed out later than that chanting "No school Monday." But there was school on Monday and there was other sobering evidence that sport was, after all, merely a diversion.

Team Captain Gene Englund had left the train and his teammates in Chicago to return to his hometown of Kenosha, where on Monday he appeared before his local draft board.

Joshua Glover
and Sherman Booth

One winter night in 1854, Joshua Glover sat down in a Racine shack to play cards when he unwittingly sparked an epic battle involving federal law, states' rights, a crusading newspaper editor and the razor-sharp issue of slavery, all topped with a burst of mob rule.

Little wonder the case against Sherman Booth remains a landmark in Wisconsin's legal memory.

A slave from near St. Louis, Glover had run away in 1852 and found work and refuge in Racine. Under the federal fugitive slave law, a runaway had no rights, and anyone who helped him could be thrown in prison. When Glover's owner learned of his whereabouts, a federal marshal and several men interrupted Glover's card game, beat him and hauled him to a Milwaukee jail.

The fugitive law was bitterly resented by many in Wisconsin. Angered by Glover's arrest—not only for anti-slavery reasons but also because of opposition to federal mandates—about 100 Racine men came to Milwaukee with the county sheriff and arrest warrants for some of those who had beaten Glover.

Joshua Glover. WHI IMAGE ID 6270

The group was spurred on by Booth, a fiery editor who had ridden through the streets calling, "Freemen, to the rescue."

In Milwaukee, the group's legal demands to free Glover were ignored by the federal marshal, who was backed by the federal judge's vow. "No power on earth," the judge said, "will impel me to yield the slave up."

But there was such power.

Joined by a large crowd of like-minded Milwaukeeans, the mob decided muscle would serve its purpose better than legalities and stormed the jail with a large timber. Glover was freed, spirited away by wagon to Waukesha and eventually taken by the abolitionists to Canada and freedom.

But even with Glover gone, the case would stretch on for years.

Booth was thrown in jail five days later for violating the fugitive law, but a Wisconsin Supreme Court justice freed him and declared the slave law unconstitutional. The rest of the court soon agreed.

Several more times federal officials would jail Booth, only to watch him be freed by the Wisconsin judges who refused to recognize Washington's opinion. Meanwhile, the nation continued to debate the central issues—states' rights and slavery—as the Civil War inevitably neared.

Booth, who eventually was pardoned by President James Buchanan, died at 92 on August 11, 1904, and was buried at Milwaukee's Forest Home Cemetery.

Belle Boyd, Confederate Spy

Belle Boyd had the courage of a soldier, nerve of a provocateur and flair of an actress, all helpful attributes for a spy. Not coincidentally, it was also said that Boyd had "the best pair of legs in the Confederacy."

Belle Boyd in a pencil sketch done 57 years after her death.
WHI IMAGE ID 46160

All of those make her the most storied Southern spy buried in Wisconsin.

She was born in Martinsburg in Virginia's Shenandoah Valley in 1843, a city alternately held by rebel and federal troops during the early days of the Civil War.

Her legend began when Northern soldiers tried to raise a Union flag over her house. Boyd's mother—and apparent inspiration—adamantly refused, and when one intruder became abusive, Belle taught him some manners.

"My indignation was aroused beyond control," she would later write. "My blood was literally boiling in my veins. I drew my pistol and shot him."

The Yankee officer who investigated the killing was soon smitten, and ruled she had done the right thing.

By most accounts, Boyd was not beautiful in the classical sense, but was blessed with charm and power over men. She joined the Confederate Intelligence Service, often supplying

Southern officers with secrets enticed from Northerners who should have known better. Even when she was arrested on suspicion of spying, a kindly general released her.

At a hotel at Front Royal, she picked up secrets by listening through a knothole from a closet over a dining room where officers were meeting and relayed the news to Confederate forces.

Her most famous exploit came in 1862, when Boyd raced from the hotel to the camp of General Stonewall Jackson, running across open fields in her blue calico dress, braving fire from each side, finally waving her sunbonnet as a signal for Jackson to advance.

Boyd was later captured and imprisoned in Washington where, still a teenager, she gained more fame for singing Southern songs through barred windows. After her release, she was sailing to Europe—by various accounts either with secrets or for her safety—when her ship was captured by the Northern Navy.

Still the spy, she converted one of her captors to the Southern cause. She later married him in London, but when he returned to America, he was arrested as a deserter; he died a few years later from the effects of imprisonment.

Boyd would marry twice more; all three husbands, curiously, were Northerners.

Boyd told—and, reportedly, enhanced—her story in a popular book, *Belle Boyd in Camp and Prison*, and for years traveled the country performing a narrative drama about her spy days. It was on such a tour in June 1900 that Boyd, after appearances in Portage and Pardeeville, suffered a heart attack in Kilbourn—now Wisconsin Dells—and died.

She was buried there in Spring Grove Cemetery, where her grave long was the site of an annual observance by Civil War veterans.

The Death of
the Death Penalty

From the earliest days of Wisconsin there were key figures who
thought the death penalty was ineffective and that no civilized
state would impose it.

But it was a man named John McCaffary who finally, and quite
involuntarily, helped make capital punishment illegal.

When it happened he was not around to take credit. McCaffary was the last man legally hanged in Wisconsin.

Hangings were not unheard of in Wisconsin during the territorial days but were not common, either. Two men found guilty
of murder—one near Portage, one near Milwaukee—were pardoned before they could be executed. But at Lancaster in 1838,
Edward Oliver was hanged for a murder in Cassville, and in 1842
a big crowd gathered in Mineral Point to witness William Caffee's
death by rope.

Abolition of capital punishment was an issue at the constitutional conventions. In 1846, a ban on capital punishment was
discussed from every angle, religious to practical, before delegates
rejected it by a vote of 68–30.

In 1849, however, its use was limited to first-degree murder
cases. Then in 1851, John McCaffary, of Kenosha, was convicted of
murdering his wife and was sentenced to be hanged—an occasion
then, as now, guaranteed to draw the curious.

Several thousand gathered for McCaffary's neck stretching,
wrote Joseph Ranney, a lawyer who has researched Wisconsin's
legal history.

"The rope was adjusted about [his] neck, and he was told it lacked five minutes of the time, during which the prisoner stood firm with clasped hands, but the movement of his lips showed he was in silent prayer."

At the appointed time, McCaffary's cap was drawn over his face, and the sheriff stepped upon a secret spring that hoisted the prisoner in the air.

While the throng watched, "He continued to struggle for the space of five minutes.

"After he had been suspended about eight minutes, his pulse was slightly reduced, and continued to beat for about 10 minutes longer, at which time life was extinct and the prisoner was let down into the coffin."

But the ugly death gave many pause, and the push to repeal the death penalty gained new life. In short order, the Legislature, at the urging of Christopher Latham Sholes, of Milwaukee, and Marvin Bovee, of Summit, abolished capital punishment.

Almost every session a bill is introduced to reinstate capital punishment, but none has attracted significant support. Wisconsin has gone without the death penalty longer than all but two states, Michigan and Rhode Island.

Golda Meir's
Milwaukee Memories

She would grow up to amaze the world, this poor Russian Jewish immigrant who became prime minister of Israel and a political giant.

But Golda Meir's first days in America were spent in her own astonishment at this strange place called Wisconsin.

Her father had preceded her to Milwaukee, where he struggled for three years before he sent word in 1905 that he had a job, and his wife and children could finally join him. Golda was then a wide-eyed eight-year-old.

"Milwaukee—even the small part of it that I saw during those first few days—overwhelmed me: new food, the baffling sounds

of an entirely unfamiliar language, the confusion of getting used to a parent I had almost forgotten. It all gave me a feeling of unreality so strong that I can still remember standing in the street and wondering who and where I was."

Her father was much changed, an American now, and his family arrived looking "Old World." That first day in Milwaukee he took them on a shopping

Golda Meir in 1973. PUBLIC DOMAIN

expedition. Her independent sister, Sheyna, resisted and a family argument ensued at Schuster's Department Store.

But Golda, who recalled the moment years later in *My Life*, was "delighted by my pretty new clothes, by the soda pop and ice cream and by the excitement of being in a real skyscraper, the first five-story building I had ever seen.

"In general I thought Milwaukee was wonderful. Everything looked so colorful and fresh, as though it had just been created, and I stood for hours staring at the traffic and the people. The automobile in which my father had fetched us from the train was the first I had ever ridden in, and I was fascinated by what seemed like the endless procession of cars, trolleys and shiny bicycles on the street."

She marveled at the stores and barbershops, at the little girls in their Sunday best, at so much opportunity, and spent her first days "in a kind of trance."

She attended the "fortress-like" Fourth Street School—now named for her—where she learned English and made friends. Her family's adjustment—to America and to each other—was troubled, but Golda prospered. When she watched her father march in a Labor Day parade she decided Milwaukee and Wisconsin were blessed to have governments that encouraged free thinking and were receptive to immigrants.

"To see my father marching on that September day was like coming out of the dark and into the light," she said.

In 1971, this woman who was now the equal of presidents and other world leaders returned to meet the students of Fourth Street School, now mostly black, not Jewish. They welcomed her like a queen, sang to her in Yiddish, presented her with Stars of David and a white rose of tissue and pipe cleaners.

And they filled her eyes with tears.

Mary Ann Van Hoof's
Vision of the Virgin

In 1950, Wisconsin Catholics were in a stir over two women. One was Mary Ann Van Hoof of Necedah, a farm wife with a fourth-grade education who said she had been visited six times—by the Blessed Virgin.

Mary had appeared from a blue mist, Van Hoof said, in a blue robe studded with white stars and holding a rosary.

And, Van Hoof revealed, on August 15, Mary would appear again.

The thought of a Juneau County farm as the next Fatima caused a faithful uproar. In June, Milwaukee newspapers predicted 10,000 would make pilgrimages to Necedah for the visit, while by August the estimate was 30,000. The simple farm wife and mother of seven had drawing power.

Van Hoof said the Virgin's messages to her had been for people to say the rosary daily, live Christian lives and work to convert godless Russia.

But some were skeptical. In June, spokesmen for the La Crosse diocese called publicity "spurious and regrettable" and said the claims were being investigated.

By August, when every available bus in Milwaukee had been chartered and extra trains scheduled, the message was stronger. Van Hoof's claims were "highly questionable" said a statement by Bishop John Treacy, who regretted the "unstable emotionalism and misguided zeal."

"Stay at home," he said, "and pray the rosary there."

Mary Ann Van Hoof on her farm near Necedah.
HANNEMAN ARCHIVE

Some trains were canceled, but the "alleged visit," as the papers put it, was still on. "I must go ahead with it," Van Hoof said, "or the blessed Virgin will punish me."

"Vision Day" drew uncounted thousands—estimates were 35,000–100,000—along with food and souvenir vendors. Some merchants added rosaries to their inventory, while Van Hoof complained that visitors were crushing her flowers and disturbing her chickens.

Even doubters acknowledged that Van Hoof seemed sincere, but true believers brought the ill and the lame to be in her presence.

"Most pathetic of the pictures in the meadow was the fenced lane leading to the shrine—the space reserved for cripples," a reporter wrote.

In front of the multitudes, Van Hoof was again visited, she said. A reporter said several women fainted, from excitement or heat, but "if anyone else thought he saw the apparition, the reporter had not heard about it . . . but it's hardly likely anyway. This is Anna Van Hoof's vision, jealously cherished."

A church spokesman debunked the "vision," saying those who said they saw something "were seeing things."

A much smaller crowd attended the last visit in October. While describing the Virgin's message that day, Van Hoof collapsed near her statue of the Lady of Fatima and struck her head.

But doubt was growing. In Milwaukee, church disapproval forced cancellation of radio broadcasts of Van Hoof sharing Mary's message, and a shrine at the farm was removed at the direction of the archdiocese.

Years later Van Hoof said she still talked regularly with the Virgin Mary, but few listened. And fewer believed.

Cream Citys Brought Baseball
to Milwaukee

When the Milwaukee Brewers switched from the American to the National League in 1998, many said baseball in the city was merely returning to its roots.

Even some who said that likely didn't know how right they were.

True, the Milwaukee Braves had played in the National League from 1953 to 1965, but the Milwaukee Cream Citys were playing National League ball back when horses and buggies carried fans to games.

Organized ball had been played in Milwaukee for several decades before the Cream City club joined the two-year-old National League in 1878. Games were played in a field at North 10th Street and West Clybourn, and the season began with a bang. Sam Weaver pitched a no-hitter to lead the Cream Citys to a 2–1 victory over Indianapolis May 9, and on May 14 1,500 fans saw the home team end the Cincinnati Reds' six-game winning streak.

But the local nine's participation lasted just one season before unpaid bills struck them out. That winter the team was ousted from the league and sold to pay a bankruptcy judgment of $125.61.

Five years later Milwaukee fielded a team in the short-lived Union League, taking over Cincinnati's franchise, and for 11 years starting in 1888 sponsored a team in the Western League, where its entry prospered under new manager Cornelius McGillicuddy.

He would go on to manage Philadelphia Athletics—and be elected to the Baseball Hall of Fame—as the more familiarly known Connie Mack.

The Milwaukee Brewers in 1909. WHI IMAGE ID 55867

In 1901 Milwaukee was one of eight teams in the newly organized American League, an outgrowth of the Western League. It
was not an altogether pleasant season. On opening day on April
25, Milwaukee's Brewers gave up 10 runs in the bottom of the
ninth and lost to Detroit 14–13, while on May 27 third baseman
Jimmy Burke set a new record with four errors in one inning.
Milwaukee finished last; the city's franchise was transferred to
St. Louis and eventually became the Baltimore Orioles.

For decades the minor-league Brewers represented baseball in
Milwaukee, winning eight pennants and three junior world series.
In the economic darkness of 1933, 1.4 million fans sought the
diversion of baseball in Milwaukee. But the city wanted a major-
league team again, and in 1953 Lou Perini moved his struggling
Boston Braves to Milwaukee's new $5 million County Stadium.

The move would give Wisconsin fans the likes of Aaron and
Matthews, Burdette and Spahn, two pennants and a 1957 World
Series victory. But after the good times, attendance sagged and
victories came harder. The Braves would leave for Atlanta in 1966,

and Milwaukee was left without major-league ball until Seattle's Pilots, an American League team, were lured here for a name change and a makeover in 1970.

Change comes today in the form of an old league and a new park. But who knows? If only the Cream Citys had gotten a new stadium. . . .

Christopher Sholes and
the Typewriter

To borrow from a later day, Christopher Latham Sholes' first typewriter was a small step for the men who built it, but a giant step for womankind.

Dozens of tinkerers were attempting to develop a writing machine in the 1860s, but the breakthrough came in a West State Street machine shop in 1867 when several Milwaukee men built the first feasible model.

It was hardly, to be sure, the little slip of a laptop keyboard on which this account was written. The typing machine built by Sholes and collaborators Carlos Glidden, Samuel Soule and Matthias Schwalbach "looked something like a cross between a small piano and a kitchen table," said the historian Richard N. Current. It typed only capital letters and was bulky and balky.

But it was a work in progress, and with the encouragement—and investment—of a former Wisconsin newspaperman, James Densmore, Sholes tweaked and refined it so much that by 1873, E. Remington & Sons began commercial manufacture of typewriters. Sholes, himself a former editor of the *Milwaukee Sentinel*, has long been awarded the title "father of the typewriter," but he always credited Densmore with breathing life into the process.

Sholes, who vastly underestimated his accomplishment's long-term worth and was eager to cash out, received only $12,000 for his initial interest. Densmore, taking the longer view, eventually profited handsomely from his share.

Women profited even more, however; no dollar estimate could touch their gain. While sales of typewriters were slow at

Sholes posing with a typewriter. WHI IMAGE ID 3218

first, it didn't take long for the machine's potential to be realized. The first demand was from stenographers and telegraphers, but the typewriter soon found its way into offices both public and private. Mark Twain was said to be the first writer to buy one, and later was the first author to submit a typewritten manuscript to a publisher—*Life on the Mississippi*.

In 1881, the YMCA in New York offered a typing course for women, and the revolution was truly under way. The typewriter offered the first white-collar job for women, and demand for typists soared. By 1888, the number of women employed as typists had grown to 60,000, and the door was open to other careers.

By the time of his death in 1890, Sholes had received additional payments for his work, but his grave at Forest Lawn cemetery was unmarked until 1919, the centennial of his birth, when the National Shorthand Reporters' association arranged for a marker "in grateful memory of the man whose genius has lightened labor and brought comfort and happiness to millions of toilers in the world's work."

Though he never boasted of his achievement, Sholes went to his grave with awareness of what he had done. In one of his letters he wrote:

"Whatever I may have felt in the early days of the value of the typewriter, it is obviously a blessing to mankind, and especially to womankind. I am glad I had something to do with it. I builded [*sic*] wiser than I knew, and the world has the benefit of it."

Old Abe, the Eagle that Went to War

Old Abe was the eagle that went to war, the feathered battle flag of Wisconsin's "Eagle Regiment," an inspiration to the men of Company C in battle after bloody battle.

Not bad for a bird once swapped for half a bushel of shelled corn.

The bird, later christened Old Abe, was a fledgling when he was found in an aerie on the Flambeau River in 1861 by an Ojibwe named O-Ge-Ma-Ke-Zhik, or Chief Sky. He took the bird to Jim Falls, near Eau Claire, where a trader named Dan McCann made the corn-for-eagle transaction.

It was the start of an incredible journey. Abe was soon given to an Eau Claire man for $2.50 (though Abe later said in an "autobiography," written with Malcolm and Margaret Rosholt, that the price was actually $3).

Whatever the amount, Abe's new owner was bound for the Civil War with Company C, Eighth Regiment, Wisconsin infantry—and Abe went with him.

He quickly became a star. The legend was born when, as the company was parading at Madison's Camp Randall, Abe held a corner of the American flag in his beak while observers cheered wildly.

Abe was carried all through the war, usually on a perch held by one of his handlers. He served in dozens of battles; Abe was known for perching on cannons, wings spread, or soaring above the fray, screaming over the sound of cannon fire and other battle sounds. Once, when his leather strap was shot off,

Carte-de-visite Centennial portrait of Old Abe for the Centennial International Exposition, February 7, 1876. WHI IMAGE ID 79581

Abe flew to another company but was later returned to Company C.

He was such an inspiration to his company that it was said Southern officers ordered Abe's capture. But even as Wisconsin soldiers fell around him, Abe survived dozens of battles and skirmishes and came home to a hero's welcome.

Peacetime only enhanced his career. Abe was presented to the state of Wisconsin and was exhibited far and wide at fairs and national expositions, including the 1876 World's Fair in Philadelphia.

He lived for years in a room at the Capitol in Madison, despite offers of thousands of dollars from private promoters eager to capitalize on a flying war veteran. School children loved him. If all the requests for souvenir feathers had been honored, Abe would have truly been a bald eagle.

What war couldn't accomplish, fire did. Abe died in March 1881 when a small fire at the Capitol unleashed smoke and fumes, but he still did not disappear. Some wanted to give Abe a veteran's funeral, but others argued in favor of taxidermy and so Abe's carcass was preserved. Abe continued to make appearances in a black walnut glass case.

A second fire at the Capitol in 1904 finally consumed Abe's remains, but not his spirit. In 1915 another eagle christened Old

Abe II was presented to the state Assembly and, again thanks to taxidermy, was given a place of honor. Today he stands above the Assembly speaker's rostrum, overseeing battles of another kind.

In World War II, the 101st Airborne Division, inspired by Old Abe, adopted a shoulder patch with an eagle's head and became the "Screaming Eagles." Abe was at war again.

Hamlin Garland and the Middle Border

The eminent writer Hamlin Garland's best works of fiction were unflinching looks at the rigors of pioneer life, where hardship and struggle greeted each day like the sun.

But for all the sacrifice and toil that he lived and described, he nonetheless loved the western Wisconsin land where he grew up, with its steep bluffs and deep coulees, small streams and picturesque farms.

"My Wisconsin birthplace had always been a source of deep satisfaction to me," he once wrote.

"That a lovely valley should form the first picture in my childhood memories is a priceless endowment."

The valley was Green's Coulee, where Garland's greatest biographical novels were set. He was born in a log cabin in West Salem, near La Crosse, in 1860 and grew up in Wisconsin, Iowa and the Dakota Territory as his parents participated in the nation's western expansion.

Portrait of Hamlin Garland from *The Writer*, 1891.
WHI IMAGE ID 2403

His nomadic years left Garland with a gritty, unromanticized understanding of life on the frontier, where harsh weather and human weakness were obstacles to progress. In 1884, he moved to Boston to become a teacher, but he soon began the literary career that would make him one of America's most respected novelists.

He wrote dozens of novels and short stories before he began his most noteworthy work, four autobiographical novels that included *A Son of the Middle Border* and *A Daughter of the Middle Border*, which earned Garland a Pulitzer Prize in 1922. These novels described the sometimes harsh pioneer existence of his forefathers, the Garlands and the McClintocks, while farming in Green's Coulee.

In 1893, he bought a house in West Salem, not far from the cabin in which he was born, to provide his elderly parents a home. He and his family lived nearby, and after he died in 1940 he was buried in Neshonoc Cemetery at West Salem. The Hamlin Garland Homestead is on the National Register of Historic Places and is open to the public in summer.

Garland spent his final years in California, but a letter to historian Fred Holmes in 1939 left no doubt his heart was still in "that lovely valley."

> It is still very vivid in my mind. I have but to close my eyes to the present, and the tiger lilies bloom again in its meadows, the mowers toss up once more the scarlet sprays of strawberries, the blackbirds rise in clouds from out of the ripening corn, and a hundred other sights and sounds, equally beautiful and equally significant, fill my inner vision.
>
> The men and women who were our neighbors in those days had a quality which made them heroic in my eyes, and as I think back to them now, I perceive that they were, in truth, a cheerful and powerful as well as an intelligent group of genuine Americans. They could laugh and they could sing. They confronted the future with confidence, for the war was over and Uncle Sam was rich enough to give every man a farm—if he would go and get it. . . .
>
> Green's Coulee belongs to the semi-mythical age of the world—to me.

When Lead Was King
in Wisconsin

Gray fever put Wisconsin on the map, at least in territorial days. Though sporadic mining had taken place for years, the real lead rush began after 1822 when the government extended its system of leasing mining districts from Missouri into the upper Mississippi region, including the rugged, lead-rich southwestern corner of Wisconsin.

The early miners, who often ignored Native ownership of land, burrowed like animals into rough pits for shelter, which gave them—and all Wisconsinites to follow—the nickname "badgers." Dozens of communities sprang up in the lead region. Many are now ghost towns, but others—Mineral Point, Dodgeville, Galena (in Illinois) and more—remain today.

Thousands of immigrants, many from Cornwall in England, arrived. By 1840, it was estimated that half of the lead in the United States came from the Wisconsin Territory.

Life was hard. In 1850, cholera ravaged Beetown and Fennimore, killing dozens and frightening many more into fleeing.

But it was nothing like the fever that had hit the lead region a few months earlier, when word arrived that bright gold had been found at Sutter's Hill in California.

It was as if a community of tired walkers had discovered horses. It was estimated that at least two-thirds of Wisconsin's thousands of lead miners headed for the gold fields in the next few years, along with hopefuls from other walks of life. The westward rush was so great that at Chapman's ferry at Potosi, a four-day backup was reported just to cross the Mississippi.

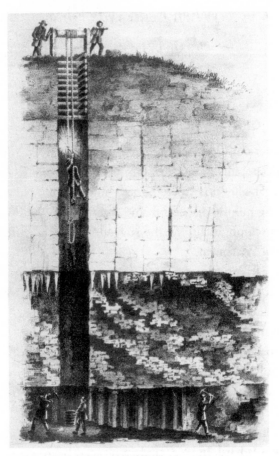

Cross section drawing of a Wisconsin lead mine, 1844.
WHI IMAGE ID 9026

"By May next," a Grant County paper noted in 1852, "Grant County will have disgorged more than a fourth of her adult population and California, like the whale that swallowed Jonah, will have swallowed this entire animal export.

"They were the bone and sinew of the country, and we parted with them as reluctantly as did King Pharaoh with the Children of Israel. . . . Grant County has invested $1,000,000 in the gold mines."

The population shriveled, and depreciation in property value was cataclysmic. Stores and farms were abandoned. Special trains were enlisted to carry converted lead miners to their new dreams, often in newly formed organizations such as the Cassville and Beetown Emigrating Company that headed west in May 1852.

The company's bylaws named supervising officers and dictated that all able-bodied members share guard duty at night, observe the Christian Sabbath and avoid open immorality.

Prospecting, however, carried few guarantees beyond hardship and hard work.

In a short time, the population of Grant County again exceeded its 1850 count, proving that departing miners were only making way for more immigrants.

But some of the residents of Grant County at the end of that decade were disappointed gold miners who had simply come home. Gold fever, like cholera, doesn't last forever.

The Klan, Briefly, Rose Again

One of Wisconsin's darker chapters was written by men wearing white. The "new" Ku Klux Klan that rose from dormancy in the early 1920s was more of an equal opportunity destroyer than its post–Civil War forebears were. This Klan, noted the historian Robert Nesbit, "took advantage of whatever prejudices came its way" against blacks, Jews, Catholics and foreigners in general, whose main failing was not finding America as early as Klan members' families had.

It was for prohibition and morality and generally supported a narrow view of righteous and comprehensive Americanism. After the Klan was dusted off and revived by an Atlanta history professor in 1915, its message spread to other states.

The Klan parading down King Street to Schroeder Funeral Home for the funeral of Police officer Herbert Dreger, December 5, 1924. WHI IMAGE ID 1902

The first klavern was organized in Wisconsin in 1920 at a quietly convened meeting aboard the US Coast Guard vessel *Hawk* in Milwaukee's harbor, and its first meeting was at the Milwaukee Businessman's Club.

The new fraternal society soon spread. Estimates on Klan strength in the 1920s vary, though several accounts suggest as many as 75,000 state residents might have belonged at one time. But while some events drew crowds of 15,000 or more—a few many thousands more—the organization never found leadership to match its base appeal.

It was strongest in Milwaukee, Kenosha and Racine but also found willing members in many other areas of the state. Crosses were burned, and parades of hooded Klan members were common for several years.

If prejudice was the common denominator, however, Klan targets were often unrelated. In Rusk County, Klansmen opposed the large number of Polish immigrants who had recently arrived. Madison Klansmen targeted Italians who lived in the Greenbush neighborhood, called "The Bush," in part because they were involved in bootlegging.

Other Klan groups had a difficult time sustaining their prejudices. At the time, there were relatively few blacks or Jews in the state (and one of those was a popular state treasurer), and too many Klan members had Catholic neighbors they actually liked and respected.

The Klan found its way into power structures in some communities, but eventually interest in this "secret society" waned. In some communities, the Klan itself was subjected to vilification. Large gatherings were still announced, but attendance lagged, and while a few scattered Klan events were recorded in the late 1920s, the group's second significant era went the way of its first.

Wisconsin and the
Columbian Exposition

It might have become the Wisconsin Tower, a brownstone rival to Paris' Eiffel Tower and a monument that would long outlast the 1893 World's Columbian Exposition.

In 1892, when state fair planners decided upon the world's tallest obelisk—a single stone 150 feet tall to be broken from a Washburn quarry and erected on the expo site—many expected huge publicity.

Sadly for history's sake, no one considered the cost of toting such a monster from Bayfield County to Chicago, and when it hit $40,000 the monolith was doomed to remain a quarry piece. A much smaller version of the intended obelisk stands today in downtown Washburn, a monument to grand, if unfinished, dreams.

Wisconsin's involvement in the world's greatest display of culture and achievement was marked by partisan squabbling over money and control (Milwaukee truly failed to capitalize on an international festival on its own doorstep, some later argued) but the state's many wonders eventually shone in grand style.

The (slightly delayed) fair marked 400 years since Columbus arrived in America. Over six months it would attract 28 million visitors, so the chance to showcase a state or country's attractions was priceless.

Still, state planners argued over how much to spend, and the opening was only weeks away when Governor George W. Peck finally released funds to cover the state's fair debts.

This smaller version of the projected 150-foot-tall single stone obelisk intended for the 1893 World's Columbian Exposition stands in downtown Washburn. DENNIS MCCANN

The centerpiece—though beer drinkers might have thought Pabst Brewing Company's gold-coated brewery replica unmatched—was the Wisconsin State Building.

Reminiscent of sprawling mansions then being built in fancy Milwaukee neighborhoods, it was built by state residents using state materials. It was to serve as a "clubhouse" for Wisconsin fairgoers as well as a showcase—much to the janitor's chagrin.

But Wisconsin was everywhere. When President Grover Cleveland hit a gold telegrapher's switch on May 1, 1893, it alerted a Reynolds-Corliss engine built by E. P. Allis & Co. of Milwaukee, which in turn made fountains flow and flags unfurl.

"The greatest show on Earth had begun, and a Wisconsin machine had started it," one account noted.

Wisconsin's display included a miniature cranberry bog, an exhibit of 1,000 jars of state grains and cereals, honey, tobacco and wool displays and a large mining exhibit cornered by 10-ton brownstone pillars. And those were only 24 feet tall!

The state also boasted a $150,000 collection of pearls from the Sugar and Pecatonica rivers (clam beds has been destroyed by prospectors by then) that later was purchased by Tiffany & Co. of New York.

And there naturally was a sizeable dairy exhibit. In all, the state took home one-sixth of all prizes given. Later, the Wisconsin State Building was bought by a Kansas banker who moved it by flatcar to Kansas City. It would become, among other things, a gambling hall.

Gaylord Nelson,
the Father of Earth Day

Hoping to rechannel the youthful energy that had so ardently targeted the Vietnam War, Wisconsin Senator Gaylord Nelson borrowed a key tactic of the anti-war movement—the teach-in.

The environment deserved—no, demanded—a day of teach-ins, he proposed in a speech in Seattle in the fall of 1969. Planet Earth, he said, should not be trusted to "indifferent, venal men who are concerned with progress and profit" and who believed the environment was an issue for "bird watchers and butterfly chasers."

So zealous was Nelson in speeches across the country that some thought his real target was the White House. But the campaign that resulted was on behalf of Mother Earth.

The activities on that first Earth Day, April 22, 1970, proved Nelson's idea of re-targeting youthful activism was sound. Thousands of colleges, high schools and even elementary schools dedicated the day to issues of pollution, toxic contaminations and recycling.

"Youth Storming to New Cause: Pollution," one newspaper headline declared. But it went beyond campuses.

Politicians rushed to seize the issue and paint themselves in shades of green. Leftists who had previously demonized big business for its war involvement had new reasons to assail "the system" for its excesses.

Like most events of the era, it was equal parts circus and be-in, debate and street theater.

A crowd gathering for the first
Earth Day march, April 21, 1970.
WHI IMAGE ID 48105

While some huddled indoors, debating the environmental danger of colored toilet tissues, others held large and loud rallies. For every politician's promise there was a doubter's sneer. Some raked abandoned lots of trash and paraded the results in wheelbarrows; others led a "Scene-Ick Tour of Greater Milwaukee."

Earth Day became an annual event; no one could deny it changed the way America viewed its nest. But Nelson insisted mere survival was not enough, that "how we survive is the critical issue."

In an Earth Day speech to the Pennsylvania House of Representatives, which suspended its rules for "a very special order of business—the business of survival," Nelson said winning the environmental war would be more challenging than winning any other war in history.

"But wish for it, work for it, fight for it and commit unlimited resources to it, nevertheless the battle to restore a proper relationship between man and his environment, between man and other living creatures, will require a long, sustained, political, moral, ethical and financial commitment—far beyond and ever made before.

"Are we able? Yes. Are we willing? That is the unanswered question."

Manitowoc's Submarines
Went to War

The Navy was so determined that its launch of the first submarine built on the Great Lakes would go well that it declared its success in advance.

The trick was, the *Peto* would also be the first sub ever launched sideways, instead of stern first. Reporters gathered at Manitowoc Shipbuilding Company on April 30, 1942, were told by a nervous Navy public relations officer that model tank tests showed the sub would list at first but immediately right itself in the narrow Manitowoc River.

"What if it doesn't?" one reporter asked. "What it rolls over and sinks?"

Germany and Japan must never know.

"As far as you guys are concerned," the officer warned scribes, "this was a great launching."

Luckily for truth's sake, it was. At 11:45 a.m. Mrs. E. A. Lofquist, wife of the chief of staff of the 9th Naval District, smacked a bottle of champagne on the bow. A second later, the 1,500-ton sub shot down the skids sideways and hit the river like a duck, swimming proudly. Several thousand onlookers cheered wildly.

Manitowoc, like other Great Lakes shipbuilders, had made car ferries, tankers and river boats. When the bleak 1930s crippled shipbuilding, the company turned to producing paper mill machinery, cement manufacturing equipment and high-speed power cranes. But when the buildup for World War II stressed capacity of military shipbuilders on the coasts, inland companies such as Manitowoc Shipbuilding were pressed into duty.

The USS *Peto* (SS-265), a Gato-class submarine named for the peto, a sharp-nosed tropical fish of the mackerel family, May 10, 1942. WHI IMAGE ID 64627

The *Peto*, the first of 28 submarines that would come from Manitowoc, was 311 feet in length and built to carry a crew of up to 85 men and 24 torpedoes. The keel was laid in June 1941. The sub was built in sections, which were lifted into place by cranes. Construction, the company noted proudly, was completed ahead of schedule.

But the Navy's pride was muted by wartime secrecy concerns. Reporters asked whether they could say how long the ship was, what armament it would carry, when it would be ready for service and, by the way, could they take pictures inside or of the hull?

No, said the Navy. No, no, no, no.

The Manitowoc River was a long way from the South Pacific, of course, and inland to boot.

The *Peto* had shakedown cruises on Lake Michigan. But, too long for the locks on the St. Lawrence River, the sub had to travel to Chicago, via the Chicago Sanitary and Ship Canal, the Des Plaines and Illinois rivers to the Mississippi and then to New Orleans.

Manitowoc's iron fish was commissioned in November and went to war, eventually being credited with sinking eight Japanese ships and damaging others.

Built for almost $4.6 million, it was sold for salvage in 1960. The historic scrap brought $36,686.01.

Ezekiel Gillespie's Fight to Vote

Simply put, Wisconsin was one of the first states to give black people the vote—but there was nothing simple about how it happened.

Ezekiel Gillespie. WHI IMAGE ID 33362

There were few black residents in Wisconsin at the time of statehood, but suffrage for blacks was an issue at the first constitutional convention in 1846.

Suffrage was absent from the original constitution, but the issue continued to simmer; in 1849 the Legislature passed a law allowing black men to vote, but the first amendment to the new constitution would take effect only if approved by "a majority of all votes cast at such election."

Voter approved the amendment, 5,265 to 4,075. However, elections canvassers refused to accept the vote, arguing the favorable vote on the referendum alone was not close to a majority of the 31,759 votes cast for governor.

Then, in 1865, Milwaukeean Ezekiel Gillespie attempted to register to vote but was turned away as a person of "mixed African blood." Gillespie, with his crusading lawyer, Byron Paine, then sued election inspectors, setting off a landmark legal battle. The case eventually reached the state supreme court.

Paine argued that suffrage for blacks was one of the causes for which Wisconsin troops had fought the Civil War.

But more technically, Paine's theory was that the black suffrage amendment had actually been approved by the 1849 amendment. He argued "a majority of all votes cast at such election" could apply only to the specific issue, not to other races such as that for governor. Interpreting "all votes cast" any other way would make it impossible to approve the referendum, Paine said.

In 1866, the three judges, all Republicans, agreed. In other words, their ruling meant that blacks had actually had the vote for 17 years before anyone knew it. Some Democrats protested the outcome, saying any black voters who attempted to exercise the right would be mobbed, but the first black votes were cast in the 1866 elections and no violence occurred.

The historian Richard Current wrote that nearly all black votes in Madison and Milwaukee were for Republicans, but the party hardly benefited from its stand on behalf of equal suffrage. There were not enough black votes to make a difference in elections, while Democrats used the issue to exploit the public's widespread fear and dislike of blacks.

In recounting crimes by blacks, Democratic newspapers would never fail to tie the actions to Republican "Negro lovers," though the word used was often more coarse than that.

"If the party division had been closer, if the Republicans had been weaker, the added burden of race prejudice might have been too much for the party to bear," Current wrote.

Ezekiel Gillespie, in addition to exercising his right as a free man to vote, went on to found St. Mark's African Methodist Episcopal Church in Milwaukee.

The Evolution of the Horicon Marsh

The Horicon Marsh was carved by glaciers, harnessed and hampered by humans, and finally given back to nature. Hundreds of thousands of waterfowl each year and thousands of humans who enjoy their visit are better off for it.

The famous avian resting place that sprawls over 31,653 acres, mostly in Dodge County, hasn't changed much in recent decades, but in the long scheme the Horicon Marsh Wildlife Area has undergone numerous face lifts.

It was dug out and shaped eons ago by a great glacier. A lake was created, which over time was turned by nature's evolutionary processes into a broad marsh that provided Native people with food and fur.

Then whites arrived with bigger ideas and the technology to give the marsh a new mission. Its location on the Rock River made it attractive as a source of water power and, in 1839, a pair of Green Bay businessmen purchased a tract of land on the river and won a license to construct a dam.

When it was finally completed under different ownership in 1846, the dam flooded upstream and eventually created a lake 14 miles long and 6 miles wide. The lake soon was filled with fish, muskrats, mink and other species and the area became a popular hunting and fishing spot. In the 1850s, steamers plied the lake with passengers and cargo.

Even then, humans' interference with what nature had wrought was controversial. When the dike was found to leak in 1852, some landowners opposed rebuilding while others insisted it be repaired. In 1854, the Horicon Iron and Manufacturing

Canadian geese at Horicon Marsh, 1972. WHI IMAGE ID 32276

Company's efforts to produce water power by raising the height of the dam led to a lawsuit by affected homeowners.

The fight wore on until 1869 when, unable to cover damage claims, the company removed the dam. It was said it took three years for water to recede and the marsh to reappear and more time for it to heal itself. But it eventually came back, as did birds, animals and the sportsmen who sought them.

Human tinkering continued into the 20th century, this time devoted to turning the marsh into farmland. Large sections were drained and crops planted, but improper drainage hampered the effort. By the 1920s, the marsh was in such disrepair that fires broke out, plant growth was hurt and wildlife went elsewhere.

At that low point, conservationists finally got the upper hand. The Horicon chapter of the Izaak Walton League pushed for restoration of the marsh. It was a long struggle, but on July 16, 1941, victory was declared when the Horicon wildlife refuge, under joint state and federal authority, was officially dedicated.

Man still controls, but nature holds sway.

The Other Return
of Douglas MacArthur

Milwaukee welcomed Douglas MacArthur in 1951 with arms that stretched well beyond city borders.

The general's motorcade from Chicago was greeted by a sign that read, "Only five miles to Milwaukee," and by others at each mile marker before it sped under a banner of red, white and blue at the county line.

"The City and County of Milwaukee Greet Our General," it said.

"Welcome Home."

MacArthur only briefly lived in Wisconsin, and his legal address was a Milwaukee hotel room. But his roots here were deep. His grandfather, Arthur, was a judge, lieutenant governor and—for four days—governor. His father, also Arthur, joined the Wisconsin volunteers and won a Medal of Honor in the Civil War.

Douglas came to Milwaukee in 1898 from the Philippines, where his father commanded US forces. Douglas and his mother lived at the old Plankinton House while he briefly attended high school before leaving for West Point, where he began the career that would make him a five-star general and commander of South Pacific forces in World War II.

Later he was involved in military and civilian control of Japan, but after he clashed with President Harry Truman over the Korean War, he was recalled in 1951. After 52 years in uniform, he had time to come home.

On April 27, 1951, Milwaukee gave MacArthur "the greatest welcome it had ever given to anyone," the *Milwaukee Journal* declared.

General Douglas MacArthur in the midst of a tickertape parade honoring his return from Korea. WHI IMAGE ID 39898

Hundreds of workers cleaned streets for the general's planned 32-mile motor tour of glory. Bunting was everywhere, flags flew, potholes were hurriedly repaired. More than 350 newspaper, magazine, radio, TV and newsreel correspondents were on hand, and special trains were scheduled to carry onlookers. Five stars marked the door to MacArthur's Plankinton suite.

Security came from the most extensive police detail in Milwaukee history at that time, perhaps 2,000 officers, firefighters and National Guard troops in all. Police set the crowd at from

800,000 to 1 million, though MacArthur's motorcade sped so quickly through some neighborhoods that not everyone saw him.

A huge throng, said to number 40,000 or more, assembled at the formal civil welcome. MacArthur spoke of the emotion with which he returned to his "ancestral home."

When he said, "It was 52 years ago that Milwaukee sent me forth into the military service, and now I report that service has ended," the crowd shouted "No! No!"

"I want you to know that I have done my best and always have kept the soldier's faith," MacArthur said.

Mayor Frank Zeidler seized the occasion to formally dedicate the courthouse plaza where they stood, and to wrap the community's arms around the famous general one more time.

"For more than a hundred years, your family has been associated with Milwaukee and has distinguished itself in local civil government, in fields of battle and military administration," Zeidler said. "Today we have in our presence the soldier after whom this square is named.

"Therefore, in the name of the people of the City of Milwaukee, I officially dedicate and designate this area, in the civic center of Milwaukee, as MacArthur Square."

And so it is yet today.

John Dillinger
and Little Bohemia

It was Eugene Boiseneau's rotten luck, but indisputable claim to a historical footnote, to be in the wrong place at the wrong time.

He was enjoying a Sunday dinner at the Little Bohemia Resort in northern Wisconsin the fateful night the FBI showed up to capture the fugitive John Dillinger. It was the night the FBI got the wrong man. Nearly every bar in northern Wisconsin makes claims to gangster customers in the old days—it's good for business—but Little Bohemia has the bullet holes to prove it.

A celebrated bank robber in the 1930s—when banks were not viewed by all Americans as innocent victims—Dillinger and his gang were on the run from hot pursuit when they reached the lodge at Manitowish Waters in April 1934.

Dillinger's Wisconsin-born girlfriend, the beautiful Evelyn "Billie" Frechette, had just been arrested by agents in Chicago, but the group that sought to hide in the woods of Vilas County included the infamous Homer Van Meter and Lester "Baby Face Nelson" Gillis.

The $1 chicken special was on the menu, according to Tom Hollatz's *Gangster Holidays*. But while the fugitives rested and dined inside, federal forces were massing nearby to try to end a spree that included murder as well as bank robbery.

A tipster had alerted them to Dillinger's presence. So on April 22, two planes of agents landed in Rhinelander, took some cars and sped off through the cold night toward a staging area nearby.

Inside, Dillinger and his boys were playing cards when agents took positions on the grounds. It was then that Boiseneau,

Dillinger's mugshot, 1933.
PUBLIC DOMAIN

a Civilian Conservation Corps worker, and his dining partners elected to leave. At the same time, two bartenders stepped outside to see why dogs were barking; they appeared to agents in the shadows to be a gang of men in the night.

Dillinger's? Worried about losing the gang—and losing face—again, agents in charge ordered the men's tires shot out. When the car did not stop, agent stepped up their fire, wounding John Morris and John Hoffman but killing the unlucky Boiseneau.

If possible, it got worse for the feds. While tragic folly ensued outside, Dillinger and most of his gang escaped the lodge through second-story windows and made their way to safety in a car confiscated at gunpoint.

Meanwhile, Baby Face Nelson exchanged shots with an agent and found his own escape. Nelson reached a nearby resort where he took hostages and later engaged in a gun battle with pursuers, killing FBI agent W. Carter Baum and injuring others.

A manhunt spread throughout the north, fueled by rumors and fantastic flights of fancy, but none of the men was captured in Wisconsin. Just months later, the "Lady in Red" would help accomplish what the FBI bungled that night, a failure that did not go unnoticed.

"Well, they had Dillinger surrounded and was all ready to shoot him when he come," Will Rogers later observed, "but another bunch of folks come out ahead, so they just shot them instead."

A small museum at Little Bohemia tells the story yet today.

The Ringling Brothers Put on a Show

The first show might not have been the greatest on earth, but its highfalutin name was all-world.

In 1883 in Baraboo, five Ringling boys who had learned show business in their back yard rented a hall for an extravaganza they modestly called "Ringling Brothers, Moral, Elevating, Instructive and Fascinating Concert and Variety Performance—One Night Only."

But then, Al, Charles, Otto, John and Alf Ringling were hardly amateurs, and a bit of bombast is good for selling tickets. The brothers had been presenting entertainment for several years and understood well the public's appetite for pleasurable diversions and the potential profit for those who could provide it.

Hadn't they raised the price of their penny circus to a lofty nickel when they added a goat to the lineup?

They were going places, they knew. So the boys perfected their singing, dancing, juggling and other skills—Al could balance a plow on his chin, a trick not seen every day—and the next spring the soon-to-be-famous Ringling Bros. Circus was born.

In April 1884, a notice in the *Baraboo Republic* announced formation of their show, and on May 19, 1884, the "Yankee Robinson and Ringling Brothers Great Double Shows, Circus and Caravan" made its first public appearance.

The performance was given on a lot where the Sauk County Jail now stands, in a ring that was merely a circle of red cloth. They had a small tent but no horses or wild animals or even dogs.

Yankee Robinson was a noted circus man at the time, and his name no doubt helped draw customers. But it was left to the

127

A Ringling Brothers poster of "Kings of the Circus World."
WHI IMAGE ID 6050

brothers to pull off this hometown debut, and their first review, in the Sauk County Democrat, rated the efforts a success.

"The performance was very credible considering the boys had never had any practice," the critic noted, "and we have not heard a single person find fault."

And so off they went, adding wagons and horses when revenue permitted, then adding camels and elephants and all the trappings of big-time circus shows. In two years they boasted a bear, hyena, monkeys, and an eagle, though they hyena had trouble living up to its "mammoth, marauding . . . prowling grave-robbing" billing. It was blind, for starters, but a circus bill was no place to let that news slip.

Theirs was a "mud show" for the first few years, rolling from town to town in wagons pulled by horses, biding time until it could move by rail. A few years later, with a genuine big top, the Ringling Bros. Circus was riding trains in style, and it wouldn't be long before it became "the greatest show on earth."

This time, the circus was as good as its name.

Senator Teasdale and Wisconsin Vice

It might not be Wisconsin's oldest profession—fur trading was—but commercial vice was a fixture in this state's rough-and-tumble years. Lumber and mining hubs such as Hayward and Hurley were infamous for lighting the nights with red, and bawdy houses long operated in Milwaukee with a wink and nod from—and no doubt a discount for—authorities.

However, in 1913 the Legislature, of all institutions, got serious about sin.

As other states were doing at the time, it named a commission to investigate the white slave trade and related issues. Senator Howard Teasdale, a Sparta Republican, was named chairman.

Vice was hardly rampant. If anything, Wisconsin was more morally upright than its neighbors; only 36 Wisconsin women were jailed for prostitution in 1910, compared with an average of 265 in bordering states.

The alternative view was that Wisconsin wasn't enforcing its laws.

Teasdale first sent questionnaires to all district attorneys. Though few were eager to acknowledge such crime was alive in their counties, one exception was Vilas County's George O'Connor. According to an account by historian Paul Hass, O'Connor said he knew of two houses, but "the women living at these places are what we call old-timers. . . . Old and practically harmless."

Teasdale next sent questionnaires to 1,400 prominent citizens across the state, though one panel member complained ministers and society women were unlikely to have solid insight on vice.

The best information came from undercover agents—including women—who were sent statewide to personally check out taverns, suspected bawdy houses, dance halls, and other possible dens of iniquity.

And they found some. Of 48 municipally tolerated brothels, 21 were in Superior, a finding that no doubt increased tourism there. An additional 440 places were found where unlawful unions could be made, which led to a series of public hearings.

"I want to know the why of this," Teasdale kept saying, though a more apt question would have been, "How much?"

The bottom line was just that; most young, undereducated women who explained why they had fallen astray said the shady side of the street paid more than the other. Their night shifts paid better than any factory or laundry.

Professionals—typically about 26, of Irish or German background, seduced at 19 by a cad and in the business voluntarily, the committee learned—testified they did very well. Daisy Allen, the most successful of 15 women at one Milwaukee house, hauled in $44.75 a week in 1909, twice the pay of a minister and three times that of a teacher.

In its prescription for solving the problem, however, the panel veered sharply from sex to booze, concluding liquor was the devil in these houses of hell. The report of the inquiry into "white slave traffic and kindred subjects" was not used to pass laws against the flesh trade but became a major weapon in the effort that led to Prohibition.

Red lights would dim, but not entirely darken, on their own.

Hammerin' Hank's
Eau Claire Days

The greatest home run hitter in baseball history began and ended his major-league career in Milwaukee.

But Henry Aaron's real introduction to organized baseball came earlier, on June 8, 1952, when a shaky two-engine commuter flight from Milwaukee deposited him in Eau Claire, the long ago lumber town whose heritage ran more to Babe the Blue Ox than Babe Ruth.

Hank Aaron, March 18, 1954.
WHI IMAGE ID 26355

Aaron was 18, a Southerner, an untraveled young black man in a then–white man's game—though he had already played in the Negro League—and the butterflies he felt could almost have carried him and his cardboard suitcase as easily as the plane.

"I'll never forget that plane," he wrote later in his autobiography, *I Had a Hammer*.

"I was a nervous wreck, bouncing around in the sky over a part of the country I'd hardly ever heard about, much less been to, headed for a white town to play ball with white boys."

He wasn't the only black man in town. He had two black teammates on the Eau Claire Bears of the Northern League—John

Covington, who later became a fellow Milwaukee Brave known as Wes, and another fellow named William Bowers.

Eau Claire was not a hateful place for black players, Aaron discovered, but it was an other-worldly place. He always felt people were watching him—and they no doubt were. But a kindly white family looked after him, which eased his off-field concerns while he tried to become comfortable on it.

He was at ease with his abilities, but odd as it sounds now, he otherwise felt on Mars. In his first at-bat, he recalled, he was more nervous about facing a white pitcher than being in organized ball.

But he singled over the third baseman's head, then singled again in his next trip and drove in a run.

"It didn't take long," he said, "to find out that the ball was still round after it left a white pitcher's hand, and it responded the same way when you hit it with a bat."

Yet the career that made him baseball's all-time leader in homers, runs batted in and total bases almost was stillborn that summer. Lonely, uncomfortable in his new surroundings, Aaron thought about packing his cardboard satchel and quitting, but his brother, Herbert Jr., warned him he would only regret coming home to nothing.

"I felt better after that, and after a few weeks I was leading the league in hitting."

His career later took him to Milwaukee, Atlanta, to Milwaukee again and to unimagined glory. But Aaron never forgot Eau Claire.

Eau Claire remembered Aaron, as well. Years later it dedicated a bronze statue of the famous slugger in his honor.

Edna Ferber
Found Her Voice

In 1903, when the so-called "petticoated press" was a novelty, 17-year-old Edna Ferber became Appleton's first female reporter. And, but for her selfish demand for an innovation called vacation, she might have stayed there.

But she pressed until an editor said yes.

"Two a year," he said. "For six months each and starting right now."

And so Ferber moved to the *Milwaukee Journal,* where for three and a half years she covered the city's underside on police and court beats. She was still a tender 22 when she became ill and returned to Appleton, where she began the literary career that, as late as 1992 by one critic's account, made her America's all-time bestselling woman author of hardcover books.

Not bad for a woman who was warned by a *Journal* editor that fiction writing wouldn't pay. In fact, it made Ferber famous and wealthy, a Pulitzer Prize–winning novelist and a Broadway playwright.

"It was no part of my plan to become a writer of fiction," she recalled. "That I was the author of a successful novel at 23 was still another incident."

That book was *Dawn O'Hara,* based on her Milwaukee days. Others included the Pulitzer-winning *So Big* (1924), *Show Boat* (1926), which became a Broadway smash, and *Come and Get It* (1935), about the raucous days of Wisconsin's logging industry. That work won Ferber few friends in Hurley, the famously woolly Wisconsin community that was her model, where some thought

Edna Ferber, pen in hand.
WHI IMAGE ID 59514

her novel was not sufficiently fictionalized.

Ferber was born in Kalamazoo, Michigan, moved to Iowa and then to Appleton, where her father ran a merchandise store. While she neither was born nor died in Wisconsin and lived most of her adult years in New York's fancy literary circles, Ferber kept her hometown in her heart and in her writing.

"I feel sorry for anyone who didn't live in a small town before the age of 16," she once said. "In a small town you can come and go with a freedom unknown to the child of the big city. You can develop into whatever it is in you to be."

"And," she also said, "though now I live in the City of Sophistication, I'll never be more than an onlooker in it. And when it comes to writing I turn back to the town with a little human awkwardness left in it."

Ferber died in her New York apartment in 1968 at the age of 80. She never married, a topic she addressed in a 1924 essay in which she called her single status as accidental as her success.

"Those years had gone whizzing by, leaping, tumbling over each other," she said of the newspaper days. "When other girls were going to school, to college, dancing, playing, flirting, laughing, buying pretty clothes, thinking of marriage—and quite properly they should have been—I was interviewing perhaps the Polish woman living near the West Allis machine shops and asking her why she had got up that night and killed her husband with a meat ax.

"Curiously enough, she always told why."

Billy Mitchell Earned His Wings

Navy Secretary Josephus Daniels was so smugly certain that Milwaukee's brash flyboy couldn't sink a battleship from an airplane he said he was "prepared to stand bareheaded on the deck" while Billy Mitchell bombed away.

He didn't, and good thing. It would have been his final wrong guess.

Billy Mitchell was a war hero who, in World War I, led the greatest air assault in history against German ground troops. He also was an unappreciated prophet, insisting to deaf ears that the future of combat was in the air. It was his ongoing disputes with bullheaded military leadership that finally ended his pioneering career, but though the Army busted him in rank, his reputation was restored by time.

Mitchell was born in 1879 to a prominent Milwaukee family. His grandfather, Alexander, was one of the founders of the Milwaukee Road and Marine National Exchange Bank, and his father, John Lendrum Mitchell, was a Wisconsin senator. At age 18 Mitchell joined the Army and within months was a lieutenant in the signal corps.

He did not begin flying until 1916, but within two years he was a brigadier general commanding an armada of 1,500 planes. Convinced that air power would change the way wars would be fought, he was the first to call for a separate air force "co-equal with the Army and Navy." But his insistence that planes could go so far as to sink ships was ridiculed by the military bureaucracy.

Uncowed, he arranged a demonstration off the Virginia coast in 1921. Using old German ships for targets, Mitchell and his fellow

General William "Billy" Mitchell in the cockpit, 1918.
WHI IMAGE ID 10623

pilots shocked their superiors by sinking the ships, though his demand for a separate air force was still not approved.

He angered his superiors by making his campaign public, and the simmering dispute finally exploded when a Navy dirigible was downed by a storm and US planes were lost in the Pacific during an ill-advised attempt at a Hawaiian flight.

Mitchell blasted "these disgusting performances" and capped it by saying: "The bodies of my former companions in the air molder under the soil in America, and Asia, Europe and Africa—many, yes, a great many, sent there directly by official stupidity."

Court-martial was inevitable. General Mitchell was convicted of conduct that discredited the military and was suspended from rank, command and duty. He promptly resigned, but continued to publicly campaign for air power. He warned of a rapidly expanding Japanese air force, calling it a threat to the American fleet.

Mitchell died in New York in 1936 at age 56; some say the bitter dispute shortened his life. At his request he was buried in Forest Home Cemetery in Milwaukee—not in Arlington National—in a service largely without military pomp and ceremony.

Beginning with Pearl Harbor, World War II validated his vision, and it introduced the B-25—known as the Mitchell Bomber. In 1948, Congress recognized his contribution by awarding his son a special medal of honor. The airport in Milwaukee carries his name.

Dust Bowl Days
in the Central Sands

The Central Sands in 1934 was a place of poor land farmed by poorer people. Decades before irrigation would bring bounty, soil in this hard-to-farm region—generally south-central Wisconsin between Portage and Stevens Point—was thin and sandy. It scarcely took a major storm to disrupt crops and lives in what the writer Michael Goc called "a flatlander's Appalachia in central Wisconsin."

Then, in 1934, a hellish storm raised suffering to new levels.

There was good rain on April 5 but then none for months. Heat came, 80s, 90s, 105 degrees one May day. It was dry across the entire Great Plains when, on May 9, a great dust storm kicked up in the west. All the earth movers in use today could not lift so much as that wind did.

"It blew for two days and one night," Goc wrote in the Wisconsin Magazine of History, "carried 300 million tons of dirt over 1,500 miles, darkened the sky from Regina, Saskatchewan, to Dallas, Texas, and then blanketed the eastern half of the United States. So powerful and so pervasive was it that one Wisconsin folktale holds that pails placed beneath the cows on that day filled with dust faster than milk."

Skies darkened; office workers lighted lamps in mid-afternoon. A weather observer in Washington (where Franklin Roosevelt watched dust settle on the presidential carpet) said the continuation of such a dust blanket "would shortly result in ice-age conditions."

A Wisconsin farmer said windblown dust "buried the fence row like snow"; a county agent said it was so bad that when he awoke on the second day he "could see the outline of my body on the bed."

In places the gale blew up fire that roared along. A writer sent to Wisconsin by the *Ladies' Home Journal* quoted witnesses who told of rabbits outrun by flames—"horrible little balls of fire." A thousand firefighters were called out.

No lives were lost but livelihoods, meager as they had been, were blown away. The storm moved a million tons of Wisconsin sand; by one estimate a foot of earth had been scraped from 20,000 acres. A federal survey found the sand region "unfit for cultivation."

Drought-ravaged farmers told of starving cows and walked cattle along roadside medians to find even scant grass. Millions of dollars of drought relief poured into the region before, on June 9, rain finally poured as well.

In the calm after the storm farmers and government agencies recognized the inadequacy of soil practices there. In the following years millions of trees were planted as windbreaks in the Central Sands and other conservation practices were employed. Many of those who planted trees by the thousands would not live to see them grow tall, but that was not the point.

The great dust storm, Goc said, "had proved to be one of those rare historical events that clearly marks a change in the mental set of those who experienced it."

Patriotism Grew
in Victory Gardens

During World War I, Wisconsin's support for the boys over there was raised in patriotic gardens fertilized by propaganda.

Many had resisted war, but in April 1917 Wisconsin became the first state to organize a Council of Defense, a vehicle for carrying out federal war policies and educating citizens on the government's aims and needs.

Other, super-patriot organizations like the Loyalty League worked to ferret out subversive thought and expose the non-supportive, regardless of any civil rights that might be involved.

But one notion Wisconsin freely embraced was that "Food Will Win the War." Food conservation was the watch-word. Citizens were urged to plant "victory gardens" where they would "sow the seeds of victory." "Food saved, men saved," went another slogan, and the National War Garden Commission said citizens who planted their own vegetables would make "every garden a munition plant."

Late that year the Council of Defense, in conjunction with the US Food Administration, urged all housewives to sign cards pledging to observe "meatless Tuesdays" and "wheatless Wednesdays." The appeal was made on a Friday; by the following Tuesday, restaurants, hotels and private homes across the state were observing it.

In Green Lake County, 100% of the housewives signed on and 80% did in Milwaukee County, but it may not be surprising in light of such overheated propaganda that would-be slackers were risking their reputations—even their personal safety.

World War I poster produced by the National War Garden Commission, 1918. WHI IMAGE ID 3548

Libraries offered recipes and exhibits of food "made from materials which patriotic boys and girls are willing to eat at this time," and "model war meals" offered such items as "Over the Top Bread" and "Over There Pie Crust."

The delights of potatoes were preached. Even children were asked to sign poetic pledges:

> At table I'll not leave a scrap
> Of food upon my plate.
> And I'll not eat between meals
> But for supper time I'll wait.

Wisconsin college students were asked to sign cards promising to have seven wheatless and seven meatless meals a week, to use at least one less pat of butter a day, omit between-meal ice cream and snacks and "to cut the use of candy at least one-third."

It was Lenten sacrifice without end, but as another slogan reminded the faithful:

"It's the FOOD bullets that are going to crush the enemy."

One story by historian R. B. Pixley showed how far and wide food patriotism reached. It involved a visitor to Wisconsin who ordered shredded wheat.

"No wheat today," replied the waitress.

"What's the matter with this state," the man asked. "I asked for meat yesterday in Milwaukee and could not get it."

"That was meatless Tuesday," he was told, "and this is wheatless Wednesday. We've got to win the war."

"By George, that's so," the man said. "Give me a cheese sandwich, and, say, put it on rye bread."

When Communists
Came to Mosinee

In the 1950s, Americans expected the Red Menace to knock on the door at any moment. Who knew the American Legion, of all groups, would let it in? But it did in Mosinee on May Day 1950, when Cold War street theater in Wisconsin made headlines in Moscow.

Fearing mere warnings insufficient, Legionnaires John Decker and Paul Thielen decided to dramatize totalitarian rule in stark fashion.

They conceived a mock Communist takeover of Mosinee, a paper mill town in Marathon County, a proposal quickly embraced by the Legion's national office and by most Mosinee leaders.

Out-of-town Legionnaires playing invading Reds would place cardboard padlocks on churches, block roads, restrict mill workers' rights and build a barbed-wire stockade for political prisoners.

There were a few skeptics—especially after two ex-Communists were enlisted as technical advisers and actors—but no dissent would stop this patriotic pageant. Even when real Communists leafleted the town in the dark of night, organizers said it only showed the Red threat was pervasive and watchfulness was critical.

More than 60 news people were on hand May 1 when a "Council of People's Commissars" went to Mayor Ralph Kronenwetter's home and put him in custody. When some photographers missed the arrest, the mayor—still in bathrobe and polka-dot pajamas—and captors re-enacted it.

Kronenwetter, said an account by Richard M. Fried, used the occasion to announce his candidacy for Congress.

However, Police Chief Carl Gewiss resisted arrest and was "shot," a script device that allowed him to go off and direct traffic.

Clergymen were detained, cars searched and drivers interrogated. Restaurants served only black bread and potato soup, books and guns were seized and the *Milwaukee Journal* showed a boy near a sign that read: "Candy for Communist Youth Members Only."

The *Mosinee Times* printed a special edition in pink ink, featuring "Our Valiant Leader" Josef Stalin on page one, but plans to erect large Stalin posters were dropped lest out-of-towners not understand it was an act.

Freedom of the press was the one right not curtailed. Even Tass, the Soviet news agency, was represented, and although some papers were critical of the stunt it drew national attention, from a two-page spread in *Life to the Daily Worker*, which wondered how a company town run by paper barons could be worse off under another system.

Alas, at the concluding rally Kronenwetter suffered a cerebral hemorrhage and died a few days later. A minister who took part also collapsed, and he died on May 7. Both deaths were cited by the *Daily Worker* as caused by the "terrorized atmosphere."

Still, the *Detroit News* predicted that "500 or more communities in the United States will adopt the Mosinee Plan for teaching Americanism." Only a handful did, however, and almost no one noticed. Mosinee had had its moment in the sun, even if it was the pink of sunset.

The Menominee—
Sovereign Nation and County

In 1961, when the federal government stopped recognizing the Menominee nation as a sovereign entity, the beautiful land of towering pines and valuable hardwoods became Wisconsin's 72nd county.

The goal of Termination, championed by some policy makers going back to the 1940s, was to remove Native nations from US government control and end their protected status, which had given these Nations control over their lands and internal affairs.

Many Menominee were doubtful about the viability of that plan. They had resisted the change when it was approved in 1954 and had successfully delayed it until 1961, when they were told that the millions of dollars they were owed by the federal government in a court case involving forestry mismanagement would be tied to their acceptance of Termination. On April 30, 1961, Governor Gaylord Nelson named new county officers and declared the partnership of Menominee County and the state's 71 others would "last forever and ever."

It was the first time that the federal government had dissolved a reservation and enabled a state to absorb it and turn it into a county. The reservation's lumber mill that became Menominee Enterprises Inc. (MEI) was the new county's main source of income, and dependence upon such a cyclical industry left many residents uneasy about the county's fiscal future. Yet today, the Menominee Tribe's industries include not only the thriving lumber mill and forest products business but also the casino and hotel

Governor Nelson signing the bill that created Menominee County.
Watching left to right are: Gordon Dickie, Bernard Grignon, Hilary Waukau,
Attorney General John W. Reynold, James Frechette, and Al Dodge.
WHI IMAGE ID 45289

enterprise, off-reservation gaming, healthcare, and an economic
development authority.

Back in 1961, however, the failures of Termination were clear.
The county was sparsely populated and had almost no tax base.
When the rush to establish such a base led Menominee Enterprises Inc. to sell lakeside lots to non-Indians and create the artificial "Legend Lake," many tribal members were horrified. Incomes
remained low and taxes were insufficient to cover critical services.
In 1965 a report called the county "a pocket of poverty."

By 1971 the Menominee were badly divided over their status.
The group Determination of Rights and Unity for Menominee
Shareholders (DRUMS), organized to fight the Legend Lake plan
and MEI corruption, marched 220 miles to Madison, where it

criticized county leaders for selling off land and mismanaging the mill. Led by Native American advocate and scholar Ada Deer, DRUMS lobbied Congress to repeal Termination. In 1973, tribal status was re-established and Menominee County was a reservation once again.

Pleasant Life Found
at Pleasant Ridge

Few go there now. The onetime community of Pleasant Ridge, founded by former slaves, has been reduced by time to fading memories and worn grave markers.

But once its attraction was magical.

"Freedom was sort of in the air," the daughter of a settler later said.

Not merely freedom, but the good life, as measured for black families then. Even as the wounds of Civil War were still raw, the rural settlement in the Beetown area of Grant County became a truly integrated community, with the nation's first school where black and white students learned, and lived, together.

"It was a beautiful place to grow up," former resident Mildred Greene recalled at age 85, "where blacks and whites were all family. We all lived and worked close together and got to know people—so much that you really loved them. Unfortunately it doesn't work like that anymore."

In Wisconsin it did once. In 1850, a former slave owner named William Horner arrived from Virginia, bringing with him freed slaves Charles and Caroline Shepard, their children, and Isaac Shepard, Charles' brother.

Land near Lancaster was cheap and scenic. Horner called the area Pleasant Ridge, and white and black residents began to clear land and build farms.

A few years later, John Greene, a Missouri slave, escaped with his family. Using wages earned and saved in slavery, he purchased

Schoolhouse of District #5 in Pleasant Ridge, 1890. People pictured include: F. J. Webb (teacher), Rina Gadlin, Bessie Hoffman, Nettie Gadlin, Cora Sheppard, Jennie Hoffman, May Hoffman, Emma Green, Oscar Gimes, and Lester Green. WHI IMAGE ID 4239

a farm at Pleasant Ridge. Greene was educated and became a community leader.

The community, which consisted of many farms but no central business district, prospered after the war. More former slaves arrived, and by the 1900s there were at least 100 black residents in the area.

Church and school were the connectors. Black and white students were taught together at District No. 5 School and black students not only attended Lancaster High School, but some went on to college, an uncommon achievement. United Brethren Church was also integrated.

Farming was done in neighbor-helping-neighbor fashion. Annual barbecue gatherings drew hundreds of residents and former residents who made food and music and danced into the night.

It was not a racial Eden, of course. Some interracial marriages took place without incident, but two murders developed from interracial romances. In 1883, black resident Samuel Gadlin was killed after a man accused him of impregnating the man's daughter.

Four white residents were accused in Gadlin's killing. He was buried in what would become the black cemetery under a stone that reads: "Murdered by the hands of a cruel murderer."

Why did Pleasant Ridge disappear? The emphasis on education left high school and college graduates no reason to return, and growth of factory jobs in urban areas lured others. By 1920, the population had shrunk considerably. In the next few decades, Pleasant Ridge, except for the markers and memories, would disappear.

Comets Brought Awe,
Tickets to Ride

The uncommon comet has long run amok in people's imagination. Halley's Comet had been said to predict everything from destruction of temples in the first century to the Black Death in the 14th.

It was natural, then, that Wisconsin would brace for its arrival on May 18, 1910—or "Fatal Eighteenth." Experts assured citizens it was harmless, but some were worried that—in an unusual occurrence—the Earth would pass through the comet's tail.

The *Milwaukee Free Press* speculated that if the two collided, the comet would vaporize everything in its path, and the light blast would blind every viewer.

According to the historical magazine *Wisconsin Then and Now,* nervousness was rampant. In Milwaukee, there was a rush to prepare wills, and more than the usual number of family reunions were reported. Several suicides were blamed on the comet's threat.

Farmers in the Fox Valley removed lightning rods from barns so as not to attract it. Along Lake Superior, some residents left their homes in fear its backwash would cause a tidal wave. And some Milwaukee girls were said to have burned their love letters, lest their deepest secrets survive them.

But the devil-may-care formed "comet clubs," and at Fatal Eighteenth parties the drink of choice was the "comet cocktail"— vermouth and apple jack over cracked ice.

That evening, Milwaukee's lakeshore was crammed with the curious when the celestial flight arrived. Alas, a bright moon hampered watching, but predictions of harm were realized. Some watchers fell off rooftops—perhaps it was the comet cocktails?—while others drove into trees while craning for better views.

Years later another comet's visit put Wisconsin in the news, or at least zany Madison lawyer Eddie Ben Elson did.

As comet Kohoutek approached in late 1973, the legendary trickster announced that a beautiful, black womanly angel had revealed to him that Kohoutek was actually an intergalactic spaceship and Elson, because of the goodness of his heart, would be its captain.

Sure, the comet would destroy Earth on Christmas Day, but 144,000 lucky passengers would be saved. And, Elson said, he was selling tickets to ride.

He printed 1,000 tickets that identified him as "Your Saviour, Edward Ben Elson, Messiah of the Odd Infinitum Church," and the story was aired nationally. But though he sat in his yard in anticipation, Kohoutek passed by.

Elson wasn't disappointed; he hadn't really wanted the world to end, he said. And the stunt did land him on the TV show *Real People*, which later sent him a plane ticket to a big guest reunion show.

Elson couldn't attend, so he found Si-Ahmed, an Algerian immigrant who resembled him, and gave Si-Ahmed the suit Elson had worn on TV. Si-Ahmed went off to Los Angeles, where he was wined and dined before the ruse was discovered.

"They're absolutely outraged," Elson said. "But what the heck. I was just up to the same old thing."

Long Fight Led to Women's Suffrage

On June 10, 1919, Wisconsin was among the first three states (with Illinois and Michigan) to ratify the 19th Amendment that gave women the right to vote.

However, it was not quite the magnanimous gesture that the state's place in line might suggest; some women in Wisconsin had been demanding the right for more than 60 years.

The suffrage movement, often interchangeable with the temperance effort, had begun even before the Civil War. Initially it concentrated on state legislatures, but while a few western states granted women the vote in order to lure residents, the campaign gained little ground in Wisconsin.

The most prominent women in the movement—Elizabeth Cady Stanton and Susan B. Anthony—were among those who

Ada James, the leader of women's suffrage in Wisconsin.
WHI IMAGE ID 9334

stumped in Wisconsin appealing for suffrage, and the Wisconsin Women's Suffrage Association was active as early as 1869.

In 1886, the men of the Wisconsin Legislature gave women half a loaf. They passed a law allowing women to vote—but only in elections pertaining to school matters.

That wasn't enough for the Reverend Olympia Brown, a Unitarian minister in Racine, who had been an ardent petitioner for full suffrage.

Why, she would ask, should "aliens, paupers, tramps [and] drunkards" be free to vote just because they were men when "teachers, church members, preachers [and] mothers of the republic" could not vote, simply because they were women.

In 1887, Brown tried to vote in Racine's spring election, arguing that the mayor and city council appointed school officials and approved school budgets.

When the city refused her vote, she sued. A judge agreed with her, but the state Supreme Court later ruled the law was not clearly defined and voided it.

After that setback the cause foundered for some time until the Political Equality League formed to support a 1912 statewide referendum on suffrage for women.

Despite the active support of Belle Case La Follette and other prominent figures, voters rejected the measure by a large margin.

By about 1915, the movement changed tactics. Instead of working state by state, it elected to push for a federal constitutional suffrage amendment.

Wisconsin native Carrie Chapman Catt became president of the National American Women Suffrage Association and launched a campaign to win the vote for women. In part because of their participation in the war effort, women found success even sooner.

After the amendment passed and was submitted to the states in 1919, journalist and suffragist Theodora Winton Youmans wrote: "The political equality of women came because a little group of women had profound conviction that the enfranchisement of women was so fundamentally bright and so absolutely necessary that it must be brought about.

"It was the burning flame in the souls of a few women which lighted and led the way."

Brown was one of the few early suffragists still alive to enjoy the hard-fought right; she voted in her first presidential election at age 85.

Good-Road Movement Paved the Way

It seems odd, in this era of superhighways, that proposing merely decent roads caused a 20-year battle. Even the arrival of the automobile in Wisconsin couldn't speed this process along.

Credit bicyclists with starting Wisconsin's "good-road movement."

In 1890, newfangled two-wheelers started showing up in significant numbers; that year, about 1,000 Milwaukeeans owned bicycles, and four years later, 15,000 state residents had picked up the fad.

There were more cyclists than good places to ride. Country rides on rutted, muddy roads could be injurious endeavors. Bicyclists formed a chapter of the League of American Wheelmen, which immediately joined commercial interests to form the Wisconsin League for Good Roads.

But bone-jarring roads didn't bother those who weren't going places. Many farmers were content with what was in place, and they certainly didn't favor paying taxes to build roads for cyclists who scared their horses.

Even when they were assured better roads would help them market their goods, improve mail and other services, ease rural isolation and even make things easier for their horses, farmers resisted higher taxes. And because of a constitutional ban on spending state tax money for internal improvements, road advocates were stymied year after year in the Legislature. Attempts to change the constitution took center stage.

The motor car didn't sputter into the good-roads debate until it was well under way. In 1899, gas-powered cars began appearing in cities; by 1902, the Milwaukee Common Council posted speed limits at a breathtaking 4 mph, and that year Robert M. La Follette campaigned in a motor car for the first time.

They bicycling fad was over, but the motor car needed roads even more. When the Wisconsin State Automobile Association formed in 1907, its chairman, James Drought, went from Milwaukee to Madison and "blazed the trail" with yellow signs and arrows on fences and posts for others to follow.

The auto club's lobbying tactics were as basic as automotive understanding was then. When a law was proposed to limit speed in cities to 8 mph, Drought drove naïve lawmakers around the Capitol so they could experience safe speeds.

Such efforts—along with an improved farm economy and a realization the auto was here to stay—finally led to a constitutional change permitting state highway spending.

In 1908—there were still only 5,600 autos in Wisconsin—voters overwhelming approved the change. In 1911, Wisconsin became the 39th state to provide financial assistance for roads. Freeways were far in the future, but ruts would soon be in the past.

Bicyclists kicked off the "Good-Road Movement" at the end of the nineteenth century when the interest in bicycles and automobiles was on the rise. Pictured here is a bicycling outing from September 20, 1896. WHI IMAGE ID 111988

The Deadliest Tornado of All

Wisconsin has an average of 20 tornadoes a year, but none has blown destruction like the devil's own breath that struck New Richmond on June 12, 1899. The dead of a dozen storms couldn't equal the loss.

The killer storm formed on a unseasonably warm late afternoon near New Richmond, then a city of 1,500 residents in western Wisconsin.

Clouds gathered and darkened, rain began to fall and some hail as well. Yet there was no immediate hint this would yield what is still the deadliest tornado in state history. Some, curious, went out to watch it approach.

Witnesses who later described watching the spinning cloud form in the distance and attack their city differed in detail but not much in the horror they felt.

The funnel-shaped cloud was described as rising and falling and sweeping across the countryside. It leveled all that was in its way and, a witness said, even "sucked up all the clouds that came near it."

It swept away entire farms so cleanly that not enough kindling was left to start a fire. Barns, houses, churches, train depots disappeared, and those humans unfortunate enough to be unprotected inside them were swept to their deaths as well or buried—dead and alive—in the rubble.

Those who did survive were left in terror of the killing storm's sound and fury.

"The roar was like that of a wild animal," a woman said later, "only a thousand times louder than any noise that I ever heard.

The aftermath of the deadly tornado. WHI IMAGE ID 70368

It hurt my ears so that I thought I could never hear again if I wasn't killed."

Fires broke out in the wind's vacuum. A man trapped on Main Street under a heavy timber as fire approached was heard screaming "Cut off my foot! Cut off my foot!" But soon the cry became "Kill me! Kill me before I burn to death!"

The extent of death and devastation became evident even as the storm passed from sight. But the actual death toll was not known until the ravaged buildings were scoured for survivors. The loss was later described in somewhat bureaucratic prose for a state committee:

"One hundred and fifteen people were killed in the storm, two lost an arm each, one lost the sight of one eye and seven lost the use of one leg and are now upon crutches. Two hundred and thirty-three persons, residents of New Richmond, registered with us as losers, representing in their families eight hundred and forty-three individuals. . . . The property loss as registered foots $624,763.14; to which must be added a large amount lost by those who made no application for aid and offered no record of losses."

But others knew the storm's wrath was beyond measure.

"No pen can describe the force of this storm, or the destruction wrought by it," a New Richmond survivor wrote days later.

"It was a slice of the day of judgment."

Clarence Darrow and the Oshkosh Strike

By the 1890s, Oshkosh was a woodworking giant, yet the workers whose labor enriched mill owners such as George Paine were themselves miserably paid.

Men received as little as $1 for 10 hours' work, and children often were removed from school so they, too, could toil.

Oshkosh, where many poor immigrants had been recruited by the mills, was ripe for the emerging union movement.

Workers organized and in 1898 met with Paine to ask for better wages, an end to replacing men with women and boys and union recognition.

Paine tossed their letter in a wastebasket, and on May 16 woodworkers voted to strike.

Samuel L. Gompers sent best wishes to Thomas L. Kidd, secretary of the Amalgamated Woodworkers Union, "in the splendid cause in which you are engaged."

It was more desperate than splendid. Most of the 2,800 woodworkers stayed home, but the promised strike benefits of $3 weekly soon disappeared. Strikebreakers were hired, and demonstrations turned violent.

"Lawlessness Prevails," a newspaper declared.

At the Paine plant, infuriated workers rushed a gate when fire hoses were used against them. In the ensuing battle, a 16-year-old striker, James Morris, was clubbed on the head and killed.

Mobs formed amid talk of lynchings; women continued to throw rocks and eggs at scabs. More than 400 members of the National Guard arrived with Gatling guns and fixed bayonets—an ominous turn of events, in that guardsmen had fired on and killed five workers in a strike in Bay View a decade earlier.

Demonstrations continued through the summer, but talks yielded no settlement. By August, Paine pressured police to arrest Kidd and two other men for conspiracy to prevent normal operation of his company, and a short time later the strike ended.

Kidd hired the prominent lawyer Clarence Darrow, who recognized the issue was no more or less than the right of workers to withhold work and that the future of labor hinged on the verdict.

His closing statement would later be described as "one of the outstanding social documents of its time, enunciating in such logical terms the rights of persons over the rights of property that it helped lead the way toward a new ordering of life in America."

It was not a criminal case, Darrow said: "It is but an episode in the great battle for human liberty . . . which will not end so long as the children of one father shall be compelled to toil to support the children of another in luxury and ease."

He blistered Paine for his malice and avarices; spoke of the suffering of children and women; and described the fight as one of right against "a paltry piece of gold."

And he told the jury: "I appeal to you, gentlemen, not for Thomas I. Kidd, but I appeal to you for the long line—the long, long, line reaching back through the ages and forward to the years to come—the long line of despoiled and downtrodden people of the earth. . . .

"I appeal to you in the name of these little children . . . who will look at your names and bless them for the verdict you will render in their aid."

After a three-week trail, the jury was out for 50 minutes. Its verdict was "not guilty."

Calvin Coolidge's
Summer White House

He was, in large part, like any other North Woods visitor, if more famously silent than most. He was there to fish, mostly, but time was set aside for relaxing, sightseeing and the unavoidable business an important man must pack with his rod and reel.

But in 1928, for President Calvin Coolidge, it was summertime in Wisconsin and the living was easy.

In 1924, while endorsing outdoor recreation, Coolidge said that "life in the open is a great character builder" and the "lead should be taken by the national government."

Now he was leading by example. It was his lame duck summer—after six years in office, he was not seeking re-election—and so the White House announced in May 1928 that he and Mrs. Coolidge would make northern Wisconsin's Superior country their summer home.

They arrived June 15 for what would be an 88-day stay at a lodge on Cedar Island near the trout-rich Brule River.

He was typically private, but even "Silent Cal" caused some fuss. Highway 2 from Brule to Superior was repaved for the visit. Security men "swarmed over the roads, testing their safety and measuring time and distances," said one account. Special phone lines were brought in to conduct the nation's business.

Not that work would interfere with fishing. The first days were so rainy that Coolidge, worried for his wife's health, considered leaving for Wyoming.

A Secret Service agent later said he warned the president leaving would give the area a black eye. And conditions did improve

President Calvin Coolidge fishing at Cedar Island Lodge, 1928.
WHI IMAGE ID 2093

so much that Coolidge—in white shirt and business suit tucked into rubber waders—fished up to four hours a day.

He was so removed from politics he skipped the Republican convention, but Herbert Hoover, chosen to succeed him, came to pay his respects.

On his 56th birthday, July 4, Coolidge was presented by local Boy Scouts with a fishing rod inscribed "From Us to You." On Sundays, the first couple attended the small Brule Presbyterian Church, led by a blind minister named John Taylor who, Coolidge later said, "is compensated by the sharpness of his spiritual sight for the lack of his physical sight."

The president did give a speech in Wausau, visited Duluth and toured the Apostle Islands. But he was hardly overtaxed by presidential duties. And that was by design; he and Mrs. Coolidge both professed better health when, on September 10, they bade farewell.

"We came here some weeks ago when summer was just beginning," Coolidge said, "and now that the first touch of the north wind is changing the foliage to crimson and gold we are returning to Washington."

He praised the Superior country as "a vigorous, enterprising, growing region, and you may well be proud of it." If that wasn't testament enough to spur northern tourism, this was: "The fishing around here, I can testify, is very excellent."

Mitchell Red Cloud's Medal of Honor

The bravery and sacrifice of Mitchell Red Cloud, war hero, brought his mother, Nellie, into a world far beyond her homeland in Wisconsin.

She was in Washington, DC, when General Omar Bradley awarded her son a Medal of Honor. She accepted appreciation and condolences from President Harry Truman, in words that were translated from English to her own language, and later there was a salute from President Dwight D. Eisenhower.

She saw VFW and American Legion posts named after her son, parks dedicated to him, a historical marker erected in his honor along the highway. She saw his photo on the cover of Life magazine in 1951 and the painting in Esquire—"Corporal Red Cloud's Last Stand."

Nellie Red Cloud, Mitchell Red Cloud's mother, standing in front of the historical marker dedicated to her son. She unveiled the marker to the public and was instrumental in choosing its location. WHI IMAGE ID 123209

And in 1984, at 87, she was the first mother to see her child inducted into the American Indian Hall of Fame in Oklahoma, where he joined Hiawatha and Pocahontas, Jim Thorpe and Geronimo.

But pain and pride walked as one. "No matter what they do," she said 33 years after Mitchell's death on a far-off battlefield, "it still hurts."

Through the years and the wars, Wisconsin has had dozens of Medal of Honor winners. Red Cloud, who died saving his company from a Chinese Communist attack on a hill in Korea in 1950, was the first American Indian.

He was born at Hatfield on July 2, 1925, and he attended the Indian school at Neillsville and Black River Falls High School before entering the Marine Corps in 1941, falsifying his age to enlist. He fought with Carlson's Raiders during World War II but, finding civilian life unsatisfactory, joined the Army in 1948.

Early on November 5, 1950, Mitchell was the first to detect an approaching enemy force. He sounded an alarm and opened fire, allowing his side time to evacuate and reorganize. Wounded, Red Cloud refused aid, instead wrapping an arm around a tree for support while firing until he died.

Mitchell, whose father had served in World War I, was the second of Nellie's sons to die in uniform. A brother, Randall, had died during maneuvers with the Army in 1949.

All the top brass gathered for the medal ceremony in April 1951. Nellie went by train to Washington, where she proudly but stoically accepted the honor.

Red Cloud was buried first in Korea, but his body was returned to Wisconsin in 1955 for a service in Hatfield that mixed modern ways with his tribe's ancient rites. A crowd of about 1,000 gathered, and all businesses in nearby Black River Falls closed. An honor guard of Ho-Chunk (formerly referred to as Winnebago) veterans fired a salute, and Nellie was presented with a folded flag, yet another honor she gladly would have forgone.

In a tribute to the Congressional Record, Wisconsin Senator Alexander Wiley expressed sympathy.

"She may speak in the Winnebago tongue more readily than in English, but the deed which her son performed speaks with a universal eloquence which no man in any tongue may match."

Underground Railroad
Went through Milton

Early Milton settler Joseph Goodrich's one-of-a-kind house was designed for security above ground and freedom below. It was one of the rare stations where the fabled Underground Railroad literally went underground.

Goodrich left his New York home with his family in July 1838 and began the long journey to Wisconsin. When they reached the southern end of Lake Michigan in July, Goodrich and two companions went on ahead to find just the right place to settle, a spot they knew would have fertile soil and a sure future. On the rich prairie at what is now Milton, Goodrich was finally satisfied with the soil his shovel overturned and so his journey ended.

He first built a cabin, which served as his family's home as well as a store and resting place for the many travelers who passed by en route to Madison, Janesville or Fort Atkinson.

The Milton House was likely a stop on the Underground Railroad during the Civil War. WHI IMAGE ID 39826

In 1844 Goodrich had two cabins but needed more room for his hotel business. He wanted a structure that would offer security against possible hostile Indian activity, so he selected as his building material a mixture of cement, stone and gravel tamped together, a mixture he called grout. On top of that, he designed a three-story hexagon, certainly a novelty on the frontier.

His creation, still known today as the historic Milton House, has long been credited as being the first concrete building in the United Sates.

Large and distinctive, it was visited by some guests with prominent names—Sojourner Truth, Grover Cleveland and boxer John L. Sullivan reportedly among them—but some guests whose names were not even whispered.

Goodrich, ardent abolitionist beyond being a successful businessman, dug a tunnel from the hexagon house to the nearby log cabin for runaway slaves to hide in during their risky flight north.

Records of how many slaves went through the tunnel do not exist, but it has been said that after slaves left Beloit, the next stop on freedom's railroad was at Goodrich's secret inn.

He continued to operate his public inn until his death in 1867, providing guests with food and shelter but not with demon rum, which he vehemently opposed.

Among his other contributions to Milton, Goodrich organized a private school that he personally supported when tuition was insufficient to cover teacher salaries. It was generally considered the forerunner of the now-defunct Milton College.

Goodrich's house, with its long residential wing off the hexagon, was converted into apartments in later decades. In 1948, part of the wing collapsed. Faced with losing its treasure, the Milton Historical Society appealed for state financial help to renovate the house and open it as a museum.

Battleship Wisconsin's
Storied Past

The first battleship named for Wisconsin was a marvel of its time. Built in San Francisco on the cusp of the 20th century, the $4.1 million *Wisconsin* measured 373 feet long and carried 2,559 tons of armor and four 13-inch main-battery guns.

When, in 1907, President Theodore Roosevelt sent his battleship fleet around the world to show US strength, the *Wisconsin* and its crew performed admirably.

The fleet came home in 1909 to learn that the British had built a much improved battleship—HMS *Dreadnought*. The *Wisconsin* and its sister ships were suddenly obsolete. A decade later, it was decommissioned and in 1922 was broken up and sold for scrap. It brought $41,812.50.

The late 1930s gave birth to a new generation of ships, fast and possessing great offensive power, with 16-inch guns capable of firing 2,700-pound shells as far as 24 miles. The final four of that class included a new *Wisconsin*. Richard Zeitlin, onetime curator of the Wisconsin Veterans Museum, called the ships "reminiscent of an exotic sports car 18 stories high."

Work began in January 1941, 11 months before Pearl Harbor. The new *Wisconsin* would cost $110 million and take 39 months to build. On December 7, 1943, in Philadelphia, Madge Goodland, wife of Governor Walter S. Goodland, christened the Wisconsin with a bottle of champagne. Ralph A. Bard, undersecretary of the Navy, was kind enough to "extol the virtues of the Badger State, its shipbuilding industry, its fishing and hunting resources and its many tourist attractions," Zeitlin wrote.

Elevated view of the battleship USS *Wisconsin*. WHI IMAGE ID 70211

Then, war. The *Wisconsin* made it to the Pacific theater for the last months of World War II, engaging its huge guns often to shell Japanese targets. On its 105,831-mile journey, not one crewman was lost or wounded, and the Wisconsin was never hit.

Korea would be different. The *Wisconsin* fired its 16-inch guns more there than it had in World War II, at rail yards, bridges and roads. In 1952, a North Korean artillery shell hit the Wisconsin, injuring three men and ripping a hole in the deck, but damage was minor.

The *Wisconsin* returned nine 16-inch shells at the offending shore battery, scoring two direct hits.

"We were never able to fire enough ammunition to suit the Marines," Commander H. C. Bruton said.

The battleship era was nearly over, however. One battleship after another was decommissioned in the 1950s; the *Wisconsin* was the last in service when it was retired in 1958.

In the 1980s, battleships were briefly in favor again. The *Wisconsin* was modernized and put back in service, at a cost of nearly $400 million. A large crowd of state officials and the ship's veterans attended the recommissioning in Pascagoula, Mississippi, in October 1988. Its big guns sounded again during the Persian Gulf War but the *Wisconsin*, the 64th and last battleship built by the US, was again deactivated in 1992. In 1998, a move began to have the ship opened to public tours.

Sam Tripp,
Notorious Horse Thief

In January 1891, the *River Falls Journal* reported the arrest of "Samuel B. Tripp, one of the most notorious horse thieves in the northwest," and recited his unlawful pedigree.

It told of Tripp's love of horses not his own, his prison stays, the time Tripp shot one of his pursuers and how, at his recent capture in Hudson, he was in possession of three horses, one newly stolen.

"The possibilities," echoed the *Hudson True Republican*, "are that Sheriff Donohue will soon take a Tripp to the penitentiary (we apologize to all good pun makers)."

No apologies needed. He was hardly the only sheriff to take this Tripp to prison, but none could cure Tripp's addiction to other people's rides. For nearly 50 years, from the 1860s to 1910, Sam Tripp the notorious horse thief, as the papers came to call him, was to stables what John Dillinger was to banks.

Tripp, born in Maine in 1843, came to Wisconsin in the late 1850s. His first theft conviction, for 55 bushels of wheat, came in Pierce County in 1862.

In 1864 Tripp enlisted in the Union Army (if his superiors had known him, the *Pierce County Plaindealer* said years later, "he would have been a valuable man to supply the army with horses.") but deserted months later. In 1870, he was imprisoned in Iowa for stealing buffalo robes; perhaps it was such inhospitable treatment that prompted his return to Wisconsin.

For some years Tripp practiced thievery here and in Minnesota. Horses, wagons, harnesses, nothing was safe when Sam

Tripp was about. In 1878, a sheriff's posse cornered him and heavy fire was exchanged but Tripp escaped, prompting one paper to accuse the sheriff of "execrably poor shooting."

But "Tripp the Desperado," as the St. Paul paper called him, was arrested and sent to Stillwater prison in 1879. After his release, he stayed out of trouble for two months before being accused of buggy theft. It was during this escape that he shot and wounded a marshal, Jones Hall, but he was later arrested in Wisconsin and returned to Stillwater.

The pattern was unbroken. He would serve time, be released, steal horses or other items, be arrested, serve time and on and on. Such was his fame that throngs would circle jails to view him, and sheriffs would double security. After his arrest in St. Croix County, he would be taken to another county because, a paper said, "authorities are afraid he will steal the St. Croix county calaboose."

In 1891, Tripp was sent to Waupun State Prison for 10 years. In 1897, he was released but the next year was imprisoned in Kansas for horse theft. He then tried Madison, where he was arrested again in 1901 under the name James Brown. But the New Richmond paper declared, "IT'S OLD TRIPP."

"He is 55 years old and is said to have stolen more horses than he has hairs on his head," a Madison paper said.

Indeed, the *New Richmond Republican Voice* offered sound advice for readers in 1905:

"LOOK OUT FOR YOUR HORSES," its headline declared.

"Sam Tripp the notorious horse thief escaped from the Hudson Jail."

Lone Rock's
Uranium Heyday

It's hard to know what made Kenneth Crook feel better—the uranium tunnel he constructed in Lone Rock in 1954 to ease his ailments, or the money true believers paid to share in his cure.

But even his magic ore couldn't cure his legal headache.

Wisconsin's uranium heyday is humorous now, but a lot of suffering citizens took it seriously when the 36-year-old farmer turned to atomic medicine.

In 1953, debilitated by a variety of stubborn ailments, he despaired of conventional treatment and went to Arizona, where he had read how mild radioactivity in abandoned mines had cured illnesses.

After 14 visits to a uranium tunnel in Tombstone, he felt improvement. Thus inspired, he and his wife packed 2,100 pounds of ore into their cars and headed for home.

He built his tunnel in Lone Rock, in Richland County, lining wallboard with leather packets of pulverized low grade ore. He painted "Uranium Tunnel" on the window and talked of the ore's marvelous healing powers. He opened for business on May 26, 1954, and, for $10 offered friends and neighbors 11 one-hour sittings.

"Within a fortnight," the *Wisconsin Magazine of History* later noted, "Crook and all the other Lone Rock tradesmen were bustling with business from the lame, the halt, and the hypochondriacal." By mid-July, his tunnel was drawing up to 200 visitors a day, and the tingling sensation that hinted of "cures" was common.

Sitting in Crook's Uranium Tunnel in Lone Rock, 1954. The pads on the visitors' laps and on the floor contain uranium ore. WHI IMAGE ID 82406

"So many say they can't feel it," a woman told a reporter, "but I feel it real strong."

A skeptical *Milwaukee Journal* story on July 26 made Crook famous, but also brought him trouble.

The *Lone Rock Journal* huffed that the big city daily should butt out, but the attorney general's office—pressed by state medical officials—soon accused Crook of violating medical practice laws.

At a court appearance, Crook was applauded by almost 150 onlookers, including a man who said arthritis had nearly crippled him before he visited the tunnel. "Now I can lick the devil out of anyone," he said.

Crook's defense was that his tunnel was merely available, that he never sold or boasted of its medical benefits. But he was hurt by witness after witness who claimed it had eased their suffering from asthma, nerves, fungus and other maladies.

On November 22, a judge ruled Crook had indeed violated the law, but the uranium boom was hardly over. By then, a dozen tunnels had been built in other Wisconsin towns by copycat quacks, including a Madison tavern owner who spent $3,500 to add a uranium room to his bar.

None did much business, but the story wasn't over. In 1955, Crook leased his tunnel to a Milwaukee chiropractor, who moved his adjustment table into an adjoining room.

He made the uranium tunnel his waiting room. It might have made patients feel better, but it eventually cost him his license.

Life in a Lumber Camp

Paul Bunyan's yarns were good, but the stories of real 'Jacks best describe the real roughhouse glory of the lumber camp. John Nelligan's account, in the March 1930 edition of the *Wisconsin Magazine of History*, spoke of an era when the eight-hour day was merely what preceeded lunch.

> At about four o'clock in the morning the chore boy, awakened by an alarm clock, or more often, by that sixth sense which warns a man that the designated hour of awakening is at hand, would crawl from his cozy net of warm blankets into the chill early morning atmosphere and start the fires—one in the cook's camp, one in the men's camp and a third in the camp office. . . .
>
> When a good healthy blaze was roaring in each of the three stoves and waves of warmth were attacking the blanket of cold which lay over the camp like a pall, the chore boy would go into the men's camp and shake the teamsters into wakefulness, being careful not to disturb the sleep of the other men. The chore boy's popularity among the jacks depended largely upon his discretion in this matter.

The teamsters would feed and harness their horses, dress themselves, wash for breakfast and often enjoy the day's first chew.

> Chewing tobacco reminds me of Ed Erickson . . . as good a man at handling horses as he later became at handling men.

Loggers posing in front of a train. WHI IMAGE ID 2170

Ed loved his chewing tobacco. Whenever he pulled his plug of tobacco out of his pocket the horses would turn their heads expectantly towards him and he always had to give each of them a chew before putting the plug back. They loved the stuff and Ed, being a gentleman, always treated them, but it ran his tobacco bill pretty high.

Reveille was at 4:35 a.m. and "come and get it" soon followed. Lumberjack hygiene was not time-consuming and a good breakfast was more important, anyway. Great stacks of flapjacks, beans or potatoes, meat, hash and oceans of coffee "with such fragrance that makes one's nose crinkle with remembrance. . . ."

Then into wool caps, flannel shirts, Mackinaw jackets and warm footwear. If the cutting was close, men would return for lunch; otherwise, it was also brought to the woods. Work was hard and ran long into the dark on many days. At night, horses were tended to, then wet socks were hung by fires to dry "where they steamed away and emitted an indescribably atrocious odor which permeated the bunkhouse atmosphere."

After dinner a few men read, mostly old papers or the *Police Gazette.*

In all my experience in logging camps I remember only one man who ever had a Bible. He was a younger fellow spending his first winter in the woods who came of pious parents. They had given him the Bible when he left home and told him to read it faithfully every Sunday he was in camp, but after watching the lumberjacks enjoy themselves doing the stag dance, the jig dance and playing games, he put the Bible aside and said, "I'll read it in the spring."

The Burning of the War Eagle

The late 1800s was the golden age of the steamboat on the upper Mississippi, before the river was tamed by locks and railroads seized the day.

Grand boats possessing beauty and speed carried passengers, cargo and entertainment between St. Louis and St. Paul. But steamers were susceptible to boiler explosions and to fires, such as the "Terrible Conflagration" in La Crosse on May 15, 1870, that claimed the *War Eagle*, a fine steamer that had won mastery of the upper river by defeating the Tishomingo in a race.

But she couldn't outrun fire.

It broke out when a cooper got too near a leaking barrel of coal oil with his lantern. In the overheated style of the day, the La Crosse *Morning Leader* told the story:

> The most terrible conflagration which has ever visited the state occurred at the La Crosse Depot this morning, by which the entire Depot and Freight Warehouses, the Elevator and contents, the Steamer *War Eagle* and nine cars, Express, Freight and other property was lost, and several lives lost.
>
> Words are utterly inadequate to picture the terrible scene—the conflagration, the consternation and the dismay. The steamer *War Eagle*, on which the fire started, blazed up like a torch in a moment, rendering escape for any difficult. . . .
>
> The extensive depot and adjoining buildings were immediately wrapped in flames. The picture then presented—the roaring conflagration, the terror, the alarm, the uncertainty, the exaggerated rumors of the loss of life, the eager crowds

The steamship *War Eagle*. MURPHY LIBRARY SPECIAL COLLECTIONS, UW–LA CROSSE

of people [with] their faces lit up by the flames, the firemen bravely at work, all formed a scene to appall the timid and awe the brave.

Words, it seems, were adequate after all.

Terrible as it was, the loss could have been worse. The train from Milwaukee had not yet arrived, or more passengers might have been on board. Despite flames and blinding smoke, passengers fled on gangways or into small boats or simply jumped overboard.

Fire spread so quickly the mail agent could only grab his money packages; the mail was lost. But the ship sank before 48 kegs of gunpowder were reached by the flames.

The newspaper reported at least four deaths: 18-year-old Mary Ulrich, "an estimable girl"; a colored barber, name unknown; an old gentleman from Kentucky and an elderly lady, whose names were also unknown. Among the injured was "one old lady, name not known, but who weighs about 200 pounds" who was badly burned before she reached the water.

Thousands of bushels of wheat and tons of freight were lost in the fires that spread across the docks and into warehouses. The ship was valued at $30,000 and the total lost was put at nearly $250,000.

"The scene presented this morning is a sad one," the paper said. "What was a hive of industry and a receptacle of wealth is now a mass of charred and blacked ruins, strewed with the debris of the great conflagration."

The paper found it curious that the "triumph of the fire fiend" was entirely surrounded by water.

Carry Nation
and the Boys at the Bar

If most temperance advocates were content to assail John Barley-corn with sharp words, one favored blades of steel.

No mere oratory for Carry Nation. The hatchet-swinging Kansan gained fame by busting bottles and busting up bars across the land, an approach that led to dozens of jailings and a few injuries as well. A sign that hangs yet today on the front of a Fond du Lac tavern recalls the time the militant Nation brought her act—and her ax—to Wisconsin.

Her publicist had gone ahead to brief reporters, who in that pre-TV age were curious about what this famous woman might look like.

"She is homely," her own man conceded. "She is homelier than a mud fence. But say, she does have a most powerful arm for swinging a hatch ax."

She arrived July 17, 1902, a summer day warm and sticky enough to give a man a taste for a beer.

Men in Fond du Lac were no different. While a crowd gathered in Lakeside Park to hear Nation speak, others gathered on downtown stools to slake their thirst.

Carry Nation in 1910. PUBLIC DOMAIN

183

The speech was unexceptional, and relatively unthreatening. Nation spoke about saloons she had smashed, chastised men in the audience for smoking and sold photos of herself and miniature souvenir hatchets.

The next day, she attended a temperance meeting, spoke to railroad workers in North Fond du Lac about the evils of drink and smoke and, when rain washed out a park lecture, moved downtown, where she asked saloon keeper E. J. Schmidt if she could speak on the corner outside his business.

Schmidt knew she would draw a crowd, and some would want a drink. He said yes.

Nation was wound up that night. She excoriated drinkers and Germans, reasoning that the latter were also all the former. Some of Schmidt's customers paid little heed, which prompted taunts from Nation, but one who had been listening really set her off. German by heritage, he responded to her angry words by buying, and presenting to her, a bottle of whiskey.

"She surprised those present," the Fond du Lac paper reported, "by drawing a hatchet from beneath her dress and smashed the bottle."

Schmidt grabbed the hatchet and strong men prevented any further damage to his bar, so the "famous incident" boasted about on the sign on the bar today might be a bit of a stretch. But bar talk is like that.

Nation had other things to do, anyway. She left for Oshkosh, which she denounced as "the wickedest city in the state, if not in the whole northwest."

John Muir's
Environmental Roots

The seed that was to grow into John Muir's conservation ethic was planted in Wisconsin, on a small farm "in the sunny woods, overlooking a flowery glacier meadow and a lake rimmed with white water lilies."

The description came in *The Story of My Boyhood and Youth*, Muir's 1913 account of early life in Wisconsin before he headed west to hike, and preserve, huge wilderness tracts.

The man who would co-found the Sierra Club was born in Scotland in 1838; he came to Wisconsin in 1849. He would later write often, and fondly, of his childhood explorations near Montello, where the John Muir Memorial Park now offers a taste of what he saw then.

Muir attended the University of Wisconsin, where he had a room that overlooked Lake Mendota, near the Muir Knoll that was later dedicated in his honor. Though he gained his greatest fame for preserving and helping to establish Yosemite and Sequoia national parks, he was also an adept inventor.

He devised an alarm clock that rolled him out of bed, and John Muir. WHI IMAGE ID 3948 a mechanical student desk he created in 1891 is on display at the Wisconsin Historical Society headquarters building.

Muir's father, Daniel, was a strict taskmaster and inspired a righteous sobriety in his son that was eased by the passing of time. Once, when reminiscing, Muir wrote a friend: "I thought of the days when I came in fresh verdure from the Wisconsin woods, and when I used to hurl very orthodox denunciations at all things morally or religiously amiss in old or young. It appears strange to me that you should all have been so patient with me."

However, Muir's greatest achievements came from looking ahead, not behind.

He became an ardent naturalist, conservationist, writer and such an activist in urging government action to preserve the wilderness that he is considered the father of the national park system.

The outdoors never failed to leave him in awe.

"No healthy man who delivers himself into the hands of Nature can possibly doubt the doubleness of his life," he wrote. "Soul and body receive separate nourishment and separate exercise . . . [but] living artificially in towns, we are sickly, and never come to know ourselves."

In 1985, Muir was one of the first inductees, with Aldo Leopold, of the new Wisconsin Conservation Hall of Fame. It aptly honored this man who never forgot the little lake in Wisconsin where "the beauty of its lilies and orchids is so pressed into my mind."

John Till, Somerset's Plaster Doctor

John Till, barefoot and unkempt but blessed with medical powers, was such a miracle healer he once used his secret plaster to reaffix a dog's severed tail.

So it was said, anyway. The tail not only healed but its wag was restored, which explained the crowd and brass band that met Till after one of his many trials for practicing medicine without a license ended in his favor. Who wouldn't take aches and pains to a man such as that?

Thousands did, pouring into the western Wisconsin town

John Till. WHI IMAGE ID 125522

of Somerset to sit for Till's one and only cure—a mysterious hot plaster concoction he would smear with a sponge on their backs and shoulders in one of three dosages: mild, strong or, for the most serious maladies, " horse treatment."

His legend took root in 1905, when farmer Octave Cloutier, whose wife suffered an infected cheek, sought out the woodsman who was purported to have healing skills. It was John Till, an Austrian by birth who had picked up an interest in folk medicines after a serious hay wagon accident as a child.

Till treated Cloutier's wife, Meline, with his plaster potion. When she recovered, Till's services were in demand.

With Cloutier as his manager, Till's reputation as the "Plaster Doctor" spread far and wide, and patients flocked to Somerset by wagon, rail and horseback. They came with palsy, paralysis, rheumatism, cancer, appendicitis, blindness and, an account by James Taylor Dunn said, "all the diseases not contagious that man is heir to."

Twelve at a time, seated on backless kitchen chairs at Cloutier's farmhouse, the needy were smeared with Till's mixture and threw their dollars into a bucket. One year he was reported to have made $80,000.

Medical societies tried repeatedly to shut him down, but Till never prescribed medicine, and juries were usually on his side. The night a band welcomed Till home hundreds of patients were waiting for treatment, though how many were tail-impaired dogs was not reported.

Skeptical newspapers tried to link several patient deaths to Till's odd remedy, but defenders said the deceased had merely been too far gone. But after several prosperous years in business, Till and Cloutier had a falling out and his salad days in Somerset ended.

He continued to practice elsewhere but was plagued by lawsuits—a Milwaukee man claimed blindness as a result of a plaster treatment—and legal problems. In 1920, the State Medical Board finally managed to make a seven-year-old conviction stick, and Till was jailed. Ten months later, Till was released after agreeing that he, his family and what money he had left would return to Europe.

Why was he successful? A doctor once suggested Till actually could make sufferers forget their problems.

When people went to him with sore stomachs, Till made their backs hurt so that they forgot all about their stomachs.

Wisconsin and the Plan for Peace

Julia Grace Wales had tried to make peace for the world. When America entered World War I in 1917, it wasn't because her Wisconsin Plan for Peace hadn't offered the world a detailed, if idealistic, alternative.

Wales, a Canadian, was an English instructor at the University of Wisconsin when Europe erupted in 1914. She was horrified by war, and her thinking on how to end it led to the plan she prepared and published.

Over Christmas break in 1914, borrowing concepts from others, Wales had fashioned her plan for averting the un-Christian war. Her plan was called "Continuous Mediation Without Armistice." It essentially called for the world's neutral nations to send delegates to an international commission or, "world thinking organ."

Talk would silence guns. The commission would invite proposals for ending the war; it would attempt to keep neutral nations from entering the war even while working with belligerent powers to stop the shooting.

She shared her idea with Hamilton Holt, a newspaper man and crusading pacifist who gave Wales wide exposure. Her plan was then shown to the Wisconsin Peace Society, which swiftly adopted it, reprinted it and brought it further attention.

A copy of what was by then called the "Wisconsin Peace Plan" was sent to Washington for President Woodrow Wilson to consider. Leading pacifists embraced it. In February 1915 it was unanimously approved at a National Peace Conference in Chicago. Senator Robert La Follette urged the president to call an international peace conference, while the Wisconsin Legislature adopted the plan by resolution and forwarded it to Wilson.

"The Wisconsin Peace Plan," declared George Nasmyth, president of the World Peace Foundation, "grows upon me every day" and Secretary of State William Jennings Bryan said, "It has created a great deal of interest."

Wales went to Europe, where a Woman's International Peace Congress also approved it unanimously. It was reprinted in three languages and distributed throughout Europe, where it received mixed response. The sinking of the *Lusitania* by a German U-boat did little to help the peace movement.

The plan continued to be debated. Wilson received thousands of telegrams urging him to pursue mediation, but he remained cool. The public similarly was uninvolved in the peace effort led by a relatively small group of academics and activists. Eventually, preparedness for war took precedence over preventing it.

Curiously, even Wales came to support war. In 1918 she wrote, "The community of nations as a whole has a duty to resist any aggressor who vitally threatens the freedom of future generations."

She did, however, hope the League of Nations would embrace mediation.

Great Chief Buffalo
Went to Washington

The memory of Great Chief Buffalo is preserved in the weedy, rundown, often overlooked Indian Cemetery in La Pointe, on Madeline Island, near the fancy marina that shelters summer guests' expensive pleasure boats.

It was on Madeline that Buffalo (or Bezhike), principal chief of the Lake Superior Chippewa Indians, died in 1856 and was buried. He was believed to be 96 years old.

Not long before his death, Buffalo had traveled to Washington as a consequence of the 1854 Treaty of La Pointe, in which the Lake Superior Chippewa agreed to accept reservation status.

For his people and his home island, that meant great change. Nearly 2,000 Indians had gathered at La Pointe when the compact was being worked out between government commissioners and tribal leaders.

Under the final terms, two reservations were set up on Wisconsin's mainland.

Indians who were Catholic were to move to Red Cliff, a few miles from Bayfield, while others went to Odanah, on the Bad River. A few Ojibwe were allowed to remain on Madeline on a tiny piece of reservation land.

A few months later, in early 1855, President Franklin Pierce requested an audience with principal Chippewa chiefs to deal with related matters. Despite his advanced age and winter conditions, Buffalo made the journey to Washington.

Buffalo and his colleagues attended a White House reception and a mechanic's fair and toured government buildings before returning home in March.

Great Chief Buffalo died less than six months later, even as Commissioner of Indian Affairs George Manypenny was at La Pointe to complete payments to the Chippewa and check on their removal to reservations.

Buffalo did not leave, however. It was said that on his death bed, Buffalo heard reports of his people settling across Chequamegon Bay at Red Cliff, where his descendants remain today.

When the White Pine
Was Limitless

Once, this state was the frontier's lumberyard. It has been estimated that the white pine cut in Wisconsin from 1875 to 1900 would be enough to build a pathway one inch thick and a half-mile wide around the equator.

No one built the boardwalk, but so many other needs existed in the developing Western Plains that the vast and seemingly limitless forests that covered much of Wisconsin largely disappeared in mere decades.

Some commercial logging had occurred before the Civil War—Oshkosh was a major milling town—but the northern lumber camps roared to life after the war.

Hardwoods were nice, but pine was the prize, and Wisconsin was mad for wide-scale lumbering. Its forests stretched beyond sight—the Chippewa River Valley alone was the proverbial empire in pine—and logs could be easily floated down the state's many rivers to mills and markets.

Or, sometimes not so easily. Huge jams were common. On the Chippewa River in 1869, a backup piled logs nearly 30 feet high for 15 miles. Daring, or perhaps foolhardy, log drivers were needed then to walk on the top of logs and open the river.

Lumbermen devised a system of tying logs together into long rafts. "The sight of a fleet of rafts negotiating the white water on the upper Wisconsin or shooting the slot in one of the larger dams was a show not to be missed," wrote historian Robert C. Nesbit.

But it was adventure with a dangerous edge. Wisconsin River rafting took 40 lives in 1872 alone.

Lumberjacks use a two-man crosscut saw to cut a pine into manageable sizes for hauling, 1880. WHI IMAGE ID 3679

The logging boom led to expansions of the railroads and to the growth of many cities, drew more immigrants to Wisconsin and made a relatively small number of lumbermen—Philetus Sawyer, Frederick Weyerhaeuser, Isaac Stephenson and the owners of Knapp, Stout and Co. among them—fabulously wealthy.

At its peak from 1888 to 1893, the industry was responsible for almost one-fourth of all the wages earned in Wisconsin. But work was hard and wages stingy; the average lumber worker in 1897 took home just $386.

And logging was inevitably a boom-and-bust business; the stumpy, debris-strewn land that was left behind by timber crews was good for little. Some optimists tried clearing and farming such lands, but most gave up after it proved both backbreaking and unprofitable.

Early on, the farsighted saw an end to the industry. Conservation was not a 19th century value; clearing land was considered progress. The renowned Increase Lapham had warned in 1867 that stripping the land of forests would cause hotter summers, colder winters, soil erosion, more damaging storms and decimated harvests.

"Under these changes of climate and productiveness, the people, being deprived of so many of the means of comfortable living, will revert to a condition of barbarism," he said.

But few listened. By 1900, Wisconsin's vast pine forest had been largely depleted, ending a rich and colorful era.

Diamonds in
Wisconsin's Rough

They were digging for water and found wealth, if only they had known. The large, bright stone that farm owner Tom Devereaux and his tenant, Charles Wood, unearthed from a well hole that day in 1876 was pretty enough, but who would think a diamond would be lurking 65 feet into the Wisconsin earth near Eagle?

Devereaux gave it to Wood's daughter to play with, but seven years later it was in the jewelry box owned by the girl's mother Clarissa Wood, when she went into Milwaukee to have a pin fixed by a jeweler name S. B. Boynton.

When he saw the stone, Boynton "took it into his hand and seemed some time looking at it," Clarissa Wood said later. But Boynton merely asked where she had found it and offered to buy the "topaz" for $1. She said no, but months later when she was in more urgent need of money she gave him the stone at his price.

Perhaps what helped tip her off to being shortchanged, said an account in *Wisconsin Then and Now*, was that Boynton immediately also bought the Devereaux farm. Before word of the dis-

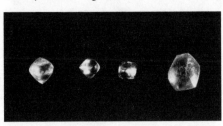

covery could spread, he organized a mining company and erected a black cloth barrier around the well so no one would see him digging for more diamonds.

An image of the Eagle Diamond (right) in 1929. IMAGE # 253493, AMERICAN MUSEUM OF NATURAL HISTORY LIBRARY

Clarissa Wood, now aware she had been scammed, offered $1.10 for the stone's return and, when she was turned down, filed suit. The case went to the State Supreme Court, which curiously ruled that the professional jeweler had not known the straw-colored stone was a diamond and thus had not committed fraud.

Boynton was not so lucky as a diamond miner. But after finding no more stones, he sprinkled store-bought diamonds on the property and sold enough stock in his mining company to allow him to head for Chicago with the Eagle Diamond.

He eventually sold it for $850 to Tiffany and Co. of New York. Later, the 15.35-carat diamond was purchased and displayed by the American Museum of Natural History.

It was not the only diamond discovered in Wisconsin. In 1886 the 21.5-carat Theresa Diamond was found by Louis Endlick near the Green Lake Moraine, but it was later broken into 10 pieces.

A four-carat white diamond found in Oregon in 1893 was also bought by Tiffany, a 6.5-carat stone found at Saukville in 1896 was sold to Milwaukee jewelers, and a gold seeker in Pierce County found 10 small diamonds over a period of years.

All Wisconsin diamonds were found along the edge of the farthest penetration of the great glaciers, and so were carried here from elsewhere. And, would-be prospectors might note, all these diamonds were found before 1900.

However, the Eagle Diamond made modern headlines. On August 31, 1964, the Eagle Diamond was among 22 rare stones, including the Star of India Sapphire and Star Ruby, stolen by Jack "Murph the Surf" Murphy and two others. The stones were later recovered in Miami.

Poor Clarissa Wood. By then the Eagle Diamond was valued at $25,000.

Jens Jensen,
Landscape Artist

Jens Jensen loved spaces that afforded the full sun of day and last light of sunset. Door County visitors who find a lakeside park with even one of those should be thankful for his vision.

Jensen is not so readily remembered as someone who bequeathed a legacy of parks and open spaces, but that is hardly his fault. In Wisconsin alone, he built dozens of estate gardens, Racine's city park system, and public landscapes in Milwaukee, Madison, Manitowoc, Sturgeon Bay and elsewhere, Susan Talbot-Stanaway wrote in *Voyageur Magazine*.

His best-known work is The Clearing in Door County, a learning atmosphere developed from light and landscape that is used yet today by students of all rank. Living spaces, he believed, yielded understanding.

"Never shall I forget a May day in the woods of southern Wisconsin when snowdrifts were everywhere," Jensen wrote.

"If you want to see the trailing arbutus at its best, where it sings of spring and sings of winter, you must see it in full bloom along a snowdrift."

Jensen (1860–1951) was from a comfortable family in Denmark, but in 1884 he and his future wife, Anne Marie Hansen, went to America. He worked as a celery farmer in Florida and a laborer in Iowa before he found, in Chicago, work and a career in public parks.

He studied plants and trees, land, light and space. By 1890, he was foreman at Chicago's largest park, Humboldt Park, and soon was designing his own spaces.

Jens Jensen. WHI IMAGE ID 11272

He was a leader in the Prairie School movement, which strove, as Talbot-Stanaway put it, "to assert Midwestern reverence for the land and Midwestern faith in The People."

While he worked for the very rich—Henry Ford and J. Ogden Armour among them—he recognized the destructive force of development on open spaces, especially when he bought land in fragile Door County. While serving on the Door County Park Board, he pushed to acquire lakeshore land for park use.

"I think the most satisfactory work I have done is in the parks and playgrounds for the public," he later said. "Private estate work is selfish—they build a wall around it and point their noses at their fellow countrymen."

The Clearing was perfect space for Jensen, "both a clearing in the woods and a clearing for the mind." He had purchased 129 acres for a summer home, but his wife preferred Chicago. After her death, he began to establish the school that exists yet today.

The Clearing struggled financially but did offer the classes Jensen had envisioned in architecture, writing, painting, and other arts. But after his death in 1951, additional support was found, and The Clearing's mission of accommodating nature was assured of longer life.

Consider sugar maples in the setting sun, which Jensen first witnessed near Lake Geneva: "These trees were in their autumn tint and the afterglow was fiery red. Its reflection in the tops of these trees produced a light that, to me, made the trees seem to be afire," he said. "Ever since that time, I have tried to place the sugar maple or the sumac in such a situation that the evening light set their tops aflame."

Karl Paul Link
Found the Cure

The line between theoretical research in a safe campus setting and the urgent needs of state residents was revealed to University of Wisconsin scientist Karl Paul Link one snowy day in 1933 when a desperate farmer came to Link's biochemistry building.

The farmer, Ed Carlson, represented not a long-term research project but an immediate plea.

What to do about his milk can filled with blood devoid of clotting capacity, and the dead heifer it had come from? What of the spoiled sweet clover that was all the farmer had to feed his cows?

Link, who had just begun to research the suspected "sweet clover disease" that caused hemorrhaging in cattle, could only advise Larson to use other feed and provide blood transfusions.

But Link, and Larson, knew it was inadequate assistance for an urgent problem.

Link was born in Indiana in 1901 and trained at top schools in the United States and Europe, earning his PhD from UW–Madison and becoming the university's first professor of biochemistry in 1930. He was already making a name for himself in the relatively new discipline when

Karl Paul Gerhardt Link with his pipe in 1958. WHI IMAGE ID 123816 he was presented with the farmer's challenge to the deliberate pace of research.

Link, with some colleagues and student assistants, began a line of inquiry that proved the link between sweet clover and the loss of clotting ability in cattle. They then isolated the anticoagulant Dicumarol, which would be a key discovery in preventing blood clots in humans.

Their research further led to development of Warfarin, the famous rat-killing substance, which was also used in developing medicines for use in treating heart disease.

President Dwight D. Eisenhower was treated with such medicine after suffering a heart attack in 1955.

Link's work brilliantly represented the ways in which campus research could touch the daily lives of ordinary Americans. And he personally embodied the often sharp clash that results when academic and personal freedoms in a university setting are pitted against political pressure to conform.

Sometimes called one of the Madison campus "bad boys," Link was faculty adviser for a Marxist student organization, spoke against "the atomic sword" and nuclear arms testing, protested the work of the House Un-American Activities Committee and even declined to have his photo taken for a campus identification card. He addressed his refusal to "the top commissar" of the university.

But it was his scientific achievements for which Link will be remembered, the credit for which he freely shared with his students.

"I think the credit for their success is three-pronged," he wrote. "They never ceased to wonder, they kept on trying, and they were on a project directed toward doing mankind some good instead of trying to destroy it."

Link died in 1987 at the age of 77.

The War to Win a College

As the 19th century moved to a close, education was at the forefront of Wisconsin's agenda, so the need for teachers was great.

The state had created five normal schools, or teacher training schools, by 1890, but all were in the southern half of the state. In 1891, the legislature authorized the Board of Regents of the Normal Schools to establish a sixth school in the northern half of the state.

It sparked a "pick me" campaign among cities reminiscent of railroading's formative days. More than a dozen cities—from Bayfield and Superior to La Crosse and Eau Claire—competed for the prestige and sizable yearly income a school would mean.

But the choice came down to Wausau or Stevens Point, which were already scrapping to become central Wisconsin's dominant

State Normal College, 1905. WHI IMAGE ID 38651

city. Landing a school could do the trick, so the competition was brutal.

Wausau's *Pilot Review* said its city "clearly outranks [any other] in natural beauty of location, and in . . . advanced municipal improvement." Any other cities had better hustle, it said, "as Wausau was playing hard for first place."

But the *Stevens Point Journal* declared it "wants that school and it wants it bad" and asked every resident to be "a committee of one to do all he can to secure it."

Regents were lobbied heavily; they were wined and dined during inspection visits the way athletic recruits are today. When they left Wausau, the *Pilot Review* said the matter was "as good as settled," but that was before Stevens Point dispatched a special train for regents.

Decision day was July 21, 1893. Voting began at 3 p.m., but ballot after ballot produced no majority. It wasn't until after midnight—and not until the 101st ballot—that a wire finally reached the winning city:

"To the boys at Stevens Point—We have won, the world is ours."

More than 2,000 people who had awaited word, and many more who joined them, began a raucous celebration with bonfires and a marching band.

The *Stevens Point Journal* wrote that the city was not celebrating because Wausau had lost—when that clearly was part of its joy—but because it won "that to which they were by right entitled."

The *Pilot Review*, seeing no reason to be more gracious than that in defeat, called Stevens Point "a city with a moral reputation which stinks worse than the Milwaukee River." The *Wausau Central*, meanwhile, declared Point of such poor character "it would be even risky to locate a penitentiary there" and said the choice clearly resulted from bribery.

Wausau, obviously, survived the loss of the normal school, which today is the University of Wisconsin–Stevens Point. And in 1994, on the school's 100th anniversary, the editors of the *Stevens Point Journal* and *Wausau Herald* officially, and finally, buried the hatchet.

Despite the availability of a weapon, neither editor was injured.

Kohler, a Community Divided

Sheboygan industrialist Walter J. Kohler Sr. wanted a model community where the workers who produced the plumbing fixtures and engines that carried his name could live in a park-like setting as nice as any suburb. His vision of "enlightened paternalism" also led him to construct what is now the posh American Club to house immigrant male workers.

But the model village would become nationally known for unhappy reasons, as the site of two family-rending strikes marked by bitterness, violence and, in one case, death.

The Kohler Company was established by John Michael Kohler and a partner in 1873, entered the plumbing ware business in 1883 and later began manufacturing engine-driven generators.

In 1934, a strike grew out of a dispute over union representation between a company-sponsored workers' association and the American Federation of Labor. It began in relative calm—lead striker Arthur Kuhn even called Walter Kohler, a former governor, "a fine man" of good character—but a mediator was unable to end it quickly.

Village officials had braced for trouble, stockpiling machine guns and other arms and wrapping several trucks in sheet metal.

On July 27, the match burned down. First, youths began breaking factory windows with stones. As the strikers paraded through town with blackjacks, slingshots and clubs, a squad of special deputies charged with tear gas and, finally, guns. Two strikers were killed and 40 wounded in the ensuing riot.

Poster urging the boycott of Kohler Company plumbing products, printed by striking Federal Labor Union No. 18545 in late 1934. WHI IMAGE ID 58466

"It was a night never to be forgotten," wrote a *Milwaukee Journal* reporter. "Such things as have happened this night are not possible. They must have been dreamed. Flaming bitterness such as this, blazing of guns such as this, charging of armed men such as this—none of it is possible in a town that has been called a model village."

The National Guard was called and ordered restored; the workers' association, which the union called company-dominated, eventually won.

The second strike—by the United Auto Workers in 1954— was so bitter some families were split all the way to the grave. It lasted six years, was again marked by violence and cost UAW $12 million in strike benefits before federal officials ruled the company had been at fault.

In such a closed and close-knit community, the strike left deep scars. On the company's 100th birthday in 1973, union and Kohler leaders reflected on its impact and lessons learned.

"They learned we can't be pushed around," said Raymond Majerus, a UAW official who, with his father and brothers, were Kohler strikers. "But we found out there is a different way of doing business with them, a good deal different than most companies."

Chairman Herbert V. Kohler Jr. similarly cited an atmosphere of mutual respect.

"We try to be pragmatic, define the problems and solve them as quickly as possible. As a result of the strike, both sides try to avoid getting locked into irrevocable positions."

The Sovereign State
of Winneconne

The saga of the short-lived but never-forgotten Sovereign State of Winneconne reads like a home version of *The Mouse That Roared*.

And why not? That is exactly what it was, a revolution with a wink in its eye.

When the state highway map was issued in 1967, the residents of Winneconne looked for their town, but couldn't find it.

Winneconne had been forgotten.

Citizens took umbrage. Was that any way to treat a proud community that had been in place for 130 years?

No, they declared, it was not. And so the village decided that if the state couldn't remember to put Winneconne on its map, Winneconne would find a way to get the state's attention. It launched a contest to determine how to get back on the map and the winning suggestion—secession—was by any measure an eye-opener.

On July 20, 1967, the Village Board voted to secede from Wisconsin, named itself the Republic of Winneconne and adopted a flag with the moto "We Like It—Where?"

Oh, yes, it further voted to declare war on the United States.

Well, why not? Rolling now, the new nation appointed secretaries of state, war and the Navy, and a restaurant owner named Vera Kitchen named herself custodian of the Kitchen Cabinet. Its air force was a single-engine Piper Club that looped in patrol overhead while the Winneconne Navy—a 35-foot-cruiser—puddled about on the Wolf River.

Having declared war, the town needed an army so it called up its own "militia," a rather rag-tag collection of

The flag of an independent Winneconne, July 20, 1967.
SOVEREIGN STATE OF WINNECONNE, INC.

black-powder enthusiasts who obligingly fired several volleys
when the Wisconsin flag was lowered and Winneconne's new
banner went up.

In his war room in Madison, a smirking Governor Warren
Knowles mused his "deep concern" about the rebellion and
hoped the National Guard would not have to be dispatched. But
it didn't ease tensions when Knowles added, "By the way, where
is Winneconne?"

By then, however, Winneconne had gone too far to turn back
and, anyway, was having too much fun.

The new government declared the dodo its official bird, poison
ivy its official flower, the skunk its official animal and the sheeps-
head its official fish. And, needing revenue, it began charging a
25-cent toll on each car crossing the Highway 116 bridge.

Perhaps because it was summer, this cold war didn't last very
long. A day later, when enough reporters had gathered to give
Winneconne the attention it was seeking, the president of the
new republic presented his demands to Knowles by telephone, a
message carried by loud-speakers through town.

Knowles agreed to restore Winneconne to the next map and,
in the interim, to erect signs so no one would miss it.

Still, someone did. In 1976, Rand-McNally left Winneconne
off its road atlas.

The Winneconne Jaycees asked Canada for political asylum.

Ripon Threw
a Grand Old Party

Ripon's claim to having sired the Republican Party is a guaranteed fight-starter in GOP circles. Jackson, Michigan, has long tried to wrest credit, as has Kansas City. It must be acknowledged, as well, that the anti-slavery feelings that inspired the March 20, 1854, meeting at Ripon's one-room schoolhouse to form a new party were simmering elsewhere.

But most historians grant that Ripon's A. E. Bovay called the first public meeting from which Whigs, Free Soilers and Democrats emerged as the vanguard of a new Republican Party.

If Jackson wants to claim the first statewide convention of Republicans, few in Ripon would quibble. Some like to say the party was born in Ripon and christened in Jackson. As *Ripon Weekly Press* editor and historian S. M. Pedrick wrote in 1915, Ripon has never said it formed a whole and complete national party that day:

"Ripon claims, merely, that here, in a frontier village, was the earnest meeting that recognized that those [anti-slavery] causes meant the casting aside of old party ties and the organization of some new party to grapple with the problems arising from the slavery question; and that the name for the new party was first suggested by a Ripon citizen and that the name was first considered as a name for the new party at the meeting above mentioned."

Bovay's urgency to form a new party grew from proposals to expand slavery to emerging states, principally Kansas and Nebraska.

Bovay had been urging creation of a Republican Party—a name with immense significance, charm and prestige, he

Warren Knowles, then a candidate for lieutenant governor, speaks from the steps of the Little White Schoolhouse. At the doorway of the school are Representative William Van Pelt (R-Fond du Lac) and Fred Goff, Madison, field representative for the state GOP, August 8, 1960. WHI IMAGE ID 105805

said—but the pending legislation forced him into action. He "went from house to house and from shop to shop and halted men on the street to get their names for the meeting," he said later. Of the 100 voters in Ripon at the time, 54 attended.

Debate lasted until "the hour was late and the candles burned low. It was a cold, windy night at the vernal equinox. But in the end all but two or three gave in and we formed our organization."

Similar meetings followed elsewhere, and a national force resulted. The schoolhouse was a residence for some time—ironically, one occupant was future Democratic governor George W. Peck. Now it is a historical site.

All the better to support Ripon's contested claim, which a writer for the *Milwaukee Journal* explained on the party's 75th anniversary. "Republicans hereabouts are willing to grant that their party has as many lives as a cat, a theory which political history has gone far to prove," he wrote, "but they are insistent that the first meow was heard March 20, 1854, in the little old schoolhouse here which bears the proud legend, 'Birthplace of the Republican Party.'"

The Faithful Foundation of St. Nazianz

For some Europeans, one of the attractions of the New World was the freedom to build new and experimental communities. In Wisconsin, that led to development of several utopian settlements, but also to a much longer-lasting venture into a religious, communistic lifestyle at St. Nazianz.

Such a unique community hardly needs legends, but St. Nazianz has a few. One is that the village's winding streets came about because when the first six settlers arrived at their new home site, a white ox appeared and led them along a winding course. Where he stopped was the site chosen for the first church.

The real story is intriguing enough. The primitive Christian community was founded by a German priest, Father Ambrose

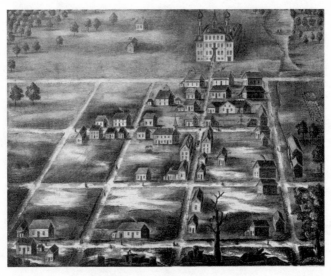

A bird's-eye view of St. Nazianz, 1860. WHI IMAGE ID 43555

Oschwald. Desiring a place to practice his vision of communal liv-ing—his strong beliefs had caused problems among his superiors—he led his parishioners to America in 1854 and came to Wisconsin, where he had heard many Germans had made good lives. They pur-chased almost 4,000 acres of wilderness in Manitowoc County and, on the heels of the six who had been sent to break ground, Oschwald and his followers moved to their crude new village.

Their inspiration was the New Testament Book of Acts: "And all that believed were together, and had all things in common; And sold their possessions and goods, and parted them to all men, as every man had need . . ."

By late 1855, Oschwald and his panel of elders had drafted rules for their new Society of St. Nazianz. All would work for the common welfare without wages, except for rare circumstances. Members of the community would eat, worship and work to-gether, and efforts were made to protect Society members from being influenced by non-members.

Oschwald even built separate dwellings for unmarried men and women who wished to practice poverty, chastity, obedience and other virtues. By the 1860s, the community numbered 200 or so, and more immigrants were arriving.

"Das Settlement," as Nazianz was often called, stabilized into a cohesive religious and social unit, according to an account in *Voyageur Magazine*. The Society began each day with early Mass. A bell would summon workers for a noon meal, followed by an-other common prater session.

The community survived under Oschwald's vision and direc-tion for almost 20 years, during which it continued to expand, especially through construction of religious buildings. A semi-nary was built and a chapel, along with an outdoor trail for the Stations of the Cross. The movement faded as original members died and outsiders moved in, but many of the early buildings still are in evidence today.

Robert's Rules
Ordered the Day

Henry Martyn Robert was trained in war and military engineering, not at running meetings of unruly citizens.

When called upon to chair his first public meeting in the early years of the Civil War, the then-captain discovered that swinging a sword was quite unlike wielding a gavel, though it might be more effective. All he knew about decorum was that "all in favor should say aye."

When some said "no," he found himself defenseless—not a position an officer enjoys. So he began looking for a way to bring order to the disorder of other public meetings.

Soon the public would know the result of his efforts as "Robert's Rules of Order," still the dominant guideline for meetings from 4-H clubs to the halls of Congress. Those rules were conceived and written in Milwaukee, though more by happenstance than because Milwaukee was plagued by out-of-control gatherings.

During the 1870s, Robert was assigned to oversee river and harbor improvements and military defenses on Lake Michigan. In the winter of 1873–74, however, he found enough down time to seriously pursue a set of rules that would ease deliberation at all levels.

He applied an engineer's order and logic to the problem, devising guidelines based on the principles of majority rule.

His *Rules of Order*, as it later became known when the book was published and widely accepted, established parliamentary procedure for committees and other bodies, describing how amendments, motions and debate were to be handled.

Finding a publisher was problematic; the topic was hardly sexy. But Robert had the type set and book printed at Milwaukee's Burdick and Armitage printing company in 1875 and produced 4,000 copies. They quickly caught on and the book, in many revised and expanded editions, eventually sold millions of copies.

"It was a task of Herculean proportions," his biographer, Ralph C. Smedley, later wrote in *The Great Peacemaker*. "It required the mind of an engineer, a logician, a mathematician, a philosopher and an idealist together with the patience of a plodding pilgrim."

Keeping the peace became Robert's passion. In the winter of 1876–77, he began speaking on parliamentary law at Milwaukee Female College—later Downer College—where he also began drilling his students on the rules. He later published other books on parliamentary practice, but none as far-reaching as his first little rule book.

Henry M. Robert retired as a brigadier general in 1901 and died on May 11, 1923. He was survived by a more orderly world.

Lucky Lindy—from Dropout to Hero

He might have been one of the University of Wisconsin's most famous graduates. Instead, Colonel Charles Lindbergh is one of its most famous dropouts, but he later received a hero's welcome and an honorary degree to boot. Lucky Lindy, indeed.

Lindbergh studied for two years at Wisconsin until he left to learn how to fly. In 1923, he took his first solo flight, joined the Air Reserves and became an air mail pilot. Of course, it was his historic New York-to-Paris non-stop flight in May 1927 that made him a worldwide celebrity.

Upon his return, he was America's unofficial king. To promote aviation, a foundation sponsored a national tour for Lindbergh and his *Spirit of St. Louis*.

On August 20, 1927, he landed in Milwaukee and was paraded before thousands on Wisconsin Avenue. He praised the city for embracing aviation and, in turn, was honored by 800 at a dinner that night.

"Lindbergh did more for us than all of our diplomats in the last 100 years," Mayor Daniel W. Hoan noted.

Lindbergh then took off for Madison, but not as the crow would fly. He dipped in salute over soldiers homes at Wood and Waukesha, then flew over Oshkosh and Fond du Lac, where phone calls to factories and businesses—along with word of mouth—brought out nearly half the city.

At first a distant speck, he flew in so low "you could hear the smooth purr of the motor, and the distant sight of Lindbergh's friendly, boyish features sent shivers of admiration up the spines

The *Spirit of St. Louis*, in which Charles Lindbergh made the first solo Atlantic crossing, arriving in Madison, August 22, 1927. WHI IMAGE ID 74130

of adults as well as the children," local historian Stan Gores, who was in the crowd, wrote 40 years later.

In 1928, Lindbergh made a farewell flight over his old mail route from St. Louis to Chicago, carrying letters with a special commemorative postmark. The involvement of Lindbergh, who was still popular enough to leave politicians envious, brought a record volume of air mail to the flight—4,278 pounds and 12 ounces. Milwaukee residents contributed more letters than any city except St. Louis.

Lindbergh returned to Wisconsin later in 1928 to receive his honorary degree from the university, where he thrilled some administrators by taking them aloft in his famous craft. And Lindy did nothing to mar his hero's reputation on that visit.

Leaving Madison, he flew to Watertown and circled a hospital where his former UW roommate, Delos Dudley, was a patient, then paused at the Janesville airport and sent Dudley a note.

"Lindbergh became a world figure overnight [but] seems to have kept human under difficulties," the *Milwaukee Journal* commented. "For that gesture is Lindbergh as we think of him. The rest is the accident of fame."

Civil Rights Grew from
Racial Wrongs

The seeds of Wisconsin's first civil rights act took root amid private slights and public insult, and flowered when the anger that resulted was channeled into political action.

Congress had passed a civil rights act in 1875, but in 1883 it was ruled unconstitutional. The matter was left to states, and a few passed laws banning racial discrimination.

In Wisconsin, rights abuses set debate in motion. In 1886 two black men were refused service at one of Milwaukee's better saloons. In 1899, Frederick Douglass was denied a hotel room in Janesville, black Civil War veterans were treated rudely at a Milwaukee encampment and black teachers were refused rooms during a Madison convention.

In September, a black Milwaukeean named Owen Howell purchased a ticket to the Bijou Opera House by messenger; when he arrived to claim his seat he was refused admission in that section and sent to the gallery. He sued.

Howell found some white defenders; in a sermon, the pastor at St. Paul's Episcopal Church accused the theater of "contemptible barbarism," according to the *Wisconsin Magazine of History*. Black residents of Milwaukee called a state convention to form a Civil Rights League and appealed for a civil rights law.

Governor William D. Hoard agreed, saying, "Wisconsin should not be behind any of the states in guaranteeing to the colored people all of those rights given to them by the Constitution of the United States."

Not everyone went along. Some newspapers, while insisting they opposed prejudice, also opposed state action to prevent it.

Howell's case was heard in the summer of 1890 before Judge Daniel H. Johnson in a courtroom crowded with black observers. After the testimony, Johnson directed the all-white jury to rule in Howell's favor; he was awarded $100 in damages plus $51.85 in costs.

William T. Green practiced law in Milwaukee and was a leader in the African American community.
UW ARCHIVES

Johnson's strong language in finding for Howell was prominent in the legislative debate that followed in 1891. Republicans pushed for a civil rights act; Democrats resisted. The original bill outlawing discrimination in saloons, restaurants, inns, barber shops and most other places was greatly watered down, then defeated anyway.

"Where is the man on this floor who will say the colored man is the equal of the white man?" Assemblyman John Winans demanded.

But times were changing. Led by attorney William T. Green, Milwaukee's black residents had taken an interest in politics, and politicians had to respond. Democrats controlling the legislature in 1893 blocked action, but in 1895 Republicans regained control. A bill was quietly introduced and passed, and on April 20, 1895, Governor W. H. Upham signed it into law.

The penalty for discrimination ranged from $5 to $100. But finally, there was one.

Richard Bong,
Ace of Aces

Just a small-town boy from northern Wisconsin, Richard Bong loved to hunt, and he learned to fly. In 1942, he went to war with a jaunty "So long, Mom, I'm off," and while fans back home kept count in the headlines, he became the "Ace of Aces" of American fighter pilots.

He downed his first Japanese planes two days after Christmas in New Guinea while suffering a single bullet to his plane.

"Not bad at all, I would say," he wrote home, but he was just warming up.

"No. 11 Falls for Lieut. Bong," a headline declared in June 1943.

Then, "State Flier gets 17th Plane to 'Lead League'" ... "Bong Bags Two More" ... "A-shooting Bong Did Go; Now 25 He Has to Show" ... and by October 1944 it was, "Bong Downs 31st Plan in Leyte Battle."

Before Bong was grounded—the military would not risk losing its greatest flying hero in combat—he would record 40 official "kills"—the common term, but not Bong's term, for downing enemy planes. He broke the record of 26 kills by Captain Eddie Rickenbacker in World War I, and at 24 was awarded the Medal of Honor, just four years after taking his first solo flight.

He was born September 20, 1920, and raised in Poplar, east of Superior on Wisconsin's northern border, where a small museum honors his memory today.

His boyhood was one of farm work, sports and deer hunting. His early plan to study engineering was set aside when he entered civilian pilot training in 1938. His first solo flight came on his 20th birthday, and soon he was flying for the US Army Air Corps.

Then came war. He was by all accounts a remarkable flier, daring and skillful enough to get his P-38 Lightning so near enemy planes his merely ordinary shooting skills would suffice. As his count climbed, Bong became a national figure whose every move landed in headlines and newsreels.

New York schoolgirls skipped rope to "How many Zeros will he get today? Let's count them up, what do you say? One, two, three . . ."

When he came home on leave in 1943 for the fall deer hunt, Bong was driven home from Milwaukee by newspapermen and surprised by a house full of people, including a brass band. On that same trip, he met and fell in love with Marjorie Vattendahl, reluctantly feeding more headlines.

"Bong Gets Warm Welcome on Reaching Home, Marge" readers were assured in early 1945. "Superior Keeps Bong, Marge Busy as Nuptials Approach."

Bong grew weary of the constant attention—he called reporters "newshawks"—and limited coverage of his wedding. Still, newsreel cameras swarmed the church in Superior when he and Marge married on February 10, 1945.

But the flier who survived so much combat would not enjoy peacetime. Assigned as a test pilot, Bong took off from a California base in an

Major Richard Ira Bong shot down more enemy aircraft than any other American pilot during World War II. WHI IMAGE ID 11017

F-80 Shooting Star, a new model jet in which several pilots had already died.

Bong was killed on that flight, one of two that made headlines around the world on August 6, 1945.

The second was by Enola Gay over Hiroshima, Japan. Days later, the same minister who had married him and Marge just six months earlier conducted Bong's funeral, and P-47 Thunderbolts roared overhead in salute when he was buried in the family plot.

The Slickster Who Sold Oil City

The barely-there community of Oil City won't soon find its way onto state highway maps, but it has earned a permanent spot in Wisconsin lore as the town that could have been Tulsa—but which was merely snookered instead.

In recent years, a hand-crafted sign has pegged the population of Oil City, founded in Monroe County in the upper reaches of the Kickapoo Valley south of Sparta, at 15 souls.

A century ago it was larger and relatively prosperous, however. Once it was downright "rich." That was in the 1860s when a sweet-talker named Tichnor arrived in the region, which had not yet been named, posing as an oil man. He persuaded residents of the area that their land was perfectly suited for producing oil and—wouldn't you just know it—within a few days he discovered oil there.

Residents, who saw it with their own eyes, were duly excited. Tichnor immediately founded Gem Petroleum Company, leased land from farmers and began offering stock to eager buyers.

Oddly, other attempts to sink wells like Tichnor's were less successful. Well after well founded gushers of pure artesian water, not unwanted but hardly black gold.

By the time the locals discovered the barrel that Tichnor had secreted in the ground and tapped for oil, the head of Gem Petroleum had headed for new hills, leaving residents sadder, wiser and poorer.

"The oil speculator was a swindler," an 1878 account conceded, "but the result was a benefit to Sparta at least." The well water their ill-fated mining had discovered proved to have valuable medical and scientific properties.

Oil City eventually had mills, a cooper shop, stores and businesses, and a school was built.

But as residents had discovered earlier, prosperity was fleeting. Surrounding communities grew bigger and Oil City finally dwindled down to a collection of houses and a little wooden structure near the stream where Oil City's healthy water flows. Residents called it "the derrick."

Peck's Bad Boy Made It Good

George Peck's "Bad Boy" was a Bart Simpson for a kinder, gentler century, when a man could become a bestselling author without Oprah Winfrey's help—and governor of Wisconsin, to boot.

Politicians have been unintentionally funny for years, but George Wilbur Peck was a newspaperman who rode humor into politics. Born in New York in 1840, he moved to Jefferson County, Wisconsin, as a very young boy, eventually joining the printer's trade in Whitewater. He served in the 4th Wisconsin Cavalry in the Civil War, finding experiences he would use in his first series of humorous writings, *The Adventures of One Terence McGrant*.

Portrait of George W. Peck when he was a Democratic candidate for governor of Wisconsin.
WHI IMAGE ID 48603

After the war, he moved to La Crosse, where in 1874 he founded *Peck's Sun*, a humor paper that struggled until he moved it to Milwaukee four years later.

He was best known for the antics of Hennery, the bad boy with a national following, who would put cod liver oil on his pa's pancakes, soft soap the steps when the deacons were visiting, slip furniture polish into the liniment bottle and torment the grocer by slipping "rotten eggs" signs into the front window. When his pa inevitably caught on, Hennery would find himself in the woodshed for a talking to with a bed slat.

If the humor seems dated today, Peck's ability to lampoon the stuffed shirts of his era was eagerly received.

"When his first issue appeared in Milwaukee, leading citizens who had almost forgotten to laugh broke out in loud guffaws and slapped their sides as they read it on the downtown sidewalks," the Milwaukee County Historical Society's newsletter said years later.

At its peak, *Peck's Sun* had a national audience and circulation approaching 100,000 copies. Jackie Coogan later played Hennery in the movies, and a spanking machine described in a Peck story became a popular attraction at county fairs.

His affability made Peck a popular speaker, and his non-partisan, non-controversial style prompted Milwaukee Democrats to offer him as mayor in 1890. He was elected easily, and his slyly winking acceptance speech ("There is nothing more pleasant in the world than to have people happy") would have made the comic-politician Pat Paulsen proud a century later.

Two years later, the "happy mayor" was nominated for governor and upset the Republican incumbent, William Dempster Hoard. Peck was the only Democrat to serve as governor from 1876 until 1933, even winning re-election to a second term.

Political life, unfortunately, did not inspire the humorist, and his publication flagged while he was governor. He would continue writing after leaving office. He often held court in the lobbies of the Plankinton or Pfister hotels and used his public appearances for such noble aims as advancing cheese as the national emblem.

"What," Peck asked sensibly, "has the eagle ever done for America?"

The CCC, America's Peacetime Army

America's greatest peacetime army, the boy foresters of the Civilian Conservation Corps, built parks and built character. If it was one of the most idealistic New Deal programs, its legacy was also among the most durable. Many Wisconsin parks we enjoy today were built with the sweat and muscle of workers who had little else to give.

The CCC was born in 1933 as a response to the Great Depression, which robbed many young men of job prospects after high school. It originally was designed to give temporary work to 300,000 young men on relief rolls. They were paid $30 a month, $25 of which was sent to their needy families. The army recruited, trained, fed and housed CCC workers in camps across the country.

By 1934, 40 US Forest Service Camps were established in Wisconsin; a year later similar camps were opened at state parks. By 1935 CCC crews were improving Devils Lake, Copper Falls, Interstate, Peninsula, Perrot, Rib Mountain and Wyalusing state parks, as well as the University of Wisconsin Arboretum in Madison.

They cut trails and roads, carried huge stones by hand to make permanent paths and staircases, cleared brush and stumps, and built bridges and shelters still in use today. Erosion controls were put in place and vulnerable bluffs stabilized, typically without mechanical equipment. An inspector once likened the building of steep trails at Perrot State Park to the "labors of the ancient Egyptians in the building of the pyramids."

Members of the Devil's Lake State Park Civilian Conservation Corps.
WHI IMAGE ID 84598

Other crews worked in city parks, such as Whitnall, Sheridan, Estabrook and Kletzsch in Milwaukee.

John E. Voight, supervisor at Whitnall, later recalled the "Chicago alley rats" in his employ who lived in tents, built roads with picks and shovels and wheelbarrows, and moved about 150,000 cubic yards of earth to build a pond near the golf course.

Eventually the CCC's stated purpose was conservation as much as making work for the poor. Crews planted hundreds of millions of trees; federal officials estimated conservation programs were advanced 25 years by the CCC crew here. At its peak, 97 CCC camps operated in Wisconsin, employing as many as 11,000 men a year. In all, about 57,000 Wisconsin men took part in the CCC.

Not everyone approved. The conservationist Aldo Leopold warned against excessive cutting of brush and developments of fire lanes in wild areas. The urgent need for work drowned out any objections, but the hungry years wouldn't last forever. By 1942, when Congress voted to demobilize the CCC during the buildup of World War II, there were just five camps left in Wisconsin.

The CCC, wrote Leslie Alexander Lacy, "was a grand experiment . . . the first genuine effort by an American government to undertake, on a massive scale, a basically practical and anti-ideological program for its dispossessed youth."

And, it might be said, for park lovers who would follow.

The Stockbridge Bible Came Home

In 1745, a band of Mahican Indians living in western Massachusetts near the trading village of Stockbridge was presented with a large, two-volume Bible.

Meant to commemorate the Indians' recent acceptance of Christianity, it was inscribed on the fly-leaf by Francis Ayscough, on behalf of Frederick, Prince of Wales. This "pious gift," Ayscough wrote, was "to remain to the use of the Successors of those Indians from generation to generation."

It is in the right hands today, but not without a journey as long and tangled as that made by the Mahicans, now known as the Stockbridge-Munsee Band of Wisconsin Indians.

The Mahicans were the only Indian tribe to officially support Colonial forces in the Revolutionary War, an effort that earned each man who served a blanket and ribbon from the Congress.

But while they were at war, settlers took some of their land. In 1785, tribal leaders moved to western New York, carrying their special Bible with them, as they would when they were relocated again and again.

After 1820, some of the tribe, now called the Stockbridge after their former village in

The front cover of the Stockbridge Bible. WHI IMAGE ID 39988

Massachusetts, reached Wisconsin and joined with a group of Munsee Indians from Pennsylvania. After several moves in Wisconsin, the tribe settled in Shawano County in 1856, still in possession of its treasured Bible.

The link was not broken until 1930. The Bible was by then being stored in an impoverished Presbyterian church when a small group of tribal members was offered $1,000 for the two volumes.

A wealthy resident of Stockbridge, Massachusetts, was developing a museum called "Mission House" at the site of the tribe's conversion and wanted to display the famous books.

Amid the hardship of the 1930s, $1,000 was a tempting sum, and four elders of the Wisconsin church—only two of them Indians—agreed to sell.

It wasn't until the 1970s, when Wisconsin tribal members were visiting Stockbridge, that the Bible's whereabouts became known.

In 1975, tribal leaders began an effort to retrieve the Bible, citing cultural and historical links to establish ownership and hinting at more modern arguments—lawsuits.

Finally, in 1990, officials of the Massachusetts museum agreed that returning it was the right thing to do.

The Stockbridge-Munsee chose 10 members to drive to Massachusetts and bring the Bible home. They took possession in a ceremony on March 9, 1991, and as they approached Shawano on the return trip, called ahead to alert members to their arrival. A crowd met them in town and escorted the Bible to the small museum on the Stockbridge-Munsee reservation where visitors can examine it yet today.

And where, two and a half centuries after it was given, it still inspires tribal members. Its return, said one member of the delegation that brought it back, "was a religious experience."

"Somehow we lost [it] and now God has given [it] back."

Galesville,
Our Garden of Eden

Many in Wisconsin believe they dwell in the finest place on Earth, but few would press the point like the Reverend D. O. Van Slyke, of Galesville, more than a century ago.

A devout, circuit-riding minister, Van Slyke not only believed but also proved—at least to his own satisfaction—that his Trempealeau County homeland was the site of the biblical Garden of Eden described in Genesis, and that Galesville had been within its walls.

The search for Eden had been long debated before Van Slyke reached his partisan conclusion, which was often mocked but never challenged to his satisfaction. Van Slyke was an ardent student of the Bible, and the more he studied the land along the Mississippi River with its bluffs and coulees and rich agricultural production, the more parallels he discovered.

There were the necessary four rivers, including the long and picturesque Mississippi, which matched the description of the Euphrates and wore a name similarly euphonic.

Surely the garden would have been neither too far north or south, he reasoned, and it would be devoid of mineral wealth and its corrupting influence. A crescent bluff along the river, unlike any in the world in his view, must have been the "Hanging Garden."

For every Bible phrase he could find a handy connection.

"'Beautiful for situation' is Galesville, the joy of all its inhabitants, if not of all the earth," he wrote in his famous 1886 pamphlet, *Garden of Eden*. "And as the hills are 'round about

Jerusalem,' so are the hills and vastly more magnificent ones round about Galesville."

Trempealeau County was "a land of milk and honey," as dairy farmers could attest. He explained the lack of apple trees by saying they had been driven out with fallen man. True, western Wisconsin was far from where Noah launched his ark at Mount Ararat, but certainly the craft would have floated eastward.

And as for snakes—"for how could you have a garden without a 'serpent,'" Van Slyke asked—wasn't Trempealeau County well known for rattlesnakes?

Those who doubted him, he said, should stand on the bluffs and examine the evidence themselves.

"Not being a believer in the speculative, vague theories of modern geologists," he wrote, "I shall leave the discussion of the geological age of our gardens to those wiseacres."

It was enough that his "calm consideration of the facts" left him with the inescapable conclusion that in Trempealeau "we have the Garden; and everything considered, not only the greatest, and grandest, and best, but the only spot on earth that answers the Bible description of that notable spot, or Garden of Eden."

If geologically suspect, he was nonetheless a civic booster without match. Van Slyke left his community a nickname for the ages.

Curds and Whey
Came to Wisconsin

That northern Wisconsin fellow who made national head-lines when he credited a foam cheesehead with saving his hide in a plane crash a few years ago actually owed his life to one Chester Hazen.

Hazen, to the surprise of his many doubters, became the father of the Wisconsin cheese industry.

New York was the center of the dairy world in the mid-1800s. Farmers here still depended on King Wheat. Some butter was being made in Wisconsin but of such miserable quality that it was dismissed as "western grease" and used on wagon wheels as often as it was eaten.

But Hazen, a native of New York who moved in 1844 to Ladoga, in Fond du Lac County, became an expert in the dairy business and became convinced he could commercially make cheese.

He began by experimenting at home. His first plant, patterned after those in New York, was dismissed as "Hazen's Folly" when it was built in 1864, but Hazen had the last laugh. Using the milk from 100 to 200 cows, including some from his own herd, he produced and sold about 185,000 pounds of cheese in 1869 for $22,940.

His net was $4,476. By 1873, his factory was using the milk of 800 cows, and dozens of other cheese plants had sprung up to seize a piece of the new market. The new America's Dairyland was born.

The "western grease" reputation was hard to shake, however.

At first, Hazen could sell his cheese only through local grocers, who often sold it without labels. Hazen was upset when he discovered a Milwaukee warehouse was selling his cheese under New York labels, still embarrassed by Wisconsin's dairy image. But Hazen, who became instrumental in dairy promotion and helped found the Wisconsin Dairymen's Association in 1872, became the first Wisconsin producer to ship a carload of cheese to the East.

It was the cheese equivalent of sending coal to Newcastle, but in the next decade, Wisconsin's rise to prominence in, and dominance of, the industry gained force.

Highway billboard advertising Wisconsin cheese for the Department of Agriculture and Markets, 1942.
WHI IMAGE ID 2039

Hazen's own cheese won a first prize at the Philadelphia Centennial Exposition in 1876 and again at the International Dairy Fair in 1878.

That event, in sweet irony, was held in New York.

Civil War
Cost Wisconsin Dearly

No one knew that war between the states would last so long, or cost Wisconsin so dearly. But many saw civil war coming.

Even before Fort Sumter fell to the enemy in April 1861, Governor Alexander Randall had asked for legislation authorizing reorganization of the militia and setting aside $100,000 for the effort.

Still, the first word that months of escalating saber rattling had led to actual warfare was met with doubt, disbelief and some confusion.

Long before the days of cable news, citizens by the hundreds gathered in newspaper and telegraph offices for official word to confirm or deny rampant rumors. When a Madison telegraph operator read aloud, from a second-story balcony, news of Fort Sumter's surrender, "it was a great shock, and the silence was painful as the people turned away and went to their homes," an observer reported.

Many clung to hope that the skirmish would not grow into war, but subsequent hostilities proved bluster truly had turned to bloodshed.

"No longer could they think simply in terms of verbally defending the government, Constitution and the laws," Walter S. Glazer wrote in the *Wisconsin Magazine of History*. "Suddenly they saw the peril to their own homes and lives."

Some state editors, politicians and civilians resisted involvement, but Randall was a forceful advocate, and many were eager

Soldiers of the 3rd Wisconsin Artillery at Camp Randall manning a cannon on wheels, 1861. WHI IMAGE ID 4225

to help preserve the Union that Wisconsin had joined only 13 years earlier.

Existing local militias were logical sources of soldiers for Wisconsin's share of the initial war effort—one regiment of 10 companies, each with 78 men plus officers.

Many of the militia groups were better trained at parading about in fashionable uniforms, and hosting annual dances, than waging battle. However, while some prospective soldiers decided their families and lives were more important than a southern war, Randall could have raised even more volunteers than President Abraham Lincoln initially requested.

Madison's Camp Randall, where university athletic teams march up and down today, was the main training ground.

As many as 70,000 troops eventually prepared for war at the former fairgrounds and marched off amid bands and flag bearers.

Civil war was bloody, bloody business. More than 12,000 Wisconsin soldiers—one of every seven who took part—would die, two-thirds from disease. By comparison, the state's loss in World War II—in which four times as many Wisconsin soldiers took part—was just over 8,000.

First Cars Brought First Car Race

In the 1870s, public interest in self-powered transportation was such that dreamers everywhere were working on contraptions that would put the horse out of work.

In 1875 that included the Wisconsin Legislature, which offered a $10,000 prize to the inventor who could come up with a machine "which shall be a cheap and practical substitute for the use of horses and other animals on the highway and farm."

The bar was set high. Such a vehicle would be required to run at least 200 miles under its own power at an average of at least 5 mph.

Tinkerers had been busy in Wisconsin even earlier. In 1873, John Carhart, a Methodist minister in Racine, and his brother designed and built a machine called "The Spark," a two-cylinder, steam-driven vehicle he unveiled on a head-turning drive on local streets.

It caused a terrible racket, but Carhart, said to have been quite a self-promoter, explained away criticism by saying, "It must be remembered that at the time there was no liquid fuel, ball bearings, or rubber tires."

Or good roads, which made the contest for the $10,000 prize a rough ride. Two steam-powered cars were entered in a race in July 1876 along a route from Green Bay to Madison.

The Green Bay entry, an unwieldy, 14,000-pound contraption, broke through a culvert near the starting line. But the Oshkosh car made it to Appleton the first day and Oshkosh the second—the Green Bay model was by then riding the rails—and reached Madison in a week.

Outing in an automobile, 1905. WHI IMAGE ID 60242

The Legislature, however, decided that the winner was hardly a practical alternative to traditional horsepower and parted with only half of the prize money. It was, however, the first governmental unit to subsidize development of the modern auto.

By 1890, Milwaukee inventors were riding about in a practical, self-propelled gasoline vehicle. But perhaps Wisconsin's most significant contribution to motor transportation came in 1908 in Clintonville.

There, Otto Zachow and William Besserdich developed the first successful four-wheel-drive car, a discovery that led to widespread production of heavy-duty, go-anywhere vehicles in Clintonville. Such vehicles would be invaluable for American troops during World War I.

Another Wisconsin contribution to highway freedom came in Hartford in 1906, where brothers George and William Kissel began their Kissel Kar Company. According to Wisconsin Then and Now, their first cars cost $1,850 without top, windshield, gas lamps, generator and horn.

In 1910, a Kissel Kar won a Los Angeles-to-Phoenix race, and, in 1922, Kissel patented a detachable top so automobiles could adjust to weather conditions. The company went out of business in 1931, but *Road and Track* magazine once described the Kissel Gold Bug as the "niftiest, raciest, and classiest American production car ever to hit the highways."

All-American Girls
Played Ball

The names of the games' honchos were familiar—solid baseball handles like P. K. Wrigley and Branch Rickey—but something about the new league was different.

Pastel uniforms, for starters, and the short flaring skirts that made sliding into second base a painful adventure.

"They wanted us to look like ladies," one member of the All-American Girls Professional Baseball League recalled years later, "and play like men."

So they did from 1943 until 1954, the decade when hardball was a game for women, too. And Wisconsin was right in the thick of it.

The league was the creation of Wrigley, the millionaire owner of the Chicago Cubs who wanted a hedge in the event men's baseball would be shut down during World War II. Players would be coached by men and there would be rules off the field as well as on.

"Only the highest type of girls play on our teams," said league president Ken Sells in announcing that Milwaukee would field a team in 1944. "The girls are properly chaperoned."

Perhaps some expected them to glow and not sweat, but the women who played baseball for fun and profit considered themselves true professionals, and they played like it. Irene "Choo Choo" Hickson of Racine later described what it was like catching for the Racine Belles:

Collage of photographs of members of the All-American Girls Professional Baseball League, as seen in the Racine Belles annual yearbook of 1948.
WHI IMAGE ID 58540

"I had to be tough, because I was 5-2 and weighed only about 118 pounds," she said, "and these big girls used to come sliding into home and try to hit me from here to eternity."

Her friend Joyce Westerman chafed at a rule—designed, no doubt, to attract male fans—that said players' hair could not be short and must be curled.

"I'd play for 10 hours, go home and pin-curl my hair, then squash a catcher's mask over it," she said. "I thought, 'This is for the birds.'"

The Racine Belles and Kenosha Comets played a number of seasons, though the Milwaukee Chicks lasted just the 1944 season. They made it one to remember, however, winning the championship before moving to Grand Rapids the next year.

The league folded for lack of sponsors, but by then men were playing baseball for more money and TV was providing Americans with other entertainment choices.

Except by ex-players, the game was nearly forgotten. But in 1988 the Baseball Hall of Fame paid homage with its "Women in Baseball" exhibit, and a few years later Hollywood followed suit with *A League of Their Own*, starring big-name actors Geena Davis, Madonna, Rosie O'Donnell and Tom Hanks.

It was a hit, and it gave players such as Alice "Lefty" Hohlmeyer, former Kenosha Comets pitcher and first baseman, a chance to relive the days of long bus rides, exhausting doubleheaders and injuries they couldn't acknowledge if players wanted to be paid.

"Boys today," Lefty said. "They get a hangnail today and they can't play."

Henry Dagget's Corset Campaign

Long before women burned undergarments in protest, one Wisconsin man joined them in a different "unmentionable" crusade.

At the end of the 19th century, a campaign surfaced to do away with corsets, those tightly laced "instruments of torture" that reduced a woman's waist to fashionable size—but at the price of comfort.

Wisconsin, according to historian Fred Holmes, played a role in the corset's development. Freeman L. Tripp, an inventive sort who owned a women's apparel store in Eau Claire, once helped women by devising a hat fastener that eliminated the need for chin ribbons.

But earlier, Tripp had added to fashion misery by patenting a whalebone corset, an invention he sold to a Chicago man for $500.

He went on to "improve" the garment in several ways, but never made it comfortable.

Indeed, it was punishing. Anti-corset crusaders complained stays were pulled so tight that while every other organ was of womanly proportion, the corseted waist was smaller than that of a girl of 10 or 12.

Wrote Dr. Arabella Kenealy in 1904, "The thing has

A corset from 1901. WHI IMAGE ID 55437

become, indeed, a national evil." If men wore corsets, it was often added, styles would change.

To the rescue of the fairer sex came Representative Henry L. Daggett of Bear Creek, who in January 1899 introduced an anti-corset resolution "relating to the health of old maids."

Newspapers, represented mostly by uncorseted males, poked much fun at Daggett, whose resolution was referred to the committee on public health, then to agriculture and finally to the Committee on Public Improvements, which suggests at least some lawmakers were having fun as well.

But Holmes said his research showed Daggett was most serious. At one hearing, he called using corsets "worse than the binding of the feet of Chinese women."

Daggett suffered for his cause. A group of Watertown women sent him a huge floral corset, and a program for the legislative ball depicted Daggett, sword in hand, attacking a monster corset. The *New London Press* claimed that Daggett's trunk was decorated "by pictures of handsome women in their nether garments" and brought more people to the train station than a circus.

The measure sparked some thoughtful response. Madison newspaperman Amos Wilder (Thornton's father), said that "misinformed young women still cramp and deform themselves into an abnormal, unhealthy and revolting parody on the beauty of the human form divine, unmindful of the official measurements of the faultless Venus de Milo (26 inches, if memory serves us right.)"

Daggett was just ahead of his time. The resolution went nowhere, but the corset, ultimately, did.

Mexican Immigrants
Found Hope in Wisconsin

Unlike some of the European groups that had earlier made Wisconsin their homes, familiar with the climate if little else, the wave of Mexican immigrants that began arriving in the 1920s faced two barriers. Both the language and weather were hard to understand.

A Mexico native who came here with her new husband in 1926 said years later she questioned her mate's sanity.

"I thought he was crazy," she said. "It was too cold. It was winter."

But there was work, as difficult, dirty and unglamorous as it often was. And however foreign the conditions and the elements, hungry workers have always pursued jobs.

Rafael Baez. HISTORIC PHOTO COLLECTION/MILWAUKEE PUBLIC LIBRARY

There were a few Spanish-speaking explorers in Wisconsin as early as the 1700s, but the first sizable influx came in the 1920s when Milwaukee industries, especially tanneries, were experiencing a labor shortage. More restrictive legislation had slowed the flow of workers from Europe, and World War I had caused reductions in the local labor force, so some tanneries recruited workers in Mexico.

In 1920, there were only 238 Mexicans in Wisconsin. But a decade later the Census Bureau recorded 2,396 Spanish-speaking men, almost 1,500 in Milwaukee.

Assimilation was often made difficult by the workers' lack of English. In some cases, they slept on cots at the tanneries in less-than-desirable conditions that would be experienced again decades later by migrant farm workers who came to pick fruit and vegetables and harvest other crops. In the 1960s, migrant farm workers challenged wages, housing and work conditions in a series of public protests that helped raise awareness of the Hispanic presence in the state.

One of the state's earliest Mexican immigrants came under quite different circumstances, however, and a few years after his arrival was already included in a biographical listing of Milwaukee's community leaders.

Rafael Baez was born in 1863 in the city of Pueblo, Mexico. Because his mother died when he was just five, Baez was placed in school early and by nine was learning to read, write and play music.

Music proved to be the right course of study. Baez was so skilled that by the age of 20 he had moved to Mexico City and won a spot in the Grand National Theater.

In 1884 Baez was discovered and recruited by C. D. Hess, whose Milwaukee opera company was making a tour of important Mexican cities. He came to Milwaukee with the company after the tour ended, and soon found a place in the city's music scene.

Baez became organist and music director for Gesu Church, one of the city's largest houses of worship, and played at other churches, as well. He also continued to compose and publish music.

Baez further found the perfect way to assimilate into Milwaukee life. On May 23, 1889, Baez married Maria Schoen, a member of a prominent German family. They had four children, which one local historian suggests was almost certainly the first Mexican-German family in the city.

The Idea Behind the Wisconsin Idea

As defined by the Wisconsin Idea, the University of Wisconsin might have been centered on the hilly end of State Street, but its borders—and constituents—stretched from Bayfield to Beloit.

The famed Wisconsin Idea, an outgrowth of the Progressive era, suggested the university's professional scholars were to serve all citizens of the state, not only those on campus.

"The expert on tap—not on top," read one description, while one writer called it "a university that runs a state."

Of course, just what policy contributions were transmitted from the academic end of State Street to the political end often depended on the willingness of politicians to accept sometimes radical ideas. Despite Wisconsin's tradition of such cooperation, not all state officials have been willing to give the scholars their ear.

But Robert M. La Follette, Madison resident and the first graduate of the university to become governor, freely embraced the concept.

After he helped his former classmate, Charles R. Van Hise, become UW president in 1903, he established a Saturday Lunch Club that

Charles Van Hise. WHI IMAGE ID 33714

joined state officials and university figures in discussion of common problems.

Many scholars were involved in shaping Progressive era policies, from the labor expert John R. Commons to the famous historian Frederick Jackson Turner, and delegations from other states came to Madison to learn how their universities could similarly become service institutions.

A major player in expanding the campus to all corners was Charles R. McCarthy, who established the professionally staffed Legislative Reference Library to assemble the best information from all sources for political consideration.

McCarthy also was instrumental in developing the University Extension, the system of offices throughout the state devoted to working with farmers, homemakers and small business owners. In rural counties, the extension agent often was a font of knowledge about modern farm practices.

Some debate whether the accomplishments of the Wisconsin Idea matched the reputation, but Van Hise's campus was known then as one of the leading "laboratories of democracy" in the country.

The Sinking
of the Lady Elgin

Rumors, the foot soldiers of grief, arrived first. The steamer *Lady Elgin* had been rammed and sunk with hundreds of Milwaukeeans aboard, most from the bustling Irish Third Ward, and a keening city's desperate need to put flesh on facts strained newspapers' presses as well as their storehouse of sorrowful descriptives.

"Yesterday morning the first premonition of the horrible news was whispered about the streets," the *Milwaukee Daily Sentinel* reported on September 10, 1860, under the headline: "APPALL-ING CALAMITY!'

"Cheeks were blanched and hearts were hushed at the tidings that the steamer had gone down with all on board. The rumor grew into a dread certainty as the dispatches began to arrive. The dreadful intelligence spread like wildfire, and soon the city was ag-itated by feelings of suspense and apprehension. The newspaper offices were besieged; the telegraph office was thronged; knots gathered at the corners and business for the moment stood still."

If business slowed for the moment, the spirt and progress of Milwaukee's up-and-coming Irish community was set back im-measurably. Many of the dead were prominent in government or commerce. It would be estimated 1,000 children were orphaned, many wives widowed, entire families lost.

In the Third Ward, the paper said, "It seemed as though sounds of mourning proceeded from every third house. Little crowds of women were congregated along the walks, some giv-ing free expression of their grief and others offering condolence. Never before has our city been stricken with such a calamity."

Sketch from the *New York Illustrated News* of the sinking of the *Lady Elgin*.
WHI IMAGE ID 6122

The *Lady Elgin* had been buoyed by high spirits when her passengers had embarked on their gala fund-raising outing to Chicago. Singing and dancing marked the moment; the party above deck was so grand that cows had been loaded below as ballast.

Among the passengers were members of Barry's Guards, mostly Irish militia led by Garrett Barry. The unit had just been stripped of its commission by Governor Alexander Randall in a dispute over state vs. federal authority in the event of civil war. However, the Irish did not want to disband and organized the excursion to raise money to obtain new rifles. Some members of German militias also were aboard, as were some city officials and firefighters.

The appalling calamity of tomorrow's headlines came on its return trip when the *Lady Elgin* was struck in the dark by a lumber carrier, the schooner *Augusta*. The cows were pushed overboard and the captain and crew worked feverishly to plug the hole left by the *Augusta*, but damage was great. In the chaos, lifeboats were woefully inadequate. Some survivors clung to the ship's floating deck but crashing waves claimed many more, some within a few yards from shore. Almost 300, maybe more, died.

For months, bodies floated along the shores of Lake Michigan. In Milwaukee, funerals continued for weeks, sometimes a dozen or more on the same day. No one was consoled that the captain of the *Augusta*, who claimed he hadn't realized serious damage had occurred, was later censured for blithely continuing on his way on that night of appalling calamity.

Houdini Couldn't Escape
Edna Ferber

When the famously elusive Harry Houdini returned to his boyhood home of Appleton in 1904, there was no escaping the hometown press. Not when the *Appleton Crescent*'s reporter was Edna Ferber, still a tender 18 at the time but destined to make a name for herself in literature.

Houdini was 30 and already known around the world. Born Ehrich Weiss,

Harry Houdini. WHI IMAGE ID 3629

he had been gone from Appleton for years—his family had moved to Milwaukee—but he freely granted the young reporter's plea for an interview when she tracked him down.

Writer and subject went to a nearby drugstore. There, according to an account by Robert Kralapp in *Voyageur* magazine, Ferber showed that while she would eventually win a Pulitzer Prize for writing, she was over her skis when faced with the amazing Houdini.

"Imagination," her florid story began, "pictures a Sampson, massive, towering with enormous hands and feet, a great shaggy head perhaps and a voice that roars and bellows and shoulders and limbs like pillars of rock."

Her imagination's problem was, Houdini was pleasant, unassuming, conventionally dressed and obviously weary from traveling home from Europe. Only his stories fit the picture she had conjured.

He recalled his first performance, a contortionist act given in a field near the railroad tracks for which he was paid "exactly 35 cents." Houdini, then making as much as $2,000 per week, threw back his head and laughed at the memory, Ferber wrote.

Houdini spoke of his parents—the mother he doted on, and his father, Meyer Weiss, who had served as rabbi in Appleton and Milwaukee.

Ferber, also Jewish, asked Houdini where he received the best treatment.

"Oh, the world is alike," he said. "When they are pleased they laugh and are pleasant, and when they think they are being cheated and are displeased then they scowl and jeer and hiss."

They chatted on, the star and star-struck scribe, about whether his performances were exaggerated (chains, locks and bolts needn't be, he said), his secrets (a great wrong to give them up, he said), even about his body.

His forearm, Ferber told her readers, was "amazing, as massive and hard as a granite pillar. His neck, too, is large and corded."

In her front-page story, she gushed like the schoolgirl she had recently been, but Houdini no doubt had led his impressionable interviewer on. When they stood to make farewells, he placed a small gift in her hand.

It was the padlock from the vending machine near his seat, which he'd quietly picked while they were talking.

"Better give it to the drugstore man," he said. "Somebody'll steal all his chewing gum."

Washburn's Boom Times

The story of many Wisconsin communities is of boom and bust. In Washburn, the booms were sometimes literal, and deadly.

In 1902, a "mysterious man with red-top boots," as the local paper called him, arrived in far northern Wisconsin, on Lake Superior's Chequamegon Bay, and began buying land. He was Major William Ramsay of the DuPont Company; he soon acquired 1,400 acres for a dynamite production plant.

Washburn was already booming, thanks to lumber, but Ramsay was proposing the country's largest dynamite plant.

Land was cleared, a power plant was built, dozens of buildings were put up—most in a ravine for safety reasons—and 11 miles of narrow-gauge rail were laid for the new "city" called the Barksdale Works. Indeed, the Town of Barksdale was created in 1907.

The first three carloads of dynamite were shipped in 1905. Production grew with the plant, which became a world model; in its first year it turned out almost 3 million pounds.

War has perverse benefits, and World War I was good for Washburn. Barksdale was the world's largest supplier of TNT and produced other explosives as well. Military officials from around the world came to inspect it.

Employment soared, to almost 6,000 at the peak, and Washburn's population—today about 2,250—soared to 10,000. Rooming houses, temporary buildings and barracks were built, as was a temporary school for workers' families. The giant plant dominated the city's economic and social picture.

Armistice Day in 1918 brought peace to the world but mass layoffs to Washburn. Dynamite for industrial uses was manufactured,

Using dynamite to break up rock, May 11, 1938.
WHI IMAGE ID 104856

but at the low point, only a handful of employees worked 12 hours a week. The Depression hurt there, as everywhere, but business improved in the late 1930s as World War II loomed.

In 1939, employment jumped to 600, wartime production grew and the facility was selected as a TNT training school dubbed the "University of Barksdale." Older residents remember living in expectation that the enemy would target Washburn for its role in the war effort.

Despite extensive safety measures, a dynamite plant was tragedy in waiting. The first explosion in 1906 took three lives and there were subsequent blasts, small and large. In 1918, seven men died when a TNT machine blew up—and in the worst accident, in 1952, eight lives were lost.

In 1971 TNT production ceased, ending Barksdale's 66-year legacy.

The Lights Went On in Appleton

Perhaps no one outside the Fox Valley thought it a race, but when word arrived on September 4, 1882, that Thomas Edison's first electricity generating plant was up and running in New York, Appleton's own plant was only a few final tweaks from readiness.

"We will start operating in the morning," said one of the builders, and he was close.

On September 30, 1882, after many false starts and a long day of tinkering, the world's first hydroelectric central station suddenly came through.

"It was getting dark when suddenly, whimsically, something happened;" wrote G. W. Van Derzee in the *Wisconsin Magazine of History*. "The carbonized filaments slowly became dull red, then bright red, then incandescent, and Glory Be—there was light!

"It is recorded that the men jumped up and down and screamed like school boys."

The Appleton Edison Electric Company was begun by paper manufacturer H. F. Rogers, who had been so impressed with Edison's first experiments with lighting a few years earlier that he had obtained the contract for an Edison central station before he had ever seen a light bulb.

Although Edison's own plant depended on steam, the tiny facility known as the Vulcan Street Plant harnessed the power of falling water in the Fox River.

It had a capacity of 12.5 kilowatts, enough to light 250 bulbs of 50 watts each, but that night it lighted only Rogers' house, making it the first residential dwelling in the world to receive electric service from a central station.

Cutaway view of the building that housed the first electrical station created to distribute incandescent light electricity, 1882. WHI IMAGE ID 28333

The generator was driven by a system of gears and belts by a water wheel operation under a 10-foot fall of water. The company quickly grew, although it did not make money, and Appleton's electrical breakthroughs had just begun.

In 1886 a new plant was built, and shortly after that the Appleton Electric Street Railway Company was incorporated. Soon, horse-frightening electric trolleys took to the streets, giving Appleton the first such mass transit anywhere and leading to the construction of trolley systems in many Wisconsin cities.

Progress does not always guarantee prosperity, however. The electric power company struggled under debts and in 1896 declared bankruptcy.

The streets car system did better, expanding into Neenah, Menasha and Kaukauna, but it was put to pasture in 1930 when bus service proved a cheaper and better alternative.

The Bilious Man's Friend
Cures All

Long before medicines came with childproof caps and government oversight, naïve sufferers often turned to fast talkers hawking mysterious miracles. One such medicine man in frontier Wisconsin was Thomas Emerson Tubbs, who could treat man or horse for any malady, often with the same prescription.

Born in Vermont, Tubbs came to River Falls in 1866. He was ambitious, by one account "a promoter on whose fingers the door of opportunity seldom slammed." He had a wagon and sled business, peddled everything from the "Babcock Fire Extinguisher" to the "Detroit Fire & Burglar Proof Safe" and owned 11 different insurance companies.

Alas, he was woefully underinsured when, in 1876, fire destroyed the "Tubbs Block" in River Falls and all of his businesses. On an up note, material in his "Detroit Fire and Burglar Proof Safe" was undamaged, so Tubbs stayed in the safe business even as he turned to his line of patent medicines.

He had long sold a medicine called "Elixir of Life," said to be as effective in treating humans with colds as horses stricken with epizootic—a condition similar to influenza. To this product Tubbs added "Excelsior Liniment," good for treating corns, rheumatism, sprains, headache, burns and toothache, and "Ready Relief to Pain," which also was touted for its equine-human one-two punch.

Tubbs advertised daily in the *River Falls Journal,* and distributed brochures in various languages so as not to allow the language barrier to cheat some poor immigrant of relief.

By the 1880s, business was so good he shed his other lines and hired agents to hawk his cures far and wide. He broadened his line to include "Magic Eye Water," "Condition Powder" and what would become his biggest success—"The Bilious Man's Friend."

Or, his ads made clear, the bilious woman:

Ho! The Bilious Woman
You all know her when you meet her,
She tells you when you greet her,
She has pimples on her face,
A disgrace to the human race,
Yet she keeps a-growing yellower every day.

She's been told her face looks badly,
We'd prescribe it for her gladly,
B. M. F. knocks off the peak,
Starts the roses in the cheek,
And she keeps a-growing handsomer every day.

Tubbs' biggest fear was the simmering temperance movement because the Bilious Man's Friend was nearly 40 proof, which might explain the friendship. But apparently no one questioned the cure, and Tubbs Medicine Company prospered.

The *Journal* estimated that if the 20,000 bottles of White Pine Cough Cure sold in 1919 were placed end to end, they would stretch more than 15 miles. By then, however, Thomas Tubbs was gone and his son, Willard, was in charge.

And there's medical irony for you. The insurance man who was underinsured had come down with an illness in 1892 that none of his medicines could touch, and he died two years later.

When Abe Lincoln Slept Here

Illinois was and remains today the Land of Lincoln, but like generations of flatlanders to follow, Abraham Lincoln spent his share of time in Wisconsin.

Not, however, in Door County or the Dells. In the tragic Black Hawk War of 1832, a young Lincoln was one of the Illinois militiamen who pursued the fleeing Indians through southern Wisconsin.

Later, however, he diminished his service—and that of a political opponent—by saying, "If he saw any live, fighting Indians, it was more than I did; but I had a good many bloody struggles with the mosquitoes."

He would return here as a candidate for president (and, later, would carry Wisconsin).

On September 30, 1859, Lincoln, by then famous because of his debates with Stephen Douglas, came to Milwaukee. A large crowd gathered at the then State Fair Grounds to listen to Lincoln speak from a farm wagon, but it was the Rail Splitter's subsequent events that make him a tourist attraction in Wisconsin yet today.

The Lincoln Bedroom in the Tallman House.
WHI IMAGE ID 34962

263

He went to Janesville, the town that still boasts "Lincoln slept here."

Not, as it turned out, all that peacefully.

Lincoln went from Milwaukee to Beloit, where on October 1 he addressed a Republican club. Learning of his near presence, the Republican club of Janesville invited him as well, and Lincoln accepted. It was said that on the journey to Janesville, he remembered the countryside from his military adventures.

After his speech, Lincoln was taken for the night to the impressive, 20-room Janesville home of William Tallman. There was conversation about current topics, including abolition, a cause dear to Tallman's heart.

Lucien Hanks, 21, another guest, recalled that Lincoln at bedtime had a carpetbag from which he pulled a "commodious" nightgown. Earlier, Mrs. Tallman had suggested quietly to Hanks that he sleep on the couch so Lincoln could have the guest room, but Lincoln was so polite as to invite Hanks to share the comfort of a bed.

"He's not a very big fellow," Lincoln reportedly told his host, "and won't take up much room . . . I think we'll get along famously, don't you, Lucien?"

However, the night's truly famous aspect was that Lincoln twitched and jerked in his sleep, snored loudly and thrashed so that Hanks couldn't sleep. He crept downstairs to the couch after all.

The following morning, Lincoln came downstairs in his stocking feet—blue, with white toes—because his boots hadn't been returned after polishing. "I don't want to cast any aspersions," he was said to have teased his host, "but when I went to bed last night I certainly had boots."

Properly shod, he attended church with the Tallmans. Their house was later opened to the public as the Lincoln-Tallman museum, a shining star in Janesville's local history.

Why It's Called Pabst Blue Ribbon

Pabst Red Ribbon? It came oh-so-close. Milwaukee's Pabst Brewing Company, as the world came to know so well, won the coveted blue ribbon in 1893 when its beer was judged "America's best" at the Columbian Exposition.

Pabst had won other ribbons in the past, but this competition was intense because major breweries were in a pitched battle for the thirsts of America's beer drinkers; winning was a major coup. Blue ribbon beer became the company's identity, and a significant part of Milwaukee's, as well, until the company eventually abandoned the city.

But Pabst came so close to being the also-ran; but for shenanigans on both sides, the story goes, it might have been Budweiser Blue Ribbon.

Captain Frederick Pabst exhibited his wares at a "spectacular thirteen-foot-square, gold-plated model of his Empire Brewery to attract attention," according to *Under the Influence*, a book about the Busch family dynasty.

In preliminary events, Anheuser-Busch won six medals and Pabst five. So judging in the ultimate category was closely watched—and much debated.

After arguments about the makeup of the panel and over how points would be awarded, the St. Louis company's beer was selected.

But judges then said they had found impurities in that beer and reversed the award.

When the irate Adolphus Busch appealed the decision, the fair commission first announced no award would be given,

then changed course yet again
and tabbed Anheuser-Busch
before Pabst persuaded the
judges, no doubt dizzy by that
point, to switch winners yet
again.

Adolphus Busch had not
become a millionaire beer ty-
coon by giving up easily, however. In early 1894, he pursued
one of the judges to Europe,
still hoping to win on appeal
and to strike any reference to
impurities.

Pabst Blue Ribbon Beer label
submitted to the state of Wisconsin
for trademark registration, 1933.
WHI IMAGE ID 91108

"You know there is no such
thing as 'fail,' when I undertake
to do anything," he wrote his son. Busch missed the judge in Berlin, however, so he followed him to France.

"At Paris I missed him again," he wrote home, "as he had left
for Montreux, and from there to Baden-Baden where I caught
up with him and by fine diplomatic talk and 1862 wines, Chateau
Metternich, he capitulated . . .

"It was a costly battle, but I think more costly to the defeated
than to us. You have no idea what tricks were resorted to. I found
out things in Berlin which I never expected. Pabst wanted to win
at all hazards and at any cost, but to no avail."

Sadly for Busch, in September 1894, almost a year after the
original decision, the commission refused to reconsider and the
ribbon stayed in Milwaukee. It turned out there was such a thing
as "fail" in his undertakings.

"Prizes," Adolphus Busch said later, in advising against entering future contests, "are not given to the goods meriting same,
but are secured by money and strategy."

James Groppi
and the Assembly Sit-In

The era of protest spawned by the Vietnam War soon engulfed other facets of Wisconsin life. In September 1969, Catholic priest and civil rights activist James Groppi and dozens of Milwaukee welfare supporters marched to Madison, where the Legislature was to meet in special session to consider reversing welfare program budget cuts.

Marchers picked up support as they neared Madison and numbered almost 1,000 when they rallied near the Capitol, where Groppi vowed the poor would be heard.

"We did not march 90 miles for nothing," he said. "We will be as nice as we can, and as mean as we have to be.

"We're tired of getting crumbs off [the Legislature's] table of abundance. We're going to knock that table right out from under them."

What followed that September 29 was an unprecedented take-over of the Assembly chambers by Groppi and supporters and an 11-hour sit-in before police finally cleared the room. The action enraged conservative lawmakers and caused Groppi's 10th arrest in a case that would ultimately involve the US Supreme Court.

Groppi didn't knock the table out from anyone in the Assembly, but he stood atop one while addressing supporters.

As marchers ringed the Capitol the following day and National Guardsmen, with bayonets fixed, kept order, legislative leaders, most of them conservative Republicans, were adamant that Groppi would pay. Relying on a long-ignored 1848 law, Representative F. James Sensenbrenner Jr. introduced a resolution

Father James Groppi at the Capitol building during
demonstrations against welfare cuts, 1969. WHI IMAGE ID 4934

declaring Groppi in contempt of the Assembly and ordering him
jailed for six months or until the session was over.

The Assembly debated more than three hours. Groppi's defenders said lawmakers were trying to be both judge and jury—
to "sock it to a priest [is] as low as you can go," Representative
Lloyd Barbee said—and his accusers said strong action was
needed or anarchy would prevail. On a 71–24 vote, Groppi was
cited for contempt.

By then he was already in jail, arrested earlier in the day on a
state disorderly conduct warrant at a church where he said Mass
and awaited his fate.

"Say a prayer for me," he said when police led him away. "God bless you all."

Ten days later, a federal judge overturned the Assembly and freed Groppi. An appeals court disagreed, but in 1972 the Supreme Court unanimously ruled that the Assembly had violated Groppi's rights.

A former Republican Assembly member decried the ruling from judges "sitting in their ivory towers in Washington [who] don't know what it's like to be under siege." But Governor Patrick Lucey, a Democrat, said that if Chief Justice Warren Burger, "not known as a wild-eyed radical," would sign such an opinion, then it represented a sound assessment of Groppi's constitutional rights.

Groppi's activism continued, even after he left the Catholic priesthood and became a Milwaukee bus driver. On the 10th anniversary of the takeover, in 1979, he said he would do it all over again.

"You always try to find the right moment," he said. "You just have to grab it."

Groppi died on November 4, 1985, at age 54.

George Poage Ran to Glory

The 1904 Olympic Games in St. Louis, celebrating the centennial of the Louisiana Purchase in conjunction with a world's fair that same year, were waged amid an undercurrent of racial uneasiness.

Black and white exhibits were mounted separately, and "colored" areas were apart from the others.

Some blacks wanted African American athletes to boycott both the fair and the games, but a Wisconsin runner named George Coleman Poage elected to participate, and in the process became the first African American athlete awarded a medal in a modern Olympiad.

George Poage was a standout athlete at the UW and the first African American to medal in the Olympics. MURPHY LIBRARY SPECIAL COLLECTIONS, UW–LA CROSSE

Poage was part of a small but vibrant black community at the time, according to an account by Bruce Mouser in the La Crosse County Historical Society newsletter. When Poage's family arrived from Missouri in 1884, there were more than 100 black residents and 29 black heads of household in La Crosse, most employed in service jobs.

A third of black males were barbers, although George Edwin Taylor was active in politics and owned and edited a newspaper in the mid-1880s.

He would later claim his was the first African American owned paper with a predominantly white readership.

So there was opportunity for young George Poage, and he took advantage.

What school records were available suggest Poage was both a good student and good athlete. He graduated second in his high school class of 25 students in 1899 and presented the salutatorian's address.

"None went on to become notable in other than a local sense," the newsletter said, "except for Poage."

It was his speed that got him noticed. He had run in high school, in one meet winning the 50-, 100-, and 220-yard dashes before removing his shoes to win second in the standing broad jump. After high school, he moved to Madison to attend the University of Wisconsin.

The games of 1904 were far smaller than today's overblown spectacles. Only 496 athletes from 11 countries competed, according to the newsletter's account, and just 20,000 spectators were in attendance for track and field events.

Many of the Americans wore the uniforms of competing athletic clubs that dominated the games. Poage was running for the Milwaukee Athletic Club—he was its first non-white competitor—when he won bronze medals in both the 200-meter and 400-meter hurdles.

His groundbreaking performance was remarked upon and, for a time, remembered. In 1913, a La Crosse newspaper would describe Poage as "one of the fastest men in [the] world" at the time and as "perhaps the greatest track athlete that was ever developed in this city."

Still, in keeping with the times, even his hometown's pride was less than colorblind. "Poage Runs Third In Olympian Games," the *La Crosse Leader-Press* reported on September 1, 1904. "La Crosse Colored Athlete Tired Near Finish."

Father Marquette's
Roughest Journey

In death as much as life, Father Jacques Marquette's story was one of long and difficult journeys. In 1673, the 36-year-old French Jesuit and the fur trader Louis Jolliet were the first Europeans to cross what would become Wisconsin and explore the upper Mississippi River.

They paddled the Fox River from Green Bay to what is now Portage, then went west on the Wisconsin River, eventually covering 2,700 miles in four exhausting months.

The school that would bear his name found no easier going. A Jesuit university had been proposed in Milwaukee as early as 1848, when statehood began but for reasons ranging from lack of funds to lack of English-speaking Jesuits, the future Marquette University did not open until 1881.

In a dedication speech, the Reverend H. F. Fairbanks said, "To this building is attached the name of one who is held in veneration by pagans and Christians alike."

Pagans, maybe. Politicians were another matter.

When Congress invited states to nominate distinguished Americans to the new Statuary Hall in 1864, the young state of Wisconsin didn't immediately reply. It wasn't until 1887 that a Chippewa Falls Republican suggested Marquette, perhaps hoping for bipartisan agreement. As the humorist George W. Peck noted, "Father Marquette belonged to neither political party. On the contrary, he was a Christian."

The *Milwaukee Sentinel* opposed the move, saying Marquette had never been a Wisconsin citizen. The Legislature approved

The statue of Father Jacques Marquette was unveiled in 1909.
WHI IMAGE ID 69550

the choice anyway, but the superintendent of the Capitol then refused to accept Marquette, again citing the lack of Wisconsin citizenship.

Marquette was in for another rough ride. His supporters wanted Catholic votes but feared offending the sizable German Lutheran voting bloc. For six years the nomination languished until, in 1893, Congress finally approved the plan. But more wrangling developed over selecting a sculptor, and by the time Gaetano

Trentanove began chipping away at his block of marble, a new wave of anti-Catholic sentiment had washed over Wisconsin.

The American Protective Association warned that Catholics were secretly out to take over America by force and called Marquette a "French tramp [and] vowed enemy of our most cherished American institutions."

Trentanove was undeterred, but after he delivered his statue to the Capitol in 1896, it brought threats and protest. Some said that a Jesuit's statue insulted the memory of Abraham Lincoln, whose images was nearby. One lawmaker warned that the Goddess of Liberty would be replaced atop the dome by a figure of St. Peter.

For years, Congress refused to accept the statue. Marquette alumni pushed for recognition, but critics demanded a real American instead. But efforts to swap Marquette for another Wisconsin figure went nowhere, and in 1904—almost 17 years after his last journey had begun—a resolution accepting the statue finally was approved.

Crossing the wild frontier hadn't been nearly so arduous.

Braves Baseball
Filled Streets with Joy

In an electric moment on a late September night in 1957, Henry Aaron lifted a 400-foot home run over the center-field fence at County Stadium to give the hometown Braves their first National League pennant.

The biggest home run in Wisconsin baseball history, it came in the biggest game ever and launched a celebration to rival that on V-J Day.

And it was only a warm-up.

Eddie Mathews, third baseman for the Milwaukee Braves baseball team, slides into home plate, July 7, 1957. WHI IMAGE ID 6225

Some say Milwaukee is not a baseball town, but no one could say it in the 1950s. In five seasons since the Braves had come to Milwaukee from Boston, they had drawn more than 2 million fans four times. They had finished third once, second twice and, thanks to "Hammerin' Hank," finally won a place in baseball's fall classic—against the New York Yankees, no less.

Some 65,000 fans gathered for fireworks at the lakefront, clogging streets for blocks to ooh and aah in celebration. The bus-stopping crowd that met players when they returned on October 4 was called unequaled in baseball history.

Fans planned World Series parties, city officials decorated light poles and hung bunting, and Milwaukee prepared for its long-awaited moment in the national eye—even more defiantly after a visiting New Yorker dismissed the city as bush league.

Then the series began. It went the limit and was settled in New York, but when Milwaukee won the seventh game, 5–0, it re-lit the celebratory fire back home.

Horns blew until they wore themselves silent. Mayor Frank Zeidler led a delegation into the City Hall tower to ring the old bell—one for each of Milwaukee's runs, then five more times for good measure. Then came the night, "the craziest, wildest night Milwaukee has ever known," the *Milwaukee Journal* said on the morning after.

"A human sea flowed on Wisconsin Ave. From the lakefront to the public museum, people were packed elbow to elbow. They shoved, drank, sang, kissed strangers and jitterbugged. They did things that they never normally would think of doing."

Revelry went beyond state borders. A Wyoming man's telegraph read: "Heaven's blessings. Urgently request mayor and council change name Milwaukee to Burdette, Wis., one day." A woman in Yakima, Washington, called the Schlitz Brewing Company and insisted on speaking to the president, Erwin C. Uihlein.

She told him she just needed to talk with someone in Milwaukee about the Braves.

A New Jersey company sent Zeidler 10 gallons of red paint "to pain the town red," not that outside help was needed. As Richard Applegate had reported for NBC-TV, "There were so many drunks on Wisconsin Ave. that it took one man 10 minutes to fall down."

If there wasn't enough to feel good about, a New York columnist reported a line he overhead from a colleague.

"You can call this 'bush' if you like," the writer had said, "but if we had a little of it in New York, the Giants wouldn't be on their way to San Francisco."

When Murrow Took Down McCarthy

By March 1954, "Tail Gunner Joe's" high-flying anti-Communist crusade had hit turbulent air. Four years after he escalated the Cold War by charging that the State Department was riddled with Communists, Wisconsin Senator Joseph McCarthy's rabid style and virulent accusations were wearing thin with many Americans.

In rapid succession, the national GOP chairman chastised his recent comments, President Dwight D. Eisenhower criticized McCarthy's handling of witnesses at hearings and the secretary of defense called claims that the Army was coddling Communists "just damn tommyrot."

McCarthy dropped a libel suit against a former senator who had called him unfit to serve, and Adlai Stevenson attacked McCarthy for his tactics and Eisenhower for not being tougher on him. After McCarthy's request for free network response time was denied, a highly-placed Republican said the administration would attempt to keep McCarthy off the front pages.

It wouldn't happen. That week, thanks to Edward R. Murrow, McCarthy would be all over the front pages— and in many living rooms, too.

On his popular *See It Now* program on CBS-TV on March 9, 1954, Murrow charged that in his hunt for

Senator Joseph R. McCarthy during the Army-McCarthy Hearings, May 24, 1954. WHI IMAGE ID 48222

Communists in high places, McCarthy repeatedly stepped over the line between "investigating and persecuting."

Acknowledging the show would be controversial, Murrow showed film clips of McCarthy's speeches—one in which he called the Democratic Party "the party of treason"—and showed McCarthy assuming various poses, including "laughing or chuckling with an almost fiendish expression," as one writer put it.

"His primary achievement," Murrow said, "has been in confusing the public mind as between the internal and the external threat of Communism."

Response was immediate and overwhelming, almost all in Murrow's favor. CBS reported 2,365 calls in four hours, all but 151 approving of Murrow. Of 1,089 telegrams, only 14 were critical. One who sent congratulations was Margaret Truman, daughter of the former president.

McCarthy's reply, filmed for TV at Murrow's invitation, was true to form.

He attempted to link Murrow to a Moscow school described as revolutionary, said Murrow had long engaged in propaganda for the Communist Party and charged that Murrow's recent remarks "followed implicitly the Communist line."

Calling the charges further examples of McCarthy's tactics of manufacturing "evidence," Murrow continued to denounce McCarthy. At Murrow's death in 1965, colleagues called his McCarthy program the greatest achievement of his career.

Commentator Elmer Davis said the program "taught everyone who works in television that the medium can show up a man's character and his record . . . by putting on the screen his own actions and words."

Later in 1954, McCarthy would further destroy his image during the televised Army-McCarthy hearings. In December, on a 67–22 vote, the Senate voted to "condemn" McCarthy, and his career effectively ended. He died in 1957.

John Savage,
Dam Builder to the World

John L. Savage's senior civil engineering thesis at the University of Wisconsin held clues to his future, for those able to decipher the title. It read: "The Accuracy of Various Approximate Methods of Calculating the Stresses in the Members of a Two-Hinged Arch."

But he well understood its importance. It was the dawn of the 20th century, and the small-town Wisconsin boy was off to design and build some of the world's greatest dams.

Savage was raised in a farm house in Cooksville in Rock County. He spent two years of high school in Evansville, two more years at the Hillside Home School at Spring Green, a private academy run by aunts of the architect Frank Lloyd Wright, and completed high school and college in Madison.

Savage soon joined the United States Reclamation Service and in 1903 was put to work on the Minidoka irrigation project in the Snake River Valley of Idaho. According to the *Wisconsin Magazine of History*, he found it to be an eye-opening service.

"When I first went out to the Snake River Valley, I saw only a river and a lot of wasteland," he said.

"After the dam was up the land changed. It got water. Farmers moved in to work the soil. Crops grew. Then came villages and towns. That's why I think this is the happiest, most thrilling work in the world."

In coming decades, it would take him around the world. Savage supervised the design of the Hoover Dam and Grand Coulee Dam, the Parker and Shasta dams, some of the first dams of the

Tennessee Valley Authority project and structures in Mexico and Australia.

In the early 1930s, he was in such demand during the rapid New Deal build-up that he was supervising the Hoover Dam and TVA projects at the same time he was called on to plan the Columbia Basin Project in parched central Washington State. In 1944, at age 64, Savage went to China to design the proposed Yangtze Gorge Dam, later delayed by China's civil war but nonetheless one of his proudest accomplishments.

Savage received an honorary doctor of science degree from the University of Wisconsin in 1934 and was awarded numerous gold medals by engineering groups. Curiously, this man who could hold rivers at bay could not keep thieves away; several times burglars made off with his medals.

Savage's retirement plans were to return to the Cooksville farm where he had grown up, he said in 1953, as well as visit "all the big dams in the west." But ill health intervened. Savage's last years were in a Colorado nursing home, where he died in 1967 at age 88.

Hasenfus Fell
into Iran-Contra Mess

The scandal that came to be known as Iran-Contra began when a Wisconsin man—just a country boy, he called himself—fell from the Nicaraguan sky and into the world headlines.

"Everyone knows my name from China to the North Pole," Eugene Hasenfus remarked ruefully a few years later.

Hasenfus was just an ex-Marine who worked in construction in his hometown of Marinette before he joined Ronald Reagan, George Bush and Oliver North on the world stage.

On October 6, 1986, while helping to arm rebel Nicaraguans—called "Contras"—in violation of US policy, Hasenfus was captured by Sandinista soldiers after his plane was shot down over the jungles of Nicaragua.

His fellow crewmen were killed, but Hasenfus was led from the crash scene with a rope around his neck—literally then, and he would say figuratively forever.

US government officials protested ignorance of the entire matter. Hasenfus maintained he was part of a CIA-directed network of flights aimed at arming the rebels, but that he did not know all of the details about who was directly running the operation.

Then, and later during congressional hearings, the Reagan administration disavowed any involvement, even as accusations swirled.

Hasenfus eventually was found guilty by a Sandinista tribunal and imprisoned for 73 days before being released, confused and not a little bitter about his ordeal.

Hasenfus returned to Marinette, where he found his life changed by his new reputation as a soldier of fortune. Out of work and in debt with hefty lawyer bills, he and his wife, Sally, later met with writers and producers, hoping for a book or movie deal that would let him tell his story and dig them out of arrears. But neither ever appeared.

"If we wanted to put drugs in it, sex in it and a bunch of other Rambo stuff in it," he said in a 1987 interview, "we would have had a movie and a book out already and it would all have been forgotten."

In June 1996, the Clinton administration rejected Hasenfus' claim to $800,000 for injuries he suffered when the plane crashed.

But Hasenfus had hinted two years earlier, after a special prosecutor's lengthy investigation concluded that the government had engaged in a cover-up of the truth, that he didn't expect satisfaction from the case.

"It's the way a wise man told me," he said. "The only way to get that would be for all sides to tell the truth, and I don't think we'll ever have that."

And, he said: "It's funny to see your name in history books when you never dreamed of it."

Unfounded Panic on the Frontier

In 1862, a Sioux uprising began in Minnesota, marked by numerous killings that many thought would spread into Wisconsin.

Only panic did, but it went all the way to the governor's office.

After settlers were killed at Acton, Minnesota, fear was felt as far away as eastern Wisconsin, which lacked only hostile Indians to justify it.

Fear was heightened because so many men were off at war. In response, General John Pope was replaced as commander of the Army of the Potomac and posted to Milwaukee, even though battles with the Sioux raged far to the west.

Terrified whites lived on and overreacted to wild rumors. And the terror of Minnesotans streaming into Wisconsin was contagious.

The chairman of the Town of Richmond, near Milwaukee, notified Governor Edward Salomon that Indians had just burned Cedarburg and were "within 5 miles, murdering and burning everything they come across."

"Farmers and villagers gathered their families into any vehicle that moved and whipped their foam-specked teams toward Milwaukee," said an account by H. W. Kuhm. "All night people poured into the city. Streets were blocked with ox carts, wagons and buggies. By morning, each train arriving from the north or west was jammed with terrified people."

Villages near Merton were deserted "except for one woman who remained behind when her husband hastily filled his wagon with his prized pigs but forgot her."

Salomon, who had been convinced the Ojibwe and Ho-Chunk would join the war, rushed arms and soldiers to attack the hostiles, and they no doubt would have acquitted themselves well if there had been any.

It was the same everywhere. On October 27, an Eau Claire woman, Lucy Hastings, wrote to relatives that:

"Our village was thrown into a terrible consternation by a report being brought to us that there was coming 300 Indians strong and were within a few miles of us burning and destroying everything before them. They news spread from house to house like wild fire, and in a short time the streets were alive with people. Every old gun was put in order, axes, shovels and hatchets, pitchforks and in some instances, lightning rods were speedily taken down and fixed into spears . . .

"Such a time I never saw and hope never to again."

Scouts, she said, went out "to learn the truth of it. If true, when within hearing distance of our pickets, they were to blow a horn and they in turn give us warning so that all the women were to flee for refuge to a large three-story building.

"The men were to protect it, but on return of our scouts it proved there was but small foundation for the fright."

In Waukesha, Kuhm wrote, "a select group of daring young men was dispatched to ferret out the rampaging Indians," but all they found was that liquor was running freely in Milwaukee.

Several days later they wandered home, as perplexed as Wisconsin's peaceful Indians.

When Fire Raged in Peshtigo

There had been warnings, enough to set Peshtigo on edge. Many fires had broken out in northern Wisconsin in the fall of 1871, fed by the dry timber slash where lumberjacks had felled forests, spurred by winds.

Fearing the worst—but not imagining how terrible it would be—officials placed extra hogsheads of water along streets, removed combustibles, even buried valuables.

A French-born priest, Father Peter Pernin, later recounted the unease:

"At one time, whilst we were still in the fields, the wind rose suddenly with more strength than it had yet displayed, and I perceived some old trunks of trees blaze out . . . just as if the wind had been a breath of fire, capable of kindling them into a flame by its mere contact."

The breath of fire blew and blew. That evening "a menacing crimson" rose above smoke in the west, "a vivid red reflection of immense extent," Pernin called it. These flames were the foot soldiers of the great Peshtigo fire.

That very day, October 8, fire in Chicago ravaged the city's business district, causing losses of $200 million.

But the fire at Peshtigo and surrounding environs was far more deadly; about 1,200 died, five times Chicago's toll, and 2,400 square miles of Wisconsin and nearby Michigan burned.

Hundreds were injured, thousands left homeless. It was, and remains, Wisconsin's worst natural disaster.

Peshtigo was a city of 1,700 by 1871 but was stuffed to overflowing when fire broke out with 200 laborers who had just arrived.

A drawing of the Peshtigo Fire by G. J. Tisdale, 1871. WHI IMAGE ID 3728

Pernin's eyewitness account describes the fire's approach as residents wise enough to seek safety in the Peshtigo River took flight. Pernin was among them, struggling to save his church's tabernacle:

> The wind, forerunner of the tempest, was increasing in violence, the redness in the sky deepening, and the roaring sound like thunder seemed almost upon us.
>
> The air was no longer fit to breathe, full as it was of sand, dust, ashes, cinders, sparks, smoke and fire . . . The neighing of horses, falling of chimneys, crashing of uprooted trees, roaring and whistling of the wind, crackling of fire as it ran with lightning-like rapidity from house to house—all sounds were there save that of the human voice. People seemed stricken

dumb by terror. The silence of the tomb reigned among the living; nature alone lifted up its voice and spoke.

Even water up to their necks offered no safety. The night air itself seemed on fire. Those who wanted to survive had to dunk their head repeatedly, a scene that almost made Pernin smile.

A woman who lost hold of the log bearing her up grabbed the horns of a swimming cow instead; it later bore her to safety.

But another terrified woman who reached the river after great struggle found herself without her infant. Pernin attempted to console her, but she threw herself to her death.

He left the river after four hours. The fire had moved on to commit further destruction; it spared the neighboring city of Marinette but not before sparks jumped to the roof of the Church of Our Lady of Lourdes and brought it to the ground. It was Father Pernin's second church.

Frances Willard, Temperance Crusader

Frances E. Willard came by her prohibitionist convictions at an early age. Still a redheaded tomboy who preferred Frank to her given name, she was making rules for the make-believe city she and her brother had created when she declared, "We will have no saloons in Fort City and then we will need no jails."

Willard devoted her life to trying to ban saloons in real-life America.

Willard was born in New York in 1839 and moved with her family to Janesville at seven. If you attended school in Wisconsin, state law requires that you already know her birthday was September 28, but the law mandating that day as Frances Willard Day is even more widely ignored today than her pet cause.

The last photograph taken of Frances Willard, a leader in the temperance movement and women's activist in the Methodist church, January 8, 1898. WHI IMAGE ID 35303

But once Willard was famous in every state in the land, and vilified in every tavern.

She was educated at a country school in Janesville that later bore her name, then at Milwaukee Female College and Northwestern female college in Evanston, where she became a professor of natural sciences.

But it was in the ban-the-booze movement of the late 1800s that Willard made her name. In 1879, she became president of the Women's Christian Temperance Union, a post she held for the rest of her life. Under her direction, and through her relentless energy, the movement grew rapidly.

For years, she toured the country, arguing that total abstinence would revive a troubled world while improving child welfare and creating a more communal life.

She founded WCTU branches everywhere she went. Often, she would speak from the rear of trains, sending word ahead to each stop so boys could run through town to gather an audience. Her leadership turned the temperance movement into a worldwide crusade and contributed mightily to the mood that prompted the 18th Amendment years later.

She also fought for women's suffrage and other social causes, and even found time to be an editor of the *Chicago Post and Mail*.

After her death in 1898, a statue of Willard was put in Statuary Hall in Washington, DC, nominated by the state of Illinois as its second and final choice—the first woman so honored.

But she never forgot Forest Home, her childhood home in the shadow of pines along the Rock River, or the little schoolhouse her father and neighbors had built.

Shortly before she died, she wrote prayerfully, "I thank Thee that wherever I may dwell, no place can be so dear, so completely embalmed in my heart."

The site became a shrine to her in following years. In 1939, a special three-cent stamp was issued in her honor. Hundreds of temperance advocates gathered to salute her in Janesville, an occasion marred only by the youth testing the loud speaker system.

He made "a mistake" and played the "Beer Barrel Polka."

Belle La Follette Was a Fighter, Too

Perhaps Belle Case La Follette deserved a snappy nickname of her own. Even Robert M. "Fighting Bob" La Follette once called his wife "altogether the brainiest member of my family . . .

"Her grasp of the great problems, sociological and economic, unsurpassed by any of the strong men who have been associated with me in my work."

She was not the woman behind this famous Wisconsin figure, but the woman beside him.

Belle Case was born in Baraboo in 1859 in a log cabin, like her future husband. She and La Follette met at the University of Wisconsin, where she had begun her studies at age 16 and where she would become the first female law school graduate.

Belle Case La Follette, photographed about the time of her husband Bob's independent campaign for the presidency, 1924.
WHI IMAGE ID 55358

She was involved in social and political issues, such as suffrage for women and pacifism, but she also influenced La Follette's writing and speaking on the topics. He acknowledged that she was his major confidant and political adviser—he was said to have referred to "when we were governor"—and she crafted some of his most important speeches.

It was not a new role for her. She had earlier helped

292 The Wisconsin Story*

him in his studies when La Follette was struggling to win a university degree.

At her urging, her husband, as governor, appointed women to public office and the university governing boards. Belle La Follette argued in her own speeches that "government is considered a men's exclusive province, a limitation that has narrowed the lives of the women, that has robbed the children, and that has reacted most injuriously upon the state."

When suffragists made appearances at more than 70 county fairs in 1912, Belle La Follette visited seven of them in 10 days.

When La Follette went to Washington, his wife continued her role as equal partner in his career. She ran his campaigns, wrote speeches, advised him on political and governmental issues, all the while pursuing her own causes at the same time.

When her husband died in 1925, there was a push to have her complete his unexpired Senate term. She declined to run, but supported her son, Robert Jr., who was easily elected. Belle La Follette then turned her energies to producing a biography of her late husband. It was nearly finished when she died in 1931.

Ground Observers Kept Eyes on Skies

It seems naïve now—as it did to many even then—but in the 1950s many Wisconsinites braced for Russian invasion with necks craned and eyes peeled.

They were volunteers in the civil defense program's Ground Observer Corps—a human force of friends and neighbors scanning the skies around the clock for the enemies of freedom.

"We're all in the front lines now," read a 1953 plea for volunteers. "Yours eyes or ears might save our nation."

Forrest J. Carleen, Minneapolis (right), district representative of the Channel Master Corporation, is presented a plaque for being "the outstanding post in the eastern air defense post" of the Madison Civil Air Patrol by four representatives, March 22, 1958.
WHI IMAGE ID 97704

The Air Force wanted GOC posts every eight miles throughout the country, each one reporting every airplane in its sights to a regional filtering station. Numerous states posts were established, but newsletters of the River Falls GOC post show it was often boring and unappreciated duty.

In early 1953 the post had 98 active observers, yet many shifts were uncovered. Some observers would work a few four-hour shifts, decide the work was silly and quit. Others wondered why River Falls should watch the sky 18 hours a day when nearby Hudson never looked up.

The answer, the newsletter editor said, was that Hudson was sloughing its duty. River Falls was doing its patriotic part.

Still, the lack of dependable workers meant a few worked overtime. A farmer, his wife and sons were credited for putting aside chores to stand and watch while Tuesday Chief Observer Glen J. Healy was cited because he, "according to him, has shot down more planes than any other observer connected with the post."

Winged lapel pins were awarded to dependable observers. William Nicholson got his in 1953 even though his membership card was run through his mother's washing machine.

The post was manned even on holidays became "enemy attackers would hardly refrain because of a holiday." Hadn't Washington himself crossed the Delaware on Christmas?

Girl Scouts were trained to stand watch, as were schoolkids and retirees with no job interferences, but as newsletter editor C. G. Stratton griped in 1955, "The community, or the nation, that depends on old people and children for so vital a function of our national defense is treading a dangerous road."

Middle-age men were sorely needed, he said. "And don't tell me they have no time for it.... Nero fiddled while Rome burned. These people, figuratively speaking, are fiddling while disaster threatens."

Still, by 1955, 44 observers worked regularly and 14 occasionally, while 47 had resigned for good reason and a discouraging 118 for no good reason. Worse, some observers were teased for even taking part.

"[The teaser] is usually the sort of fellow who cheated on gas rationing during the war," Stratton said. "So don't be surprised if I am jailed on account of assault and battery."

But the River Falls post watched on, if not every hour. One month, despite many vacancies, it reported 209 planes, a number exceeded by only nine of the 549 posts reporting to Minneapolis.

That none were enemy craft hardly mattered. The GOC gave way in 1958 to higher-technology defenses.

Frank Lloyd Wright's Spring Green Days

He was hailed at his death as perhaps the greatest of Wisconsin's native sons, but the world-renowned architect Frank Lloyd Wright and his state were often estranged.

His hometown paper, Spring Green's *Weekly Home News*, said of his passing: "In the death of Frank Lloyd Wright, the bell tolls for Spring Green as well."

But years earlier, that paper had called him "either insane or degenerate." And when he arrived in Spring Green in 1911, his neighbors asked the sheriff to evict him.

The proudly unconventional Wright invited such reactions by his often scandalous conduct.

He was born in Richland County in 1869 (some accounts say 1867) to a Welsh family of preachers and teachers. His mother, Anna Lloyd Jones, came from a Spring Green family that owned the land where Wright would later build his famed Taliesin— Welsh for "shining brow."

He studied engineering at the University of Wisconsin, studied architecture in Chicago under the great Louis Sullivan and later went off on his own, becoming more famous with each major project.

His personal life was another matter. In 1909, he left his family and took up with a married neighbor. Their arrival in Spring Green posed, as newspaper editor W. R. Purdy put it, "a menace to the morals of a community and an insult to every family therein."

Wright replied that he had no intent to bring scandal; he expressed respect for Spring Green's dignity and pledged to make the community proud.

Wright met spectacular success and spectacular tragedy. In 1914 a deranged servant set fire to Taliesin and killed his lover, her two children and several workers. His next marriage also ended badly but his third marriage, to Olga (Olgivanna) Lvanhovna Lazovich in 1928, would last until his death in 1959.

Spring Green eventually came to appreciate Wright's worldwide influence.

At his death, it was observed that while he had designed numerous houses, several churches and the noted S. C. Johnson Company office building in Racine, no major government-financed examples of his work existed in Wisconsin. Even a planned Madison civic auditorium was abandoned for almost 40 years before Monona Terrace was completed in 1997.

The odd relationship did not end at his death. In 1985, at his wife's final wish, Wright's remains were exhumed from his grave at Spring Green and moved to Taliesin West at Scottsdale, Arizona, where Olgivanna was buried.

When some in Wisconsin protested, architect and son-in-law

William Wesley Peters found a certain irony.

"Wisconsin as a state," Peters said, "never gave Mr. Wright recognition, not on the campus, not in major public buildings."

For his considerable ego and unorthodox style, however, Wright was not without a sense of humor. When a Johnson Wax executive called to say the roof on Wright's design was leaking right over his desk, the world's best architect had a solution. "Move your chair."

Frank Lloyd Wright in 1930.
WHI IMAGE ID 1921

Morgan and Elizabeth Martin, Green Bay Pioneers

If Morgan L. Martin arrived in early Green Bay with designs on carving a comfortable living from its frontier opportunities, future wife Elizabeth Smith Martin arrived in 1835 with sick misgivings.

Traveling with her uncle aboard the steamer *Thomas Jefferson*, she was greeted by cannon fire from Fort Howard, and the rough settlement she would call home caused her heart to sink. She saw "oceans of sand" and a "green, slimy" river "breathing of malaria."

"Ah!" she wrote in her diary. "Was it for such a land as this my uncle deserted the dear old town on Lake Champlain, with its ten thousand beauties and blissful associations? Alas! . . . How gladly would I turn back—back to my childhood's home."

No surprise, then, that she didn't stay in Green Bay on that occasion.

But two years later she would return and, soon after, marry Martin. The couple immediately began to establish Hazelwood, a home that included perhaps the most famous dining room table in Wisconsin history.

If legend can be accepted, it was on that table where the final draft of Wisconsin's constitution was drawn up.

Morgan Martin's lengthy and varied resume testifies to the adaptability and can-do spirit of pioneers, though failure as much as success prompted some of his career moves.

A New York native, Martin came to Green Bay in 1827 to found, with his cousin James Doty, the first law practice in Wisconsin. In 1829, he and Doty—and perhaps Henry Baird—traveled from

Morgan L. Martin, 1866. WHI IMAGE ID 2786

Green Bay to Prairie du Chien, becoming the first non-Indians to cross Wisconsin.

He made a fortune investing in property, including a partnership with Solomon Juneau in platting Milwaukee's east side. He was a member of both the Michigan legislative council and Wisconsin territorial council, was the Wisconsin Territory's representative to Congress and president of the second constitutional convention. He served in the Wisconsin Assembly and Senate and, after service as paymaster in the Civil War, was an Indian agent and judge.

The Martins built Hazelwood—now a historic house museum—despite financial setbacks in a bank panic. However, Martin suffered more significant losses from a failed effort to build a canal and lock system on the Fox River from Lake Winnebago to Green Bay. In 1866, Martin was declared bankrupt.

Martin resumed his law practice in 1870 and his last years were filled with learning, fishing and family. He and Elizabeth helped create Lawrence College, and he was involved in the State Historical Society of Wisconsin, which he had also helped form.

Elizabeth, who endured long and lonely periods when business or politics called her husband away, eventually came to appreciate her Green Bay home. She later contributed memory pieces to the *Milwaukee Sentinel* describing the ennobling aspects of those early hardships.

In 1888, the Historical Society's Reuben G. Thwaites would write: "No one who has carefully studied the beginnings of Wisconsin greatness can but recognize that all honor and praise are due the memory of master spirits like Martin, who moulded [*sic*] the nascent commonwealth intelligently and well."

Anger in the Milk House

Clearly, Gundar Felland should have gone to a school social, as planned. Instead, in October 1933, the Dane County farmer took food and coffee to men taking part in Wisconsin dairy farmers' third milk strike of the year.

At the picketing site, Felland was shot dead by a Madison man, who then waved his gun and shouted, "Come on, I'll give it to all of you."

It was a violent year in America's suffering Dairyland. The Depression was hard on everyone, but farmers were beyond frustrated.

In desperation, many organized to attempt to raise milk prices and vowed to strike if necessary. They elected as their leader Walter M. Singler, who vowed: "Farmers by uniting can turn this nation upside down. We must prove that it is not money, not gold, but food that is essential."

Wisconsin farmers also formed a chapter of the national Farmers' Holiday Association headed by Dunn County farmer Arnold Gilberts, who declared, "We'll solve our problems with bayonets, and I don't mean maybe."

The first strike in February accomplished little. A few cheese and butter plants were shut down, but shippers used other routes, and striking farmers were dispersed by tear gas and clubs. A truce was quickly called.

Gilberts wasn't done. In asking for a second strike he said, "I want to see a holiday so terrible that it will darken the sky and go down as the greatest tragedy in history, so your children and

The Battle of Durham Hill during the milk strike, showing sheriff's deputies and National Guardsmen (sworn in as special deputies) charging farmers with bayonets, May 18, 1933. WHI IMAGE ID 3245

mine can read what happened in 1933 when agriculture went on a rampage."

The other side was ready; 2,500 National Guard members were made available, and shipments of tear gas were sent to Wisconsin. In May, farmers began seizing milk trucks and dumping their loads, then disappearing.

A highlight was the "Battle of Durham Hill" in Waukesha County, where Sheriff Arthur J. Moran summoned newspapermen, laid down a tear gas screen and sent bayonet-toting Guardsmen to drive striking farmers back.

The strike failed, but when prices did not improve, a third holiday was set for October. It lasted four sometimes-violent weeks. In addition to the killing of Felland, two farmers committed suicide—as strikers attempted to keep food from reaching markets. Milk was dumped and cheese plants were dynamited; trucks were hijacked and numerous shots fired.

But there was some humorous ingenuity. On Madison's Lake Monona, a crafty farmer attempted to row a boatload of milk to market under cover of darkness; pickets launched their own boat, seized his milk and poured it into the lake.

In Marshfield, a resourceful youth decorated his car with paper streamers, tied tin cans to the bumper and painted "Just Married" on the door. With his girl beside him, he drove unmolested through picket lines—with his load of butter for market.

But Felland had died in vain. The strike petered out, and on November 18 a truce was called.

Justice for the Workers

At the turn of the century, Wisconsin workplaces were often dangerous places, and employers had little incentive to make them safer.

Industrialization had made machinery bigger and more complex. The advent of chemical processes in manufacturing posed new threats, yet workers who were involved in accidents on the job or suffered occupational diseases could be compensated only if they successfully sued their employers and proved negligence.

Legal phraseology then, according to a *Wisconsin Blue Book* account, spoke of the law of master and servant.

Out-of-work plaintiffs could rarely afford the time and legal costs for such recovery efforts. Increasingly there were calls, here and in other states, for government to establish a fair compensation system.

Wisconsin, as it often did in that period, led the way in creating policies that became national models.

The key, again, was turning to University of Wisconsin experts for a solution. After considerable study, John R. Commons, the nationally famous labor expert, drafted legislation to create a state-directed insurance fund for compensation without requiring finding of fault.

The public already believed employers should pay for their injured employees, and of course labor was on board. By injecting incentives for employers, and by exempting farmers and the smallest workplaces, Commons eventually drew all sides together.

The law, by making employers responsible for injury, offered strong incentives to make workplaces safer.

Safe workplaces, in turn, made for more profitable companies, benefiting employers and consumers.

The nation's first compensation act became effective May 3, 1911. Even more was accomplished, however.

Again with Commons in the lead, the state created the first Industrial Commission, which was given broad power in overseeing safety conditions and defining "reasonable" standards.

At the same time, Wisconsin passed the first modern apprenticeship law and adopted other labor laws, including regulations over employment of children and women.

All of the groundbreaking legislation was signed by Governor Francis E. McGovern, the former Milwaukee district attorney who supported the policies of Robert M. La Follette and who was in office when many of the era's progressive reforms were passed.

History Was Key to Reuben Gold Thwaites

When Wisconsinites look back on the state's history with fondness and curiosity, it is appropriate to recall the man who pointed the way. He was Reuben Gold Thwaites, who wrested history from the hands of scholars and shared it with the common people.

Thwaites was not the founder of the State Historical Society of Wisconsin. He was its second secretary, but for 26 years—from 1887 until his death in 1913—Thwaites was the forceful leader who expanded its size, mission and status in state life.

This portrait of Reuben Gold Thwaites from 1899 was used as the basis for a painting by John Johansen resides in the Society collection. WHI IMAGE ID 62768

Before Thwaites, Wisconsin's historical society—and most others—were closed circles, collecting manuscripts, documents and other papers for use by generally restricted memberships. Thwaites, a former newspaper editor, wanted the secrets of the past unveiled for everyone.

So he threw open the doors. Influenced by, and a participant in, Wisconsin's progressive era, Thwaites believed the state's historical collections could play as large a role in public education as the library and school.

It should be as open to the man on the street, he said, as to the professor on the hill.

"We are missing a golden opportunity in the education of the masses," he said in 1891, in pushing to expand the society's museum.

He greatly increased the society's catalog, collected the works of Wisconsin authors and state newspapers and tracked down Wisconsin manuscripts in every dark corner.

He worked to establish local societies, helped communities apply for Carnegie library funds, founded the Wisconsin Library Association and was president of the national group. He was instrumental in recognizing state historical treasures, leading to the development of dedicated sites we enjoy today.

"Energy, thy name is Thwaites," a colleague once said. His labor resulted in a historical society that was a national model. As the 20th century opened, Thwaites could say, "This Society [has] moved away from its traditional moorings as an exclusive, almost an aristocratic retreat for the learned alone, and carried on its work of self-popularization."

At his death, the governor, Supreme Court justices, university regents and legislators attended a memorial service at the Capitol, where eminent historian Frederick Jackson Turner returned from Harvard to laud Thwaites for turning over "a new type of state historical society" to his successors.

"Happy, thrice happy, they, if in the times to come their names shall be spoken with the respect and affection with which we speak the name of Reuben Gold Thwaites."

Iron Brigade Was Story of Valor, Loss

The Iron Brigade won its name from bravery displayed and its fame from blood spilled. Composed of three Wisconsin regiments—the Second, Sixth and Seventh Wisconsin Volunteers—as well as a regiment each from Indiana and, later, Michigan, it was the only all-western brigade in the Army of the Potomac.

It served in every major campaign, fought in the Civil War's fiercest battles and, said historian Alan T. Nolan, was "frequently at the vortex of the fighting and uniformly fighting with desperate and telling gallantry."

Such valor resulted in terrible sacrifice. It was the sad fate of these mostly farm-boy soldiers in "The Black Hat Brigade" to gain so much admiration for losing so many men.

The Second Wisconsin alone suffered the greatest percentage of losses in the Union Army, while the Seventh had the most men lost in battle of any northern regiment.

The brigade's first commander was Rufus King, the Milwaukee newspaperman, followed by West Point graduate John Gibbon, a man from North Carolina who took charge in 1862.

Its fighting career began in earnest that August at Brawner Farm, on the eve of the Union defeat at Second Bull Run, when the brigade admirably stood up to Stonewall Jackson's larger, stronger force.

"It was a stand-up, give-and-take encounter," said one account.

"The opposing armies faced each other at a maximum distance of 70 yards, exchanging volley for volley at that deadly distance. There was no lying down, no cover or entrenchment, no maneuvering. Neither side advanced; neither side retreated.

[When it ended] the dead of both lines lay where they had fallen in even rows."

It was much the same at Antietam, at South Mountain (where they earned their new name when General George B. McClellan observed their courage and said, "They must be made of iron!") and in the celebrated railroad cut at Gettysburg.

Rufus Dawes, a Wisconsin colonel, later described the tragic battle:

> I ordered my men to climb over the turnpike fences and advance (into) the heavy fire, which they began at once to pour upon us from their cover in the cut . . . many were struck on the fences, but the line pushed on . . .
>
> "Forward, charge!" was the order I gave. With the colors at the advance point, the regiment firmly and hurriedly moved forward, while the whole field behind streamed with men who had been shot and who were struggling to the rear or sinking in death upon the ground. The only commands I gave as we advanced were "Align on the colors! Close up on the colors!"
>
> The regiment was being so broken up that this order alone could hold the body together. Meanwhile, the colors fell upon the ground several times but were raised again by the heroes of the color guard.

Of 420 men who started at the turnpike fence, about 240 reached the railroad cut. After the war, at a soldiers' reunion in Wisconsin, Gibbon offered the highest praise.

"I was not a Wisconsin soldier and have not been honorably discharged, but at judgement day," Gibbon said, "I want to be with the Wisconsin soldiers."

First Train Had Rocky Ride

In May 1954, more than 500 rail buffs gathered for a train ride commemorating the 100th anniversary of the first passenger run from Milwaukee to Madison.

"In the interest of complete reporting," a train riding reporter acknowledged the next day, "it must be set down that the locomotive struck a cow along the right of way between Palmyra and Whitewater."

It was less tragedy (except, perhaps, for the cow) than nice timing. The run wouldn't have been historically appropriate without a snag or three.

Train travel developed in fits and starts in Wisconsin. By the 1830s, even as canal advocates were chasing their doomed-to-fail dreams, railroad supporters were looking for a way to connect Milwaukee to the Mississippi River.

Transporting lead and furs from the frontier to the developed eastern cities would make someone rich, it was widely believed, so the territorial legislature was swamped with petitions. There was much squabbling over proposed routes, but in 1848 authority was given for a rail line beginning in Milwaukee and stretching to Waukesha.

In February 1850, the company became the Milwaukee & Mississippi Railroad Company, and on September 12 the first rails were spiked down. It wasn't easy going; one account describes how a set of tracks crossing the Menominee Valley sank one night and had to be dug from the marsh.

The Mississippi River was still a distant dream when the first train rolled on November 20. Just five miles of track had been

MILWAUKEE & MISSISSIPPI

RAIL ROAD COMPANY.

BYRON KILBOURN,	-	-	*President.*
W. TAINTOR,	-	-	*Secretary.*
W. P. FLANDERS,	-	-	*Treasurer.*

This road is laid with the best of T rail so far as completed. Trains for freight and passangengers leave the Depot on Second Street, regularly every morning and afternoon.

E. D. HOLTON, Sup'tdt.

Milwaukee, Feb. 15th, 1851.

H. J. GOFF,
CONFECTIONER AND MANUFACTURER OF

CANDIES.

Advertisement for Milwaukee and Mississippi Railroad Company, 1851.
WHI IMAGE ID 64016

laid, but a locomotive and two cars filled with dignitaries chugged from Milwaukee to Wauwatosa.

It was Westward Ho! from there, over obstacles physical and financial. When the tracks reached Waukesha the following February, 250 men and women—accompanied by a band and much hoopla—rode the 20.5-mile route for the first time, reaching mouth-dropping speeds of 25 miles per hour.

"So opens the first link of the iron chain which is to connect us with the Mississippi," a newspaper crowed, rosy-eyed at the achievement. "May two years hence see it stretched across the state."

Instead, it took seven. Rails passed through Eagle and into Milton, then up to Stoughton and Madison, where in 1854 a crowd of 2,000 met the first train.

Then the line stretched west through Boscobel and to the river. When the locomotive finally smoked into Prairie du Chien in April 1857, one of its passengers was Solomon Juneau, Milwaukee's first citizen. The iron chain's last link had been completed.

The lead boom was long over. But Milwaukee & Mississippi, the forerunner of the huge Milwaukee Road, was a key link to America's West.

When Fond du Lac
Snubbed the President

Any city welcomes a sitting president, even—as La Crosse showed in 1990 with President Bill Clinton—a president under fire.

But until cooler heads prevailed, Fond du Lac once canceled a parade and told President William Howard Taft to take a hike.

It was in 1911 when Taft, who loved to travel, was on a 48-day national tour.

Fond du Lac wanted in. Initial plans were to make Taft the chief draw at the county fair, but the schedule didn't work. Still, a Milwaukee visit was set for October, so feisty Fond du Lac Mayor Frank J. Wolff's bid was accepted. Other Fox Valley cities were also scheduled, but Wolff bragged Taft had favored Fond du Lac with almost three hours—far more than any other place.

No idea was too big. Planners wanted special trains to bring in 10,000, even 20,000, guests. A hall would be hired. Thirty-five horse soldiers were to escort Taft's car, and one newsman predicted hundreds of cars would follow—even though there were only 445 in the entire county.

Bands and banner were ordered, and Mayor Wolff placed ads in nearby cities. Planners even hired a daredevil pilot to drop 1,500 cards over nearby—and rival—Sheboygan, reading: "Fond du Lac Invites You To Meet President Taft."

But trouble loomed. Wolff heard Appleton was suddenly getting another hour, Neenah had been added to the tour, and Oshkosh was getting more time.

It could only come out of Fond du Lac's moment in the sun. Wolff summoned his committee, griped that the city might get but a short speech from the rear of the train and impulsively decided to advise Taft of their disappointment.

His telegraph concluded: "All arrangements have been abandoned. Give all your time to Oshkosh and Appleton."

The *Fond du Lac Reporter*, jumping on the canceled bandwagon, published a special edition, and the story went national.

Saner sorts jumped in to save the day. The postmaster wired his apologies and a new invitation; local Republicans worked behind the scenes to smooth the waters, and pressure grew on Wolff to reconsider. Finally, he gathered his committee for a private three-hour meeting, after which a new wire was sent.

It cited a "misunderstanding" and "hasty action," renewed the bid and promised Taft a hearty welcome. In Salem, Oregon, Taft's party issued a release calling the incident "the most interesting connected with the recent travels of a president," and accepted.

On October 26, Taft did arrive. The parade was grand, the music patriotic, and the warm greeting was heartfelt. Young brothers Robert and Albert Jones even presented the rotund executive with a three-and-three-quarters-pound spud they'd dubbed the "Taft Potato."

"If I'd have known what a grand reception we were going to receive in Fond du Lac," Taft's secretary told Wolff, "I'd have arranged to stay here all day."

It no doubt gave Wolff ideas.

World War I Met with Resistance

If America was divided on the question of entering the First World War, Wisconsin was fractured. In the end, it would acquit itself admirably, both in battle and at home. Early in the war Wisconsin had a higher percentage of volunteers to draftees than any Midwestern state; it led all states in National Guard preparedness and every Liberty Bond quota was exceeded.

But before the war, Wisconsin's reluctance to participate struck many critics as unequivocally treasonous.

This was one fight Robert M. La Follette, then in the US Senate, wanted no part of. He feared—and he was largely correct—that it would bring an end to progressive reforms.

Even as the nation's early neutrality veered toward preparedness for war, he vehemently opposed American entry; he and his wife, Belle Case La Follette, were visible, vocal—and often scorned—pacifists.

Milwaukee Socialists were also adamantly opposed to the war. And Wisconsin's large German population raised loyalty doubts among those who wore their patriotism on their sleeves.

Criticism was pointed when La Follette would note that it would be America's poor and powerless who would die, or when he demanded to know how a war to save democracy could be joined without a popular vote.

"La Follette is acting as a German because there is a large German vote in the Wisconsin constituency," a Chicago newspaper wrote. A *Life* magazine cover showed the Kaiser pinning iron crosses all over La Follette for voting against US entry.

His was not the only "no" vote. Nine of 11 Wisconsin members of the House of Representatives also voted "no."

They were not unrepresentative of sentiment at home. When Monroe voters, on the eve of war, were presented with a referendum on American entry, they voted 954–95 against war.

They were also among the first to show that Wisconsin's misgivings would not translate into noninvolvement. When war was declared three days later, Monroe residents held a rally and parade in support of their government.

And war it would be. Wisconsin supplied doctors and nurses for the effort; its farmers increased food production, factories hummed 24 hours a day and residents abstained from meat and wheat one day a week to conserve supplies.

Wisconsin sent nearly 125,000 men into the military in World War I, and its 2,649 casualties ranked fourth highest among the states.

But even after the war, its leaders continued to make waves. In 1919, Mayor Daniel W. Hoan, who had angered many by his war opposition, earned national attention for refusing to invite Belgium's King Albert to Milwaukee during a State Department–sponsored post-war tour.

"I should go to my grave in everlasting shame were I to boost one iota the stock of any king," Hoan declared.

"I stand for the man who works, to hell with kings."

Black Hawk's Tragic Last Stand

Wisconsin's last Indian battle came in territorial days, but it set in motion the development that led to statehood a few years later.

The Sauk and Fox Indians had yielded to white encroachment for years before most tribal members ceded their land and moved to Iowa in 1829.

Black Hawk left later, and most reluctantly, but after a hard winter in 1832 he led a force of about 1,000 men, along with women, children and the aged, across the Mississippi intent on driving out usurpers and replanting their old fields.

The plan was almost certain to fail, wrote historian Norman Risjord, "but it was hardly a declaration of war."

But war would come. General Henry Atkinson had just arrived with a large force to keep restless tribes from acting up, and the Illinois militia, which included young Abraham Lincoln, also activated its units.

A painting of Black Hawk by Robert M. Sully, 1833.

WHI IMAGE ID 11706

Black Hawk soon realized the fighting help he had expected would not materialize and, as he wrote in his autobiography, his band was exhausted and hungry.

But when his men went to an Illinois militia camp with a white flag, they were fired upon. Several Indians were killed, and Black Hawk's band, unable to surrender, was on the run. They moved up the Rock River and through the Four Lakes area, now Madison, before reaching a hillside near Sauk City.

There they made a desperate stand. His people had been eating roots and bark to stay alive, and some had died along the trail. When soldiers approached, he wrote, "We were now compelled to fight or sacrifice our wives and children to the fury of the whites. . . . I was mounted on a fine horse, and was pleased to see my warriors so brave. I addressed them in a loud voice, telling them to stand their ground, and never yield it to the enemy."

His men were forced back, but the battle allowed women and children time to cross the Wisconsin River and head for the Mississippi. Their flight was slow; by the time they reached the Mississippi more of the old and young had died.

In a shameful episode, another effort to surrender was ignored. Black Hawk's party was fired on by a steamboat, the *Warrior*. The following morning, the Indians attempted to give up once more.

"The whites paid no attention to their entreaties," Black Hawk wrote, "but commenced slaughtering them. In a little while the whole army arrived. Our braves, but few in number, finding that the enemy paid no respect to age or sex, and seeing that they were murdering helpless women and little children, determined to fight until they were killed. As many women as could commenced swimming the Mississippi with children on their backs. A number of them were drowned and some shot before reaching the opposite shore."

Almost a century and a half later, the Wisconsin Legislature officially apologized for that "battle" on the Bad Axe River. As part of 1998 sesquicentennial activities, the restored Wisconsin Heights battle site was opened for interpretive tours.

"Rock River was a beautiful country," Black Hawk wrote. "I loved my towns, my cornfields, and the home of my people. I fought for it. It is now yours. Keep it as we did."

State Slogan Grew
from Civil War Gamble

It was a bloody national nightmare by any measure, but the Civil War did inspire Wisconsin's favorite slogan and give birth to its flag.

The call of "On, Wisconsin!" was uttered for the first time near Chattanooga, Tennessee, at the battle of Missionary Ridge, and involved a young Wisconsin officer named Arthur MacArthur Jr. (whose son, Douglas, would gain a bit of military fame as well).

Leading an unauthorized assault against Confederate positions on November 24, 1863, MacArthur picked up the flag of the 24th Wisconsin infantry and cried, "On, Wisconsin!"

Sufficiently stirred, the men advanced to battle.

General Ulysses S. Grant, watching the attack through field glasses, told an aide to promote MacArthur if the attacked succeeded—but to court-martial him if it failed.

It did not fail.

MacArthur, just 19 at the time, was later awarded the Medal of Honor.

Many units in the Civil War viewed flags as almost as important in battle as bullets, but Wisconsin was without an official state flag when the fighting began.

It had had a state seal since territorial days. The first showed a miner's arm grasping a pick over a pile of ore, but such a narrow theme hardly served the state when mining declined and other pursuits gained favor.

The next version was too busy, reflecting a farmer, an American Indian, a pyramid of pig iron, a sailboat and steamboat, a sheaf of wheat, the old capitol and a flour mill, all over the frontier motto, "Civilitas successit barbarum."

In 1851, a new seal was developed by Wisconsin's new governor, Nelson Dewey, and noted Milwaukee attorney Edward G. Ryan, who met each other on a New York street and worked out the design while sitting on the steps of a Wall Street bank. It bore a plow representing agriculture, an arm and hammer for manufacturing, a crossed shovel and pick for mining, and an anchor representing navigation.

A sailor and a man holding a pick represented labor by land and sea, and the seal included Wisconsin's nickname, "the Badger state," and the motto "Forward."

But a seal could not easily be carried into battle. So in 1863, after fielding requests for flags from regiments in the field, the Legislature ordered that the seal be printed or embroidered in color on a dark blue field, with regimental designation printed beneath the seal. The United States coat of arms was printed on the other side.

The seal was modified slightly 30 years later—an improved drawing of a badger was among the changes. Specifications were codified in 1913, and the flag went largely unchanged until 1979 when, concerned that Wisconsin's flag did not sufficiently stand out from others, the Legislature added the word "Wisconsin" and the statehood date "1848" in white letters, centered above and below the coat of arms.

The author of the changes had complained that Wisconsin's flag and New York's were almost indistinguishable, perhaps because of that session on the Wall Street steps.

Carl Schurz Had Lincoln's Ear

Carl Schurz came to America searching not merely for personal freedom, but for "the chance to gain full legal citizenship."

He found it in the young state of Wisconsin, where he became a giant in the large German-American community, an influential political figure and a man so rhetorically gifted that Abraham Lincoln referred to him as one of America's greatest orators.

He was born in Liblar, Germany, in 1829. At the University of Bonn, he became involved in the Prussian democratic revolution of 1848, but when the revolution was defeated he fled the country. He returned to help free a fellow revolutionary from the notorious Spandau prison and later lived briefly in England before coming to America.

Like many of his countrymen, he gravitated to Wisconsin, but he decided against living in Milwaukee because it had "too many Germans." Instead, Schurz and his wife, Margarethe—she would gain her own fame for starting the nation's first kindergarten—settled in Watertown, where he entered the business world.

But he wanted full citizenship, so he entered politics. He was elected to the city council and county board, but his silver tongue was already setting him up for greater achievements.

Hating slavery and finding Democrats uninterested in attacking its evils—or in cleaning up their own corruption—Schurz joined the nascent Republican Party. Although he lost his first bid for the Assembly, he was nominated for lieutenant governor in 1857, in part to lure German votes to the ticket.

Alas, while his oratory won him the nickname "that tremendous Dutchman," it did not win him the nomination. Schurz

Carl Shurz, 1879. WHI IMAGE ID 3926

moved to Milwaukee in 1858, entered a law practice and became a university regent, but by then he was traveling the country giving speeches for Lincoln, the candidate he believed would undo the awful institution of slavery.

Lincoln was so impressed with his supporter's skills that he read his inaugural speech to Schurz in advance.

Lincoln named Schurz his minister to Spain, where he chafed in Madrid while civil war raged at home. Soon Schurz returned to America, was named a brigadier general and continued to urge Lincoln to declare that slaves were emancipated.

After the war, Schurz became a newspaperman, eventually owning a German-language paper in St. Louis.

But he stayed politically involved. In 1869 he was elected a United States senator for Missouri; later was secretary of the interior under President Rutherford B. Hayes and wrote several books. In 1905, Schurz was awarded an honorary degree from the University of Wisconsin, capping a career of full legal citizenship. He died in 1906.

The "Merci" Train Came to Wisconsin

In February 1949, a boxcar arrived in Madison filled with trees, a poem, paintings, spinning wheels, bells, lace champagne and so much more.

Filled, mostly, with gratitude.

The "40 et 8," as the rail cars sent to every state were known, was a thank you from the people of France for American relief efforts in the aftermath of World War II.

The "Merci" train, as it was called, was actually repayment in kind.

In 1947, at the urging of newspaper columnist Drew Pearson, Americans launched a people-to-people rebuilding effort that resulted in the Friendship Train, with 700 carloads of food, fuel and clothing for French and Italian people left in need by the war.

The French were so grateful that, at the suggestion of French war veteran and railroad worker Andre Picard, they decided to fill their own rail cars with thank-you gifts for Americans.

They took boxcars that had been used in World War I to transport soldiers to the front lines. These were they famous "Forty and Eights," so-named because their suggested loads were 40 men or eight horses, but not, as many thought, 40 men and eight horses at the same time. It was enough that men would sometimes climb in immediately after horses had departed.

The boxcars were filled with gifts big and small, valuable and largely worthless. There were miniature mannequins in historic fashions, bicycles, dolls, wedding dresses—even a black lingerie donated anonymously "for a beautiful blonde."

French Gratitude Train boxcar (Merci Train) carrying gifts for the state of Wisconsin, February 13, 1949. WHI IMAGE ID 57739

The cars arrived in New York on the merchant ship *Magellan* on February 3, 1949, to a hero's welcome. Planes flew overhead while whistles and bells sounded. There were 49 boxcars, one for each of the 48 states and one for Washington, DC, and Hawaii to share.

The Wisconsin car was first displayed at the Capitol and later presented to the State Historical Society by an ambassador of the French government. Later, with the help of the American Legion organization named for the Forty and Eight, the French car was put on display at State Fair Park in West Allis.

In 1969, the car was moved to the Mid-Continent Railway Museum at North Freedom, near Baraboo, where it remains on display today, one of 42 remaining examples of friendship between two nations.

At least Wisconsin got to enjoy its gifts. By the time that single shared car reached Hawaii, which had donated two carloads of sugar to the relief effort, its contents were being enjoyed back in Washington. Hawaiians were left with packing straw.

"Bowie Knife" Duel Never Drew Blood

Before war between North and South, there was a legendary near-duel between hot-headed congressmen from Wisconsin and Virginia. The saga of Bowie Knife Potter and his "Pryor engagement" may have had its silly aspects—it helped laugh dueling out of political favor—but it served as an uncanny prelude for the brewing enmity that would soon split America.

At another time, the argument that nearly led to congressional bloodshed might have been shrugged off as an impolitic moment.

But in 1860s America, compromise was a rare thing. Nearly every Washington discussion was colored by the emotional and volatile issue of slavery.

In this sneak preview of national events, East Troy Republican John Fox Potter was the Northerner, a Maine native who had moved to Wisconsin in 1838. He was a man of culture and good manners, although his outspoken support for abolition was one reason he was elected to Congress in 1857.

Indeed, an account by W. B. Hesseltine said Potter quickly "brought a biting sarcasm into debates on the slavery issue."

His southern counterpart was Virginian Roger Pryor, "an ardent fire-eating Southerner"

One of the knives presented to John F. Potter by the Republicans of Missouri, 1860. WHI IMAGE ID 45547

who had a reputation for strong oratory and, when his words alone were insufficient to draw blood, for dueling with pistol and sword.

"Frequently in his speeches he alluded to his career as a duelist and expressed his willingness to meet his Yankee antagonists on the field of honor," Hesseltine wrote.

Fists were as important in that atmosphere as Robert's Rules of Order. On one occasion, Potter emerged from a fight with a black eye but fared better than a Southern colleague who came out without his wig.

Then came the fateful day, April 5, 1860. During a fiery speech condemning slavery, members began hurling insults and accusations. Potter and Pryor were among those involved, and, while order was eventually restored, the bad blood flowed anew when Potter later inserted more strong words in the official record.

Pryor could take no more. He demanded "the satisfaction usual among gentlemen" and left it to Potter as the challenged party to select weapons.

Although he likely had never even held one, Potter chose Bowie knives of equal size, weight and length.

Pryor's second called the terms vulgar, barbarous and inhumane, but Potter refused to budge. When the talk heated up, police intervened and placed both men under arrest to preserve the peace.

There never was a duel, of course, despite the urgent efforts of Washington reporters to stoke the flames. Potter earned national fame, and knives of all sizes were sent him from around the country. The Missouri delegation to the Chicago convention presented him with a seven-foot Bowie knife.

For the rest of his life he was known as Bowie Knife Potter, but his eventual demise was hardly that glamorous.

Potter died in 1899 from injuries suffered when he tripped and fell at his East Troy home while trying to avoid stepping on his pet cat.

Watertown's Delectable
Stuffed Geese

The American diet has gone lean and light to the extent that the era is lost to history, but once stuffed holiday diners could thank Wisconsin's stuffed geese.

Not just any geese. These were Watertown's famous stuffed geese, giant ganders that were specially selected by growers and fed almost to the point of explosion.

At the turn of the century, Watertown stuffed geese—especially pâté made from their equally oversize livers—were prized holiday treats on fancy restaurant menus across the land.

Goose-stuffing was an old world practice brought to the Watertown area by German immigrants. An account in *Wisconsin Then and Now* said commercial goose stuffing was being practiced as early as 1886 in the Watertown area. One year a Watertown stuffed goose was sent as a Christmas gift to that famous knife and fork man, President William Howard Taft. At the industry's peak, more than 150,000 pounds of stuffed geese were produced annually.

That wouldn't be as many geese as one might expect. These were monsters, even allowing that the 48-pounder reportedly enjoyed by Taft may have grown some in the retelling. On average, stuffed geese were marketed at between 24 and 30 pounds dressed, twice the size of normal geese, with livers weighing one to three pounds.

Raising such heavyweights was possible through a process called "noodling" and through careful selection of likely candidates.

Large ganders with long necks would be put in confined quarters so they couldn't exercise off their extra pounds. Around November 1, in order to time their readiness for the holiday season, the farmer would prepare special noodles from a paste that often included corn meal, wheat flour, oats or barley.

At feeding time, the noodles would be softened in boiling water and the noodler, wearing gloves and taking care not to be injured by the feisty fowl, would grab the goose, open its bill, insert the noodles and see that they were swallowed.

"The art," the story noted dryly, "was in determining the maximum number of noodles a bird could take without stuffing it to death."

They were fed day and night because the heavier the goose, the higher the price. The lard produced in the processing was also prized. But during the Depression, demand slackened, veteran noodlers left farming and few young farmers picked up the practice.

About the last evidence of Watertown's reign as America's goose capital comes from its high school sports teams—the Watertown Goslings.

Janesville Tankers'
Cruel Death March

In the peaceful 1920s and 30s, tank duty made for social soldiers. The men of the National Guard's Janesville Tank Company trained weekends and summers but had time for dances and parades and boys' nights out.

Then the rumble of guns in Europe turned weekend warriors into combat soldiers. For these tankers, who would suffer in the infamous Bataan Death March, war truly would be hell.

By 1940, as war loomed, the unit had 112 enlisted men, from auto workers to tradesmen, even juniors in high school. The United States was rushing to assemble an armored force to rival Germany's, but that would take years. Until modern tanks could be built and soldiers trained to run them, National Guard units were needed for one thing.

Insufficiently trained and equipped, they were nonetheless to buy time until the larger armored force was ready to fight. One general, according to an account written by Thomas Doherty, later called them the "lost children" of the armored force.

In November 1940, Janesville's tankers were sworn into the Army as Company A, 192nd Tank Battalion, and boarded trains for Fort Knox. After almost a year of learning to operate tanks and their weapons, the 192nd was sent not to Europe—as most had expected—but to the Philippines.

"Arrived in Phil safely," one soldier cabled home. "Everyone from Janesville fine. Put this in the [Janesville] *Gazette*."

Pearl Harbor fell days later, and no one would be fine for some time.

Japanese planes had crippled US air defenses, the US had sent men to distant places but was not able to adequately arm or supply them, and from the start, the odds were against the Americans.

Fighting was at night and in unfamiliar jungles, but for four months the Janesville men fought next to other American and Filipino units. Many survivors would feel betrayed that General Douglas MacArthur had been recalled to Washington in March and that promised support never arrived, leaving the "Battling Bastards of Bataan" to their awful fate.

On April 8 they were told to destroy their weapons. Before news of Bataan's fall reached loved ones at home, the death march was on.

Captives suffered terrible atrocities. Men were indiscriminately killed and disease and hunger went untouched.

Of 100 Janesville tankers who arrived in the Philippines, 94 were alive when the march began, Doherty wrote. Five would die in May, eight in June, 14 in July, many others later in internment camps.

By war's end, 40% of Americans in Japanese captivity died, but fully two-thirds of Janesville's men would die. The 64 victims included five sets of brothers and five of seven officers. But the stories of some survivors revealed scars that lasted lifetimes.

In April 1947, a crowd of 15,000 watched 28 survivors march to Janesville's Corn Exchange to unveil a marker. Remains of some of the dead wouldn't come home for several years.

Increase Lapham, Weather Pioneer

Increase Lapham once said Wisconsin citizens were better informed about the geography of their state than residents of any other.

"And for this," he wrote, "they are largely indebted to me—or at least to my maps and books."

If less than humble, it was no more than right.

Lapham, a New York native, was the fifth of 13 children of Rachel and Seneca Lapham, an engineer on the Erie Canal. Increase was himself brought to Wisconsin by Byron Kilbourn in 1836 to work on the Milwaukee and Rock River Canal, a high-blown dream that never came to fruition.

Once in Milwaukee, however, he found the work of a dozen lifetimes in as many disciplines. It might even be easier to list the firsts not credited to Lapham than to name his accomplishments.

He was Wisconsin's first scientist, compiled the first reports about state plants and shells and was the first to chronicle the state's geography. He was the first to record Wisconsin's Indian mounds and served as the first state geologist. As he noted, he was the first to map

Increase Lapham. WHI IMAGE ID 2219

Wisconsin, a work he updated regularly while traveling with his little horse, Adelaide.

He was most famous, though, as the father of what was to become the National Weather Service.

He had long taken a deep interest in the elements, recording weather observations daily for years to create his own base of knowledge. Nothing escaped his notice. In 1841, shortly after arriving in Milwaukee, Lapham's notes read:

"Apr. 1, first vessel from Chicago arrived. Apr. 4, grass begins to grow. Apr. 5, frog music commenced . . . kingfishers first observed. Apr. 7, snakes seen. Sept. 15, Mary I. Lapham 2 years old today."

When his scientific work took him away from home, his wife, Ann, would record conditions four times daily.

Lapham believed that the study of weather would lead to accurate predictions that would make the Great Lakes safer for shipping. For years, he charted storms on his own to demonstrate his theories until finally, in 1869, his efforts prompted the government to create the weather bureau. On November 8, 1870, he was in the bureau's Chicago office to help prepare and release the nation's first forecast. It called for high winds throughout the Great Lakes, and sure enough the wind blew strong.

Not merely the first weather forecast, then, but also the first correct one. Lapham declined to become the bureau's director—it was part of the Department of War, which conflicted with his Quaker principles—but he accepted an observer's role and earned his first pay ever for scientific labors. Lapham then served as state geologist, but after a political appointee replaced him he moved to a farm near Oconomowoc and continued his personal studies. One day in 1875, he pushed off in his little rowboat to do some fishing. Out on the lake, he suffered a heart attack; his body was found in the boat that evening.

It was a full life, yet Lapham is most known today for doing something about what others only talk about.

Goodell Won Women Right to Practice Law

Rhoda Lavinia Goodell was a journalist, temperance advocate, lawyer and fighter for women's rights—the need for which was evidenced by her petition to practice law before the Wisconsin Supreme Court.

A practicing lawyer in Rock County, Goodell prepared her own argument for admission. But she had to enlist a male colleague to present it in court.

He, and she, were turned down. But Goodell was hardly the shy and retiring woman Chief Justice Edward G. Ryan sought to keep at home, and she would eventually prevail.

In 1871 Goodell had moved to Janesville from New York, where she had edited an abolitionist newspaper with her father. After three years of study, Goodell was accepted to practice law in Rock County but soon was denied the right to appeal a case to the Wisconsin Supreme Court.

Goodell did not belong to the state bar, a membership automatically given to male lawyers. When she was refused admission, Goodell sued and in December 1875 won a hearing before the three-member Supreme Court.

Her case was built of bricks of common sense. There was

Lavinia Goodell. WHI IMAGE ID 111556

no legislative restriction against women practicing before the court, she said. It was commonly understood the use of masculine language in the law referred to women as well, and the fact that women had been admitted to the University of Wisconsin law school implied admission to the bar of the Supreme Court.

Refusing women, she said, meant "a great injustice is done to one-half the community by shutting them out arbitrarily from an honorable and remunerative field of industry."

Ryan's denial was so inflammatory that some later said it actually advanced women's causes.

Ryan noted Goodell was "a lady whose character raises no personal objection; something perhaps not always to be found in women who deny the ways of their sex for the ways of ours."

Still, he said, letting her practice law would be "a sweeping revolution of the social order."

"The law of nature destines and qualifies the female sex for the bearing and nurture of the children of our race and for the custody of the homes of the world . . .

"And all life-long callings of women inconsistent with these sacred duties of their sex, as is the profession of law, are departures from the order of nature, and when voluntary, treason against it."

"The peculiar qualities of womanhood," Ryan went on, "its gentle graces, its quick sensibility, its purity, its delicacy, its emotional impulses . . . are surely not qualifications for forensic strife. Discussions are habitually necessary in courts of justice which are unfit for female ears."

Goodell went back to her Janesville practice but, supported by male lawyers from Rock County, fought on. In 1877 the Legislature voted that "no person shall be denied a license on account of sex," and in June 1879, Goodell, over Ryan's continued objection, was admitted to the bar of the Wisconsin Supreme Court.

But women would soon lose their strongest legal advocate. Less than a year later Goodell died of cancer. She was 40.

Dreamers Wanted Canals, Not Railroads

Had the dreamers prevailed, Wisconsin might have become Venice with cows. Unfortunately for them, the early dreamers who sought to build canals across Wisconsin at the dawn of statehood would have likely needed more money—and luck—than existed at the time, so audacious was their scheme.

But perhaps vision always outruns means. Canal advocates drew their inspiration from the recently completed Erie Canal that linked the Hudson River with Lake Erie, a huge engineering achievement and economic boon to the eastern region.

"Ducks," as canal supporters were called, took a dim view of railroads that were just arriving in Wisconsin, but had high hopes for boat traffic that would link Lake Michigan ports with the riches of the lead mines in southwestern Wisconsin.

As with the iron rails that eventually were built, communities located along any proposed watery route expected great prosperity to flow past, so competition was fierce. While others planned a canal linking the Fox and Wisconsin rivers, noted Milwaukeean Byron Kilbourn and some business associates concocted a plan to dig a ditch from Milwaukee to the Rock River at Watertown, then westward to the booming lead region and the Mississippi River.

There were skeptics, but Kilbourn lobbied for his ditch before the territorial legislature in Belmont and, later, in Burlington. On January 5, 1838, Governor Henry Dodge signed a bill establishing the Wisconsin & Rock River Canal Company.

Kilbourn won land grants for well over 100,000 acres for his ditch. The territorial legislature approved construction bonds and there was established a Board of Canal Commissioners, but ultimately this pie-in-the-sky canal plan ended in failure.

Underfunded, poorly managed, facing opposition from other developers and political figures, the company stopped construction after only a short stretch had been dug in Milwaukee. The positive outcome was a dam on the stretch that began providing power for businesses in the area.

Attention then shifted back to the Fox-Wisconsin plan, which continued to be pursued with little success for a few years.

By the time the new state of Wisconsin ended its flirtation with canals in the 1850s, the railroad's potential had clearly taken hold. The dreamers had moved on, and the same battles that had been fought over water routes moved on to dry land.

Nelson Dewey,
Wisconsin's First Governor

Nelson Dewey is best remembered for building a sprawling estate, parts of which survive today, but Dewey's dreams of surrounding it with a grand city were beyond his reach.

Born December 19, 1813, Dewey was a Connecticut Yankee who found his place not in King Arthur's Court but in the new territory of Wisconsin. He was 23 when he traveled in 1836 by stagecoach, steamer, sailing ship, horseback and on foot for five weeks to reach his new home. But by the time Wisconsin became a state 12 years later he had done well enough to become its first governor.

Dewey made his home in Cassville, on the Mississippi River in the then-bustling lead region. His land development company was intent on creating a major city at Cassville that might even become the territorial capital, but after the selection of Madison instead, Dewey began a career in politics.

He was elected Grant County Register of Deeds in 1837, was named justice of the peace and admitted to the bar, and became district attorney.

Dewey then served two terms in the Territorial Assembly, where Whigs and his Democratic Party were fighting for power.

At the same time, Dewey had formed a law and real estate company with a partner, J. Allen Barber, and became quite wealthy. He was a well-known and respected figure, and when a divided Democratic convention needed a candidate for governor in 1848, Dewey was the compromise choice.

He defeated the Whig, John H. Tweedy, and on June 7, 1848, at just 34 years old, Dewey became Wisconsin's first governor.

Dewey presided over the transition from territory to statehood by taking the middle road between political extremes. But he served, as historian Robert C. Nesbit put it, "two unexceptional terms . . . during which he did nothing to advance his own career."

Nelson Dewey. WHI IMAGE ID 55243

In 1854 he revived his plans to build up Cassville, acquiring buildings and attempting to attract investment. Just north of Cassville, Dewey built a "palace in the wilderness," a 2,000-acre estate with a house as modern as the times allowed.

Dewey's house at his "Stonefield" estate had 20 fireplaces and a hot air furnace, and was surrounded by miles of stone walls and roads with arched stone bridges.

But Cassville drew few settlers, and when Dewey's investment in a railroad failed—and his fabulous home burned to the ground in 1873—he was forced to surrender his property.

He returned to his law practice and later ran for public office several more times, losing bids for lieutenant governor and the state Senate. On July 21, 1889, Nelson Dewey died, Nesbit said, "in relative obscurity and poverty" at his home in Cassville.

The Gubernatorial Showdown of 1856

The custom is to have but one chief executive at a time, but for a rollicking period in 1855–56 Wisconsin had a two-headed—almost three-headed—governorship.

In seeking re-election, Governor William Augustus Barstow, a Waukesha Democrat, had to face charges of mismanaging state funds, corruption and bribery involving railroad lobbyists, a platform of scandal that limited his margin of victory to just 157 votes.

On January 7, 1856, he was inaugurated amid pomp and circumstance. And, lacking a mandate, Barstow brought with him seven companies of militia, along with several thousand supporters, many of them armed. Barstow was taking no chances.

Republican Coles Bashford, meanwhile, went quietly to the Wisconsin Supreme Court to argue that his party had been denied rightful victory by rigged voting.

On January 10, Bashford went to the governor's office and demanded it be turned over to him, which set off a lengthy legal battle. Eventually, the Supreme Court determined Bashford had been elected and was entitled to serve.

But Barstow wasn't finished. On March 21, 1856, rather than let the Republican be sworn in, Barstow stepped down so his lieutenant governor, Arthur MacArthur—grandfather of Douglas, the future general—could take the oath of office. He would serve just four days, but one of his few official acts was to order arms and ammunition stored at the Capitol removed to lessen the chance that the power struggle would lead to violence.

The game of gubernatorial musical chairs ran on. On March 25, Bashford went to the governor's office and advised MacArthur

LEFT TO RIGHT: Barstow, Bashford, MacArthur. WHI IMAGE ID 117531, WHI IMAGE ID 2537, WHI IMAGE ID 38937

he was taking over, preferably without force but with force if it came to that.

When MacArthur asked whether Bashford was serious, Bashford's attorney, Timothy O. Howe, was said to have replied: "My advice is that Mr. Bashford hang his coat on a nail and proceed in the performance of his gubernatorial duties. I would not, of course, advise him to lay violent hands on so distinguished a man as Governor MacArthur."

MacArthur replied that he felt the threat amounted to virtual force, but decided he would submit. He retired and returned to his duties in the state Senate; he also became a respected judge, toastmaster and, later, president of the Society for the Prevention of Cruelty to Animals and Children.

As it turned out, Bashford's single term was marked, as his predecessor's had been, by allegations of rampant corruption.

In 1858, after he left office, the Legislature approved an investigation of the railroad land grants approved under Bashford's rule; 72 officials, including Bashford, were implicated, but no legal action was taken. Still, wrote historian Fred Holmes: "It was an epoch fogged with political trickery and legislative chicanery. The low level was reached by the wholesale bribing of the legislature of 1856."

And it came at a time when governors still hung their coats on a nail.

"Julius the Just" Was Dairy Defender

To his admirers he was "Julius the Just;" to detractors "Just Julius." But by any measure, Julius P. Heil was one of Wisconsin's most colorful governors. And when he had his way, the color was that of cheddar cheese.

Born in Germany in 1876, Heil was raised on a farm near New Berlin, and though he would become a leading industrialist, he never forgot his farm-boy beginnings.

At 14, Heil worked in Milwaukee as a drill press hand; he was a conductor on street railway lines and traveled the world for the Falk Corporation supervising the installations of welded street car rails, work that led to the company he would later form with three employees. It would eventually employ more than 3,000.

His business credentials and civic activities helped him become the Republican candidate for governor in 1938, and for two terms he worked to undo the accomplishments of the La Follettes who had preceded him. His brusque, even impolitic, style often drew criticism; his political enemies viewed him as dictatorial and would greet him with "Heil Julius."

The people, opined Madison's *Capital Times* in 1939, "will not stand for signing away dictatorial powers to any man, let alone to a clowning, garrulous politician."

But Heil met criticism head-on. When a student called him a "brainless idiot" in a university paper, Heil said, "I'm going to have that young man brought before me and if he doesn't belong to the state of Wisconsin I'm going to kick him out."

Wisconsin was sacred to Heil, especially the dairy industry he gained fame for promoting. He toured the South to smooth

Governor Julius Heil squirting milk from a cow, perhaps on a parade float, in 1940. His button reads "Drink More Milk." WHI IMAGE ID 99734

resentment at the Wisconsin oleo tax. He promoted giving cheese as a gift, arranging it so that packages of cheese could be mailed anywhere in the United States for $1.

In 1940 he sent cheese to the nation's governors at Christmas. The response so pleased him he said they would get 2 pounds of state cheese every month for two years. He installed a milk bar at the Capitol, milked a Guernsey cow on a float in a Milwaukee parade and suggested factory workers be given milk during working hours.

"Mother," he once told Eleanor Roosevelt, "you're going to get a package of cheese every week while I'm governor of Wisconsin."

"She was tickled pink," he said later.

He had little use for Madison, preferring to work and live in Milwaukee. In his second term he was criticized for alleged "playboy" tendencies and for ignoring his duties in favor of hob-nobbing with Hollywood celebrities and visiting royalty.

A famous Heil moment was recalled in a story published upon his death in 1967. It involved his introduction of Crown Prince Frederick and Princess Ingrid of Denmark to a Madison audience.

"Girls and boys," he said, "let's give a big hand. Ain't she a beaut!"

And Heil did give her a hand, the story said—a pat on her posterior.

It was not reported whether she, too, was tickled pink.

Peace in Europe Brought Joy to Streets

The longed-for news that World War I had ended on November 11, 1918, was shouted to Milwaukee in blaring headlines, and shrill whistles woke the sleeping populace to read them.

Of course, not all hostilities ended on Armistice Day. The *Milwaukee Sentinel* boasted for days that it was first with the news of peace. The *Journal* responded that, because the *Sentinel* had prematurely announced a surrender three days earlier, many Milwaukeeans didn't believe it this time until they read it in the *Journal*.

However, the *Sentinel*'s overeagerness had provided a night of practice celebration and when the "greatest news the world had known in centuries" (as the *Journal* put it) arrived, the town greeted it with abandon.

Streets filled with raucous, anything-goes celebrations. Chorus girls from the Gayety Theater, accompanied by a band from the Randolph Hotel, paraded up and down Grand Avenue singing "The Star-Spangled Banner," while half-dressed hotel guests trailed along.

A group of Italians celebrated in a motor truck belonging to Vincent Catalano, pausing only briefly when it collided with a bakery wagon. Another group marched through downtown making music with cow bells, tin cans, horns and other noise-makers. Even women's rights advanced that night: the *Journal* noted that at 6 a.m., Henry Wehr's watering hole "was lined two deep with celebrants, several women placing their feet on 'the rail' beside the men and taking 'theirs' in the true spirit of democracy."

One man adorned his car with a string of sausages and a placard that read, "All that is left of the Kaiser." Harley-Davidson

An impromptu Armistice Day street parade in Menominee, November 11, 1918. WHI IMAGE ID 103411

employees marched together in celebrations, as did uniformed city health inspectors behind a big "To Hell with the Kaiser" banner. Others dragged effigies of the Kaiser behind their horn-tooting autos.

At the Milwaukee Orphan Asylum, a boy dressed as Uncle Sam led a parade of cheering children. As day broke, church services were held for those still sober, but many businesses closed for the day so employees could celebrate peace.

Some overdid it, of course. A dozen or so women employees of Briggs & Stratton were injured when their overloaded car tipped over in front of the plant. The next day, all the drunken and rowdy revelers who were arrested made for an unusually large police court calendar, including "nine gorgeously bedecked women, somewhat rumpled after a night in the central police station," who were charged with giving their all during the celebration—but for a price.

After the period of war and restraint, letting loose was expected. But one letter to the newspaper, alluding to the casualties, offered perspective:

"[I]n all that crowd of horn-blowing and shouting people, how many are giving a thought to the price we paid? The Gold Star Mothers were not in jammed, downtown Milwaukee today.

"(Signed) Sober."

Chester Thordarson's
Icelandic Retreat

Today Rock Island is largely given over to ghosts and summer hikers, but once this lonely spit of land off Door County was home to a wealthy and inventive man's vision of a grand Icelandic village.

Chester Thordarson was of both islands, born in Iceland in 1867—his first name was originally Hjortur—but master of 777 acres of Rock Island most of his adult life.

He came to America in 1873, living with his family in Milwaukee, De Forest and Shawano before eventually landing in Chicago. He yearned for education; at 18 he enrolled in a fourth-grade class of 10-year-olds, enduring embarrassment in order to learn.

His interest was electricity, which would make him rich. He left the Chicago Edison Company to form his own and went on to produce high-voltage transformers, one of which earned a gold medal at the 1904 St. Louis World's Fair.

But his passions were his thousands of books and his Rock Island estate, which he began to acquire in 1910.

Carol Lohry Cartwright wrote in the *Wisconsin Magazine of History* that Thordarson might have been drawn by the Icelanders on nearby Washington Island, but it may also have been that rugged, wooded Rock Island simply resembled his homeland.

His proprietorship was uneven. He often said he wanted to develop a preserve for plants and wildlife but later sought to be allowed to drive off or shoot every deer on Rock Island.

It seemed his ban on outside hunters had led to too many deer that fed on his prized plants.

The Thordarson estate, including the boathouse and a stone-paved path with benches. WHI IMAGE ID 48564

He conducted experiments, including a test of "electrocul-ture," which involved stringing a network of wires over a field of fruit trees. Thordarson was confident he could make everything grow nicely without direct sunlight.

His first buildings were basic, but during the 1920s he launched an aggressive building program.

Four stone buildings in Icelandic design, other stone struc-tures and elaborate landscaping resulted, all part of what Cart-wright called his "romantic vision of an Icelandic village."

He built a greenhouse on a fieldstone base and a boathouse-great hall said to be reminiscent of the Icelandic parliament building.

He moved his vast collection of books—between 10,000 to 11,000 titles, including many rare books—to the great hall while he was building a library.

He proudly entertained visitors—a special cabin was built for Chicago Mayor William Hale "Big Bill" Thompson, who came often—and one guest who enjoyed Thordarson's tour called him "a picture of dreams come true."

He was fond of Wisconsin's university, which awarded him an honorary degree, but not sufficiently fond to donate his library to it.

However, the UW purchased it for $300,000 in 1946, shortly after Thordarson's death, to help establish Memorial Library's rare books collection.

In 1964, the state purchased his estate from his heirs for $175,000 to create rustic Rock Island State Park. Only camping and hiking are permitted, but evidence of Thordarson's dream remains there today. It isn't Iceland, but it once came close.

When Protest Came to Campus

After students and police clashed in 1967 in the first truly violent Vietnam War protest, Paul Soglin (a student leader and later Madison mayor), later recalled that a young woman surveyed the bloody scene and said, "I now consider myself a radical; would someone please tell me what that means?"

It meant that the war had come home to Madison, because she was not alone. The perceptions and politics of many students were changed—even radicalized—by the protest that had ended in riot, as police and campus authorities similarly confronted a new reality. Demonstrations that rose up over campus recruitment by Dow Chemical Company, maker of napalm used in Vietnam, were the unmistakable harbingers of an era of student unrest that would climax years later in the deadly bombing of a campus laboratory.

University of Wisconsin–Madison students clash with riot police during campus demonstration to protest Dow Chemical involvement during the Vietnam War, 1967.
WHI IMAGE ID 2289

A protest of Dow's presence on the University of Wisconsin campus in October 1967 was not a surprise. Disruptions during its last recruiting visit had led to 19 arrests, and the dean of students had threatened expulsion or other discipline if the interviews were disrupted.

Still, the dean told an investigating panel later, the violent melee that resulted when club-swinging police charged protesters at a sit-in was a shock. The investigation lasted for months, and legal issues growing out of arrests eventually reached the Supreme Court.

Hundreds of students were in the Commerce Building, singing songs of protest and flexing the new muscles of activism, when police armed with tear gas and clubs moved in to enforce their orders to clear the building.

Soglin later noted wryly that students who had been in front of him were suddenly scarce.

"And then there was nobody between me and the cops," he said. "I remember thinking, 'This is it.'"

He was beaten on the neck, back, legs and spine. It was the same throughout the building as police went after students, who hurled back names and rocks, glass and spit. Outside, the crowd, and the sense of danger, grew. A police inspector later said police were fighting for their lives in "one of the most vicious demonstrations I've ever been in."

The next day, newspapers reported more than 75 injuries, including 10 or more officers, and the arrests of 11 protestors.

Aftershocks would ripple over the campus for months.

About 1,500 marchers demanded an end to the police action to disperse peaceful protests. State Attorney General Bronson La Follette angered law-enforcement groups by labeling the police response "brutality." Impatient regents demanded stronger discipline of protesters. Angry legislators railed against "dirty hippies" and "communists" on campus.

"We should shoot them if necessary," Senator Leland McParland, a Cudahy Democrat, suggested. "I would. I would. Because it's insurrection."

Threats aside, campus life had changed. By February 1968, a survey found that 75% of students endorsed organized protest as a "legitimate means of expressing student grievances." Only 7% disagreed.

Strange Bedfellows,
and Hogs in the Basement

Modern legislators who find themselves wined and dined in Madison should appreciate those hardy pioneer politicians who paved the way.

An account from Madison's earliest days, when the future capital existed mostly on paper and statehood was still in gestation, reveals how early Wisconsin politics literally made for strange bedfellows—and also close ones.

The territorial legislature was ready for Madison before Madison was ready for it. The future city was essentially a wilderness when workers arrived in 1837 to begin work on a capitol building and such other government structures as would be needed. On July 4, 1837, the cornerstone of Madison's first capitol was set amid appropriate celebration.

"The festivities continued for three days, as long as it took for the whiskey to give out," according to the *Wisconsin Blue Book*.

But when the territorial legislature arrived in 1838, construction was lagging.

A special committee that examined the problem found of Madison's hotels: "at the Madison House there was one

Sketch drawn by George Harrison of the Wisconsin State Capitol, the third capitol in the state, the first Capitol in Madison.
WHI IMAGE ID 6969

room that would accommodate four persons; and at the American Hotel, eight rooms, sufficient to accommodate twenty-six persons."

Food was similarly lacking in charm.

"Though we paid metropolitan prices, it cannot be said that we had exactly metropolitan fare," wrote Judge J. G. Knapp. "But men were remarkably accommodating in those early times, and without a grumble could eat 'hog and hominy' or 'common doing' when 'chicken fixings' could not be had, and they would occupy a 'field bed' when they were required to sleep 'spoon fashion' . . .

"At the Madison House, only six men were placed in a room sixteen feet square . . . Happy were those men who could find places in private houses where four men might find two beds in a cold room ten or twelve feet square."

Worse, their capitol was not ready for them, either. Two rooms were hurried into use, but when heaters were turned on, the green wood dried and shrank, leaving gaps in the boards as wide as a man's hand.

The basement was undone, but not unusable. The building's contractor, James Morrison, took advantage of the open space to keep his herd of hogs out of the harsh weather, which inspired in Ebenezer Child, the down-to-earth representative from Green Bay, an idea for quieting his long-winded brethren.

"When members of this ilk would become too tedious," he said, "I would take a long pole, go at the hogs and stir them up; when they would raise a young pandemonium for noise and confusion, the speaker's voice would become completely drowned, and he would be compelled to stop."

In late December—whether to escape the cold or the hogs or to find more pleasing spoon-shaped sleeping partners—lawmakers declared a one-month recess and went home.

When Ice Came in from the Cold

At least one ice age in Wisconsin had nothing to do with great glaciers. What we take for granted now was once a thriving industry, for how could one enjoy a cold beer on a hot day if someone hadn't thought to store ice when nature made it?

The ice harvest was the winter equivalent of making hay while the sun shone. In the 1880s and 1890s, it was also a profitable industry that turned frozen lakes into seasonal factories as busy as any in town.

Individuals had often cut ice in winter for personal use, but the advent of nationwide rail service created new appetites for ice among industries that shipped perishables—most notably breweries.

About 1880, according to James P. Krudwig's account in *Voyageur* magazine, breweries used an estimated 1 million tons of ice

Oshkosh Pure Ice and Coal Co. horse-drawn wagon, September 20, 1926. WHI IMAGE ID 88275

a year in the 1880s to distribute their beer, while twice as much was needed to cool and serve it.

Milwaukee's Best (later Pabst) Brewery was the biggest single user. In addition, ice was in demand for shipping meat—Chicago's Swift and Armour used refrigerated cars—as well as fruits and vegetables.

At first, ice was ice, but as pollution concerns arose, harvesters sought pure sources. Wisconsin and Maine, Krudwig said, made the nation's best ice.

Ice at a foot thick was preferred. Some companies used farmers and their horses, who otherwise would have been idle in winter.

Best Brewery established a permanent ice plant on Pewaukee Lake that was soon sold to Armour. It was 1,200 feet long and 200 feet deep and could hold more than 175,000 tons.

It had railroad service, too, and during peak ice season crews worked day and night cutting heavy blocks and hauling them into storage.

Ice plants were also built near Madison's cornerstone lakes and the frozen surface of Green Bay. Miller Rasmussen Ice Company in Green Bay operated 40 heavy sleighs to haul ice from harvesting fields, but home delivery of ice was still grunt work.

A manufacturer of weights and barbells later had a booklet that claimed many great weightlifters had been icemen who hauled heavy loads up and down stairs.

The work was sometimes hazardous, of course; Miller Rasmussen co-founder L. P. "Shorty" Rasmussen fell into Shawano Lake while harvesting ice during the unseasonably warm winter of 1921, caught pneumonia and died a week later.

But the ice industry proved as ephemeral as ice ultimately is. By the early 20th century, technology made the manufacture of artificial ice more practical, and the market began to melt.

In 1920–21, the same warm winter that took Rasmussen's life also cost more surviving ice harvesters their livelihoods.

Index

Van Hise, Charles R., *250*, 250
Van Hoof, Mary Ann, 91–93, *92*
Van Slyke, D. O., 234–235
Vattendahl, Marjorie, 223
Vega, Marylois Purdy, 66
victory gardens, 140–142
Vietnam War, 349–350
Vilas County, 129
Virgin Mary, 91–93
Voight, John E., 230
Voigt, Edward, 77
Voree, 40–41
voting rights, 118–119, 153–154

Waldmeir, Pete, 23
Wales, Julia Grace, 189–190
War Eagle, 180–182, *181*
Washburn, 257–258
Watertown, 326
Wausau, 203–205
weather, 331
Weaver, Sam, 94
Weller, Steve, 23
Westerman, Joyce, 244
white pine, 193–195
Whittlesey, Asaph, *5*, 5–6
Wilder, Amos, 247
Wilder, Laura Ingalls, 47–49, *48*
Wiley, Alexander, 166
Willard, Frances E., *289*, 289–290
Williams, Daniel Hale, *61*, 61–63
Wilson, Woodrow, 189–190
Winans, John, 221
Winneconne, 209–210
Wisconsin, 169–171, *170*
Wisconsin & Rock River Canal
    Company, 334–335

Wisconsin Capitol Fire (1904),
    73–75
Wisconsin Dairymen's Association,
    14
Wisconsin Dells, 7–9
Wisconsin Idea, 250–251
"Wisconsin Peace Plan," 189–190
Wisconsin River, 1, 27–29
Wisconsin State Automobile Asso-
    ciation, 156
Wisconsin State Building, 111, 112
Wisconsin State Capitol, 351–352
Wolff, Frank J., 312–313
women, and typewriters, 97–99
women's athletics, 243–245
Women's Christian Temperance
    Union, 290
Wood, Charles, 196
Wood, Clarissa, 196–197
Woodruff, 38–39
work safety / compensation,
    303–304
World Series, 275–277
World War I, 16–18, 135–137, 140–
    142, *141*, 189–190, 314–315,
    343–345
World War II, 170, 222–224, 322–
    323, 328–329
World's Columbian Exposition
    (1893), 110–112
Wright, Frank Lloyd, 296–297, *297*

Youmans, Theodora Winton, 154

Zachow, Otto, 241
Zeidler, Frank, 124, 276, 277
Zeitlin, Richard, 169

About the Author

Dennis McCann spent most of his professional life traveling Wisconsin and the Midwest for the *Milwaukee Journal* and *Milwaukee Journal-Sentinel*. A Wisconsin native and graduate of the University of Wisconsin–Madison, he is the author of three Wisconsin Historical Society Press books—*Badger Boneyards: The Eternal Rest of the Story*, *This Superior Place: Stories of Bayfield and the Apostle Islands*, and *This Storied River: Legend & Lore of the Upper Mississippi*. He and his wife, Barbara, a retired teacher, reside in Bayfield.